TEXTUAL SPACES

Habent sua fata libelli
EARLY MODERN STUDIES SERIES

GENERAL EDITOR

Michael Wolfe
Queens College, CUNY

EDITORIAL BOARD OF EARLY MODERN STUDIES

Elaine Beilin
Framingham State University

Raymond A. Mentzer
University of Iowa

Christopher Celenza
Johns Hopkins University

Robert V. Schnucker
Truman State University (Emeritus)

Barbara B. Diefendorf
Boston University

Nicholas Terpstra
University of Toronto

Paula Findlen
Stanford University

Margo Todd
University of Pennsylvania

Scott H. Hendrix
Princeton Theological Seminary

James Tracy
University of Minnesota

Jane Campbell Hutchison
University of Wisconsin–Madison

Merry Wiesner-Hanks
University of Wisconsin–Milwaukee

Mary B. McKinley
University of Virginia

TEXTUAL SPACES
French Renaissance Writings on
the Italian Voyage

RICHARD E. KEATLEY

The Pennsylvania State University Press
University Park, Pennsylvania

Library of Congress Cataloging-in-Publication Data

Names: Keatley, Richard E., author.
Title: Textual spaces : French Renaissance writings on the Italian voyage / Richard E. Keatley.
Other titles: Early modern studies series.
Description: University Park, Pennsylvania : The Pennsylvania State University Press, [2018] | Series: Early modern studies series | Includes bibliographical references and index.
Summary: "Examines how French Renaissance travelers consumed and represented Italian space through writing and the imagination. Includes writings by Rabelais, Montaigne, and Du Bellay as well as lesser-known French travelers, illustrating how the material and imaginative aspects of travel joined to form a space of desire in the French imagination"—Provided by publisher.
Identifiers: LCCN 2018016444 | ISBN 9780271081298 (cloth : alk. paper)
Subjects: LCSH: Travelers' writings, French—Italy—History and criticism. | French prose literature—16th century—History and criticism. | Italy—Description and travel—Early works to 1800.
Classification: LCC PQ613.K43 2018 | DDC 840.9/3245—dc23
LC record available at https://lccn.loc.gov/2018016444

Copyright © 2019 Richard E. Keatley
All rights reserved
Printed in the United States of America
Published by The Pennsylvania State University Press,
University Park, PA 16802-1003

The Pennsylvania State University Press is a member of the Association of University Presses.

It is the policy of The Pennsylvania State University Press to use acid-free paper. Publications on uncoated stock satisfy the minimum requirements of American National Standard for Information Sciences—Permanence of Paper for Printed Library Material, ANSI Z39.48-1992.

Per Pina
il più bel viaggio della mia vita

CONTENTS

Acknowledgments ix

Introduction 1

1 Montaigne Inside and Out 9
2 Textuality, Sexuality, and Political Geography: André de la Vigne and the French Conquest of Naples 32
3 Space, Travel, and Work 51
4 The Topographical Narrative 70
5 Spaces and Places of the *Voyage d'Italie* 105
6 Mapping Montaigne's Rome 146

Conclusions 172

Notes 175
Bibliography 207
Index 230

ACKNOWLEDGMENTS

This work could not have existed without the help, encouragement, and advice of many friends and colleagues. To begin with, I want to thank my three advisors, whose advice I did not always heed: Claude Blum, Deborah Losse, and Edwin Duval.

I am especially grateful to scholars whose invitations to speak on their respective campuses have allowed me to better understand my own ideas and receive constructive feedback, including Tom Conley (Harvard), Frank Lestringant (Paris IV–Sorbonne), Jacques Pothier (Université de Versailles–Saint-Quentin-en-Yvellines), Rosella Mamoli-Zorzi, Stefano Maso, Stefano Campostrini (all three of Ca' Foscari University of Venice), Philippe Desan (University of Chicago), and Concetta Cavallini (Università degli Studi di Bari Aldo Moro).

I received a Beinecke fellowship while still at Yale University, as well as a research fellowship from the Renaissance Society of America to study rare volumes in the Bibliothèque Nationale de France. A special thanks goes to the ATLANTIS program of the Department of Education, whose grant, while unrelated to the work of this book, allowed me to spend invaluable hours in the Biblioteca Marciana in Venice, and to Georgia State University for sending me, in the company of many marvelous students, to explore many of the places visited by Montaigne and the other travelers studied here.

Thanks go also to the many librarians who have helped in the Bibliothèque Nationale de France, the Marciana in Venice, the Augusta in Perugia, the Biblioteca Nazionale in Naples, the New York Public Library, the Houghton at Harvard, and the Beinecke at Yale. My studies have been a pleasant and rewarding journey thanks to you.

I thank the following colleagues who have read versions of this work and given much-needed moral support: Concetta Cavallini, Marina Coslovi, Brenton Hobart, Leslie Marsh, Jeff Persels, Marcello Simonetta, and Juliann Vitullo. Thanks especially to Audrey Goodman and David Payne for their input and friendship and to Philippe Desan, George

Hoffman, and Eric MacPhail for their comments on earlier versions of this manuscript.

To Pierre-Yves Le Duc, whose art and work ethic are an inspiration to us all, *mando un caro saluto*.

INTRODUCTION

In the spring of 1589, a young French traveler, nearing the end of his year long journey through Italy and arriving in the remote Christian outpost of Malta, found his surprise visit was somewhat suspect. His crossing from the mainland had been adventuresome. He sailed in a Spanish galleon from Naples to Messina, singing on deck with the sailors and arriving in the great trading city of Palermo. From there he took a felucca, one of the small, single-sailed vessels that worked the coasts of southern Italy, sailing back to Messina and down Sicily's eastern coast. He describes shores plagued by pirates and backed by a hostile, symbolic landscape, skirting the mythical traps of Scylla and Charybdis (Straits of Messina) and sailing past black, amorphous, ashen stones belched from the mouth of the formidable "Mont Gibel" (Etna). After brief stops in Catania and Syracuse, his vessel followed the sparsely inhabited coast of the southern part of the island. They overnighted in caves "creusees d'impétuosité de mer, dans lesquelles se peuvent cacher les galliotes turcquesques qui coustumierement attendent les vaisseaux des passans d'un cotté ou d'aultre" (carved out by the sea's force, where Turkish corsairs can hide awaiting vessels that pass through in either direction). Delayed by contrary winds and followed by a suspicious ship they managed to keep at a distance, the traveler and his companion finally arrived "saintz et sauvés (*sic*)" (safe and sound, or sainted and saved)[1] on April 13, 1589, where they were quickly brought to meet the Grand Master of the Order of the Knights of Malta, Cardinal Hugues de Loubenx de Verdalle.[2] When asked the purpose of their visit, our traveler responded with words that had become a leitmotif of his journey up to that point; he replied that he had been driven to this remote location by "le seul desir de voir l'isle et la bonne compagnie qui y estoit" (139) (the sole desire to see the island and the good company that was there). Verdalle welcomed the visitors and invited them to stay as long as they liked but later summoned our anonymous traveler to his chambers to ask him yet again what he was doing there and if he had any message from the king, to which our traveler "faict la mesme response" (gave the same answer).

Verdalle's questioning underscores the ambiguous status of Renaissance travelers, whose political profiles are often masked by pleasant ramblings through Italy in the pursuit of the "desir de voir" (desire to see things). Traveling as official or unofficial representatives of the government or working for high-ranking patrons, these travelers are called upon to navigate a network of sociopolitical influence in which the issues of national, religious, and personal identity all come into play. Like the explorers of the New World, travelers to Italy embody the social, political, and religious tensions of their countries of origin.[3] They practice and learn the art of politics and study law in the universities of Padua, Pavia, Ferrara, and Bologna or the arts of horsemanship and fencing needed for members of the soldierly class.[4] At the same time, the narratives, poems, and descriptions that emerge from this political experience generally give short shrift to these practical concerns, preferring, like the author of the anonymous *Discours viatiques*, to narrate their adventures; record archaeological, architectural, and anthropological singularities; and wander for the "desir de voir." The political content of the narrative of travel to Italy thus acts as a disguised motor of aesthetic production, lying in the background of an experience expressed in literary terms and modeled on forms of textual production. Literary form thus communicates the inherently metaphorical, metaphysical aspects of travel in a larger sense, one that reflects a personalized *mythos* embedded deep within the traveler's psyche.[5]

Philippe Desan has recently described the relationship between Michel de Montaigne's lifelong engagement with politics and the writing of the *Essais*.[6] Among other things, Desan illustrates the important role Montaigne's Italian journey played in Henri III's jockeying for power with Pope Gregory XIII.[7] These considerations provide social and political context for the writing of the 1582 edition of the *Essais*, but more importantly, they explore the links between Montaigne's aesthetic and literary activity and his politics, building on George Hoffmann's analysis of the intersections between Montaigne's practice of writing and his public career.⁸ If the *Essais* elicit questions regarding the relationship between public and private modes of expression, the *Journal de voyage* exacerbates many of these same problems due to its apparent lack of concern for the politics. Whether written as a private notebook or addressed, like the *Discours viatiques*, to an intimate friend, the travel account, like the *Essais*, creates a private space within the public square of literary expression, an "arriere-boutique" of intellectual and aesthetic interrogation whose relationship to political action is difficult to define due to its repressed nature.

THE WAR OVER SPACES: FRENCH AND ITALIAN WARS IN THE SIXTEENTH CENTURY

This book examines how political, social, and economic concerns come to bear on the aesthetics of literary production. We will see that Renaissance travelers' expressed escapism and that their gluttony for space and experience appear as expressions of a performed leisure in the sense studied by Virginia Krause,⁹ using contact with the cultural spaces of Italy as a form of symbolic capital whose resonances are inherently sociopolitical. The examination of antiquity, analysis of the structures of Italy's modern cities, and wandering toward unnamed, undiscovered lands stem from the tastes and representational needs of a social class whose behavioral models skirt the borders between traditional, chivalric models of behavior and the demonstration of the intellectual, social, and political ability needed to get promoted.¹⁰ Crossing mountains, tracing the steps of Cicero, and sounding the depths of volcanic caves in the pursuit of curiosity become rhetorical performances within the political context of late sixteenth-century France and its ongoing contentious relationship with Italy.

France's engagement in Italy began calamitously in 1494 with Charles VIII's attempt to wrest the Neapolitan throne from King Ferrante d'Aragona and ended sixty-five years later with the French renunciation of its territorial claims in Italy with the signing of the Treaty of Cateau-Cambrésis. During this period, France's kings and nobility often focused their attention more on their neighbor to the south than on affairs at home. The Italian Wars not only served as a training ground for the nobility, offering the chance to serve one's country, but also led to the importation of the technology and culture of Renaissance Italy into

France. While the French conquests in Italy were doomed to be ephemeral, as the Italian historiographer Marino Sanudo boasted,[11] the impact of the sixty-year engagement on the technology, culture, and politics of France was profound and long-lasting.[12]

Travelers to Italy after the signing of the Treaty of Cateau-Cambrésis thus moved through an altered political landscape in which French influence had been replaced by that of a global Spanish Empire. French travelers' perceptions were often influenced by the particular political circumstances of the states they visited: positive in cities with strong French sympathies, such as Ferrara or Siena,[13] nostalgic or critical in places where Spanish control had replaced French influence. More often than not, however, French travelers learned to navigate a new, increasingly complex reality, such as in Turin, where a highly strategic marriage guaranteed pro-French sentiment while the city itself recalled France's defeat at the hand of Duke Emmanuel-Philibert (reigned 1553–80).[14] Much of the rest of Italy had become a Spanish protectorate, with the kingdom of Naples and the coastal states of the Presidio outright Spanish possessions. The Duchies of Milan, Republic of Genoa, all objectives, at one time or another, of the expansionist aspirations of the French monarchy, were now, like Mantua, the Grand Duchy of Tuscany, and the Republics of Lucca and Genoa, under Spanish protection or control.

These smoldering political tensions, fueled by the historic cultural relationship between French and Italian culture, helped transform Italy's cities and territories, once the object of explicit territorial ambitions, into spaces of desire, where nostalgic rumination and aesthetic memory are elaborated in interesting ways.

THE SPATIAL (TEXTUAL) DISCOURSE

If the political and national implications of geographical space are apparent, the translation of the individual's experience into a coherent discourse is less straightforward. Space is subjective, embodying political, economic, and social values that are then interpreted by the viewer.[15] The psychological, historical, and political factors that make up the "accidental whole" of perceived space are thus reexpressed in what Henri Lefebvre calls "created space."[16] At the same time, the geopolitical spaces of Renaissance Italy are themselves textually determined so that the traveler, prepared through reading and research, comes to interrogate the textual spaces, adding vision and firsthand experience to his humanistic preparation conducted through reading. The travel narrative thus pits the textual culture of Renaissance humanism against the practical, lived approach of an emerging spatial discourse characteristic of the age of geographical discovery, challenging and negotiating what Numa Broc calls a "textualized" image of the world.[17]

The "weight of the library" evident in the description of the New World and Middle East[18] reaches a point of paroxysm in the writing of Italy.[19] The use of an antiquarian lens to describe space, characteristic of the humanistic reading of geography as the theater of history, marks the French vision of Italy with the anachronism of looking at one thing while imagining another and anticipates the Orientalist view in which the visualized present is seen as the sign of an incipient absence.[20] The need to annex the Italian landscape into the French identity thus leads to the creation of a heterotopic space, transforming spatial discourse into a means for expressing French national interests. Textual authority provides the illusion of coherence, correcting the cognitive dissonance of visual recognition while deferring meaning in a game of infinite textual referencing.[21] The omnipresent emphasis of vision in the Renaissance travel narrative can thus be seen as an attempt to overcompensate for a lack of access to visual documentation. At the same time, literary representation problematizes the iconicity of spatial citation by appropriating personal experience into discourse centered on the traveler. More so, perhaps, than the exploration of *terrae incognitae*, travel through the "known" spaces of Italy forces a confrontation between words and reality.

SCOPE AND ORGANIZATION OF THIS STUDY

This book begins and ends with an analysis of two moments in Michel de Montaigne's journey through Italy as represented in his *Journal de voyage*. In both of these instances, we can see the complexity of Montaigne's thoughts regarding Italian spaces, his French homeland and fellow countrymen, and the intersection between public service and personal enjoyment of travel. As Montaigne enters Italy after a pleasant stay in what he calls "Germany," we see how his longings for "other" spaces are fueled by conflicting thoughts of his homeland and of his unannounced purpose in Rome. The Alpine passage also marks Montaigne's entry as an active voice in the discourse of the *Journal*, whose narrative was maintained by a personal secretary. Montaigne's vision of travel is indicative of his class and political status, while the voice of his servant, alert and trained in the art of mimetic and political representation, seconds and helps construct his master's self-image.

My next two chapters deal with two examples of secretarial writing of the French experience of the Italian Wars. André de la Vigne's *Voyage de Naples* and *La Ressource de la Chrestienté*, written at the opening of the Italian Wars, use topographical, allegorical, and poetic space to justify Charles VIII's plan to take Naples and glorify the king's actions while in Italy. La Vigne's techniques range from the allegorical use of sex to represent landscape to the bombastic use of the poetic arsenal of the *grands rhetoriqueurs* to replicate the spatial order of battle. La Vigne is also an early example of authorial self-assertion in the age of printing. His writing of the spaces of official discourse, moreover, contributes to and conditions his own assertion of self-identity. Sixty years later, Joachim Du Bellay subverts the secretary's voice in his bitterly sarcastic "vers secretaires."[22] Written as French aspirations to an ultramontane empire come to a close, Du Bellay's *Regrets* describes courtly intrigue, dissemblance, and moral debauchery, reflecting an evolution not only in the French engagement in Italy but also in how the author uses the Italian journey to stage a version of himself. By concentrating on the narrative elements of the *Regrets*, including the sometimes neglected *sonnets courtisans*, this chapter shows how the spatial narrative redirects Du Bellay's satirical Roman lament back onto the French political scene, transforming the *voyage de Rome* into a *voyage d'Italie* and positing Du Bellay as an experienced court servant.[23]

My fourth chapter examines the use of antiquarian discourse as a narrative device and spatial frame. The narrative use of topographical description displaces the universalizing pretense of descriptive geography and antiquarian discourse to the personalized context of the traveler's discourse, anticipating Montaigne's call for "des topographes qui nous fissent narration particuliere des endroits ou ils ont esté" (topographers who would give us a personal narrative of the places they have been).[24] François Rabelais plays with this idea in his dedication of Giovanni Bartolomeo Marliani's *Topography of Ancient Rome*, the first true guide of Rome's antiquities, as he praises the Milanese humanist for his "graphic view" from the hills of Rome. Marliani in fact offers a new approach to space modeled on Pausanias's *Periegesis*, or "walking around," of ancient

Greece. Marliani's ability to accompany his reader through space and time makes the *Topography* the first Roman guidebook to allow a truly spatial approach to visiting the city. He "narrates," as his translator Ercole Barbarasa points out, the past and present in a single spatial narrative. Guides such as these allow French travelers to use the symbolic backdrop of Italy as a space for explorative action, as is the case with Joseph Catin, who uses Benedetto di Falco's *Descrittione dei luoghi antichi di Napoli* to cast himself as an astute observer, accurate writer, and audacious explorer in the mold of the elder Pliny. Catin uses topographical spaces as rhetorical points, misplacing Vesuvius and Virgil's tomb in his creation of an aesthetic space that is topographical and metaphorically coherent. Jacques de Villamont, author of the most popular travel account of the late sixteenth century, uses space in a more openly textual and political way. Presenting his *Voyages* through a series of frames—political, theological, and personal—he reframes himself for the modified political scene at home. Villamont's publication of his private "treasure" allows him, like his contemporary Michel de Montaigne, to offer himself as a political and geographical middleman in Henri IV's attempts to regain control over war-torn France.

Chapter 5 examines Italian spaces from the point of view of the French traveler of the late sixteenth century making his way toward Rome. Using travelers' comments and itineraries, period maps and guides, and modern geographical and historical sources, it traces a prototypical French traveler from his crossing of the Alps through Savoy and into Piedmont and southward to Rome. Equally important to the antiquarian vision of Italy are the immense technological and cultural changes that transformed Italy's cities into wonders of innovation, commerce, and art. The building efforts of Italy's various leaders—the Medici in Florence, the Savoy in Turin, the papacy, Spanish viceroys of Naples, and so on—provide various, competing visions of the political, technological, and social use of urban space. French travelers' political melancholy for lost spaces thus joins with a desire to understand, record, and remember the structures of the modern Italian city. Their expanding itineraries illustrate a desire for spatial exploration, while the visions of specific places begin to coagulate around fixed ideas or themes—Milan's (lost) grandeur, the heterotopic space of Rome's wasteland transformed by the glory of the New Rome, or Venice's status as the longest-lived republic create visions of what one is supposed to see while on tour in Italy. The interaction between public and personal space can be seen in Montaigne's famous reticence in admitting why Florence should be considered, above other cities, as "la belle." In my analysis, this aesthetic reaction relates to Montaigne's insistent observation and memory of Franco-Florentine relations and his resistance to the new order of Medici hegemony over a mythologized space.

No destination can compare to the importance of Rome, a city Montaigne describes with characteristic ambiguity and reticence. Montaigne seems to resist not only Rome's call as he heads down the descending landscape of the Via Francigena and Via Cassia but also the debunking of an imaginary city, whose vision is at once fictional and a lived reality. Montaigne's philosophical considerations on Roman glory or vanity can be informed, moreover, by a topographical understanding of his stay in the Eternal City. This chapter maps Montaigne's movements as closely as possible, offering a detailed understanding of the material aspects of the Roman journey. After comparing Montaigne's arrival in Rome with those recounted in other French accounts following the same route, I describe Montaigne's neighborhood in *Le quattro porte* district of the Campomarzio. The extremely detailed maps, or rather portraits, drawn and printed around the time of Montaigne's visit allow an understanding of where Montaigne lived, giving (two) possible positions for the location of Montaigne's apartments "vis à vis de Santa Lucia della Tinta" (across from Santa Lucia della Tinta). The second half of this chapter provides an idea of Montaigne's daily activities. Using sources such as the *Roman Missal* of 1570 and Pompeo Ugonio's *Historia delle Stationi di Roma* (1588), I argue that Montaigne spent considerable time attending the ritual masses of the Lenten season while participating in a political, antiquarian tourism that gave him a deep understanding of Roman space. These experiences, the creation of an "arriere-boutique" in the Campomarzio combined with a political sociability centered around wanderings of Roman spaces, contributed to Montaigne's vision of Rome as a "sepulcher" and a second, if somewhat distant, home.

Chapter 1

MONTAIGNE INSIDE AND OUT

As Montaigne entered the Bavarian Alps on his way to Italy, his engagement with the landscape became more intense and detailed. The rolling hills and vineyards that had accompanied him from his home in the Périgord region of southern France and through western Switzerland, where he ambled along on horseback eating grapes, gave way to an implicitly transgressive contact with wild forests, soaring mountains, raging streams, and tight passes that became the focus of his *Journal de voyage*. A change occurs abruptly, just outside Munich, as the so-called troop, which included Montaigne's brother Bernard de Mattecoulon, Charles d'Estissac, another unnamed gentleman, and their servants, headed due south into the Duke of Bavaria's hunting forests, which were populated by flocks of red animals that ran around "comme moutons" (48) (like sheep [904]).[1] After spending the night in Königsdorf, "chetif, petit village" (ibid.) (wretched little village [ibid.]), they began to climb, following the course of the Loisach River to the banks of the Kochelsee and over the Kesselberg Pass into the "belly of the Alps":

> Le samedi bon matin, nous en partismes; et après avoir rencontré à nostre main droite la riviere Yser et un grand lac au pied des monts de Baviere, et avoir monté une petite montaigne d'une heure de chemin, au haut de laquelle il y a une inscription qui porte qu'un Duc de Baviere avoit fait percer le rochier il y a cent ans ou environ, nous nous engouffrasmes tout à fait dans le ventre des Alpes, par un chemin aisé et commode et amusément entretenu, le beau temps et serein nous y aidant fort. A la descente de cette petite montaigne, nous rencontrasmes un

très-beau lac d'une lieue de Gascongne de longueur et autant de largeur, tout entourné de très-hautes et inaccessibles montaignes; et suivant tousjours cette route, au bas des monts, rencontrions par fois de petites plaines de prairies très-plaisantes, où il y a des demeures, et vinsmes coucher d'une traite à Mitevol. (48–49)

(Early on Saturday morning we left here; and after coming upon the river Isar on our right and a large lake at the foot of the Bavarian mountains, and climbing for an hour's ride a little mountain on top of which there is an inscription saying that a Duke of Bavaria had had the rock cut through a hundred years ago or thereabouts, we plunged right into the heart of the Alps by an easy, comfortable, and delightfully well-kept road, the beautiful serene weather favoring us. On descending the little mountain we came upon a very beautiful lake, a Gascon league in length and as much in breadth, wholly surrounded by very high and inaccessible mountains; and still following this route at the foot of the mountains, from time to time we came upon several patches of very pleasant meadowland, on which there are houses; and without stopping we came on to sleep at Mittenwald.) (905)

The travelers' first encounter with the Alps shows the challenge of capturing this spatial experience in textual form, with the resultant description, apparently mimetic and well-orchestrated, veiling a subjective reading, or "creation" of space. More a composition than a sequence of events, the passage shows an aesthetic appreciation of the landscape, while the nobleman's appropriation of space becomes an exercise of reading, movement, and writing. The travelers enter into communication with the land. In the animated descriptions that follow, earth, sky, and water pass by and around the travelers, mixing in vivid images characteristic of a subjective interaction with the landscape.[2]

The secretary's reading transforms a pleasant climb into a liminal passage into the "Alps' belly," a symbolic penetration that moves them toward their destination and suggests their conquest and domination of space. Moving through a mountain that a Bavarian duke "avoit fait percer" (had pierced through) some one hundred years earlier, the travelers see and "meet" (rencontrer) personified lakes, mountains, and valleys that are described as humanized objects.[3] As they continue down the mountain, the pleasant fields and streams pass by homes and accompany them to bed in Mittenwald.

If the travelers seem to bury themselves in the Alps and spatial confusion, it is also this "nous" that rewrites or "creates" space.[4] The traveling subject ("nous") is repeated rather overinsistently, as if at risk of being overcome or in an attempt to control the emotional struggle of traveling through space. "*Nous* en partimes . . . *nous nous engouffrasmes* tout à fait . . . le beau serein *nous* aidant fort" (*We* left there . . . *we immersed ourselves* completely . . . the beautiful weather helping *us* a lot). Querlon's edition of the *Journal*, printed before the loss of the original manuscript, records a further example of this doubled subject, adding the apparent lapsus of "le beau serein nous **NOUS** y aidant fort" (the beautiful weather helping us to us [?] a lot).[5] This redoubling of the land-subject only makes sense in a reading that emphasizes the embedded subjectivity of a "culturally signified geography," which provides a communicative means of resistance and subjectivity through the representation of space.[6] The redundant, agrammatical repetition conflates what "we" receive with what "we" project onto the space around us. The Montaigne/secretary couple, in other words, reacts to landscape in a way that reflects modern sensibilities to the subjective nature of space as the traveler inserts his or her self into the landscape, "finding," "meeting," and "discovering" a space that at the same time "discovers itself" and moves "all around" in a pluri-dimensional, present, yet "inaccessible" experience.

At the same time, we should not forget that Montaigne and his companions are not on a metaphorical journey. Not only are they engaged in a literal expression of national power and individual social engagement but the spaces they inhabit—France, Italy, the Kesselberg Pass—are also real places whose shape and transformation by man allow the real communication of power over and through space. The analysis of these material aspects of travel allow for a better understanding of its imaginative aspects. The Kesselberg Road did not include a tunnel but was a significant work of engineering transportation, having connected the cities of Bavaria to the market and trading port of Venice.[7] Montaigne's citation of an "inscription" underlines the importance of the written word and of the assertion of nobility's control over space. The actual marble plaque, now housed in the Bavarian National Museum, is as much a piece of civic propaganda as the road itself was.[8] Montaigne probably had no idea what the sign actually said, given its cryptic abbreviation, in

German, in a heavy gothic script. His reading of the mountain's "piercing" by "some" duke is, in fact, a good interpretation for someone who repeatedly complains of the lack of adequate translators and his subjection to the interpretation of "un belistre de guide" (32) (some poor blockhead of a guide [892]). Montaigne deciphers the year, written in Latin, and recognizes the arms of the Dukes of Bavaria—two rampant lions in the upper left and bottom left corners, with diagonal lozenges in the remaining square—allowing him to impose his own textualized version of the pass.[9]

The spatial discourse that progressively invades Montaigne's *Journal* as he moves closer to Italy is thus worth examining closely. At stake is not only our interpretation of the interaction between Montaigne and his secretary (the secretary and *his* lord)[10] but also the dialogue between Montaigne's inner self and the spaces around him, whose textual manifestations embody issues of power, politics, and personality.[11] This chapter examines the confluence of thoughts and anxieties motivated by Montaigne's experience of space that contribute to his projection of emotion and desire onto the "entre-deux des Alpes" (in-between spaces of the Alps).[12] Beginning with his home, itself a space of conflict on a number of levels, it then examines the road leading from Périgord, through France, and into Montaigne's "Germany." During his journey from the Périgord to Paris and toward the Swiss border, Montaigne pays close attention to the spaces around him and their relationship to questions of French national and Montaigne's personal social identity. Another significant element of this spatial maelstrom is Montaigne's mythologized image of Italy, a space associated with his personal, cosmopolitan tendencies; the education he received from his father; and his idealistic view of the accomplishments of ancient Rome. These factors all come together as Montaigne draws nearer to Rome, approaching a new phase of his life and putting an end to his enchanted journey as the wanderer reenters the workplace of Franco-papal political engagement. Most importantly, they underline the importance of the performance of travel, as Montaigne heads to Rome on a diplomatic mission but continues to display the behavior of a leisured traveler.[13] This return to work, after crossing the utopian spaces of Switzerland, Germany, and Austria, thus gives rise to Montaigne's hidden issues, inciting and justifying his proclaimed "passion du mespris de son païs, qu'il avoit à haine et à contre coeur" (32) (passion, a certain scorn for his country, which he regarded with hatred and indignation [892]).

CONFLICTED SPACES

Montaigne's itinerary from the Dordogne to the Swiss border took him through some of the areas most hardly fought over in France's Wars of Religion. Passing from his home in the Périgord, through southern and central France, and then eastward through Champagne, Bar, and Lorraine, Montaigne would have witnessed firsthand the state of strife consuming his homeland. His route through the Huguenot-controlled south to the king's camp at Saint-Maur-des-Fossés, north of Paris, where Montaigne presented the monarch with a copy of the first edition of his *Essais*, was also as politically symbolic as it was physically dangerous. Montaigne's journey can nonetheless be seen as providing relief from the conflicted spaces of his homeland.

Montaigne's home—his château located on the border between the Guyenne and Périgord—embodies a number of the personal and political tensions implicit in the essayist's declared retreat from public life into "the lap of the learned virgins." Located on a promontory rising near the confluence of the Lidoire and Dordogne Rivers, this castle, with its yellowish stone, aging towers, and courtyard overlooking vineyards and forests, has come to represent a *locus idoneus* for literary contemplation—an ideal retreat for writing a book.[14] Montaigne himself had conceived of it in this way, commemorating his retreat there with a dedication to his dead friend Étienne de la Boétie and a ceremonious plaque underlining his need for freedom, peace, and leisure.[15] As George Hoffmann has pointed out, however, Montaigne's depiction of his home may have been more wishful thinking than reality.[16] Montaigne continued to engage in politics from a spot located on the borderlands between Protestant and royal forces, even as he constructed a vision of his home as a space separated from the work of the public. The essayist asserts a form of "performed" leisure characteristic of his conflicted social status as an emerging member of the *noblesse de robe*.[17]

Links between this form of leisure, the writing of the *Essais*, and Montaigne's psychological need to travel are also embedded in Montaigne's description of this idealized retreat.[18] While Montaigne describes his library as a place of rest, the images he uses imply a certain movement of the mind:

> Chez moy, je me destourne un peu plus souvent à ma librairie, d'où tout d'une main je commande à mon mesnage. Je suis sur

l'entrée et vois soubs moy mon jardin, ma basse court, et dans la pluspart des membres de ma maison. Là je feuillette à cette heure un livre, à cette heure un autre, sans ordre et sans dessein, à pièces descousues; tantost je resve, tantost j'enregistre et dicte, en me promenant, mes songes que voicy.

(C) Elle est au troisiesme estage d'une tour. Le premier, c'est ma chapelle, le second une chambre et sa suite, où je me couche souvent, pour estre seul. Au dessus, elle a une grande garderobe. C'estoit au temps passé le lieu plus inutile de ma maison. Je passe là et la plus part des jours de ma vie, et la plus part des heures du jour. Je n'y suis jamais la nuict. (828)

(When at home, I turn aside a little more often to my library, from which at one sweep I command a view of my household. I am over the entrance, and see below me my garden, my farmyard, my courtyard, and into most of the parts of my house. There I leaf through now one book, now another, without order and without plan, by disconnected fragments. One moment I muse, another moment I set down or dictate, walking back and forth, these fancies of mine that you see here.

[C] It is on the third floor of a tower; the first is my chapel, the second a bedroom and dressing room, where I often sleep in order to be alone. Above it is a great wardrobe. In the past it was the most useless place in my house. In my library I spend most of the days of my life, and most of the hours of the day. I am never there at night.) (628–29)

Montaigne removes himself "pour estre seul" (in order to be alone), "reculer de la presse" (retreat from the crowds), "estre a soy" (be with himself), and "se cacher" (hide). He constructs a space in which he can "se faire particulierement la cour" (court himself). This retreat and self-courtship, moreover, involves a constant agitation and inability to stand still. He "turns aside" ([se] destourne) from the duties of his estate, family life, and politics to a place where he can look to himself, wander through books, and write. This rambling method, as we shall see further on, not only characterizes the writing of the *Journal de voyage* and *Essais* but is also characteristic of his approach to space and travel. Montaigne seems to need spatial and intellectual dispersiveness to feel at home, to get lost in order to find himself. The most telling detail in this description, however, is his reference to the martial origins of his watchtower, emasculated as the "most useless part" of his dwelling.[19] Writing and travel thus provide way to escape from politics, providing a means for reclaiming a previously lost aspect of his martial identity.

By negotiating his own space, defined through letters, isolation, and the desire to move around, Montaigne sets himself apart from the struggling spaces and material reality of his isolated castle located at the epicenter of the Wars of Religion.[20] Set off from the country road connecting Castillon and Sainte-Foye-la-Grande, his home was both within the administrative influence of Catholic Bordeaux and surrounded by Huguenot-controlled Périgord, a fact that allowed Montaigne to serve as a go-between in the courts of the French and Navarrois kings. Pulled in both directions at once, Montaigne's home thus resembled many of the conflicted spaces that included the contested Protestant "places de sûreté," the cities of Cahors, Périgueux, and Montségur,[21] and even the embattled capital of Quercy, which remained under a precarious royal control.[22]

The itineraries leading from Bordeaux to Paris, as described in Charles Estienne's *Guide des chemins de France*, would have taken Montaigne through even more disputed territory. A departure from Bordeaux would have led through the center of the Protestant resistance, passing the strongholds of Cozes, Cognac, Taillebourg, and Pons.[23] The most direct route from his home to the Bordeaux-Paris road would have been to head north through Angoulême, a city rife with the memory of the Huguenot massacre of Catholic priests, and Poitiers, famous for the siege by the Protestant Admiral Colligny in 1569. A third, and more probable, route headed northeast, passing rapidly through Protestant-controlled Périgueux before connecting to the Cahors-Limoges road.[24] This safer route passed through royalist Limoges before reaching the royal fortresses of Guéret and Issoudun.[25] Read symbolically, Montaigne's movement from his conflicted homeland to the royal siege of La Fère thus maps out a route of political and ideological affiliation, taking him from Protestant territory toward King Henri III's efforts to retake essential French cities.[26]

The first surviving page of the *Journal* in fact places Montaigne at the siege of La Fère, where "Monsieur de Montaigne depescha M. de Mattecoulon en poste avec ledit escuyer, pour visiter ledit Comte, et trouva que ses playes n'estoient pas mortelles" (3) (Monsieur de Montaigne dispatched Monsieur de Mattecoulon posthaste with the said groom to visit the said count, and found that his wounds were not mortal. [867]) While not explicitly mentioned, Montaigne's presence at the battle underlines his royalist affiliation and political engagement as a knight of the Order of Saint Michel and Ordinary Gentleman of the King's Chamber. It was at nearby Saint-Maur-des-Fossés that Montaigne presented his book to the king and would have received instructions regarding his journey to Italy.

From La Fère, Montaigne headed toward the imperial territory of modern-day Switzerland, crossing a number of political borders characteristic of the fluid and changing affiliations of the emerging French nation-state.[27] After a brief stop in Mours,[28] he visited Beaumont-sur-Oise, a fortress and small town where Charles d'Estissac joined the eastward-bound troop. The travelers' itinerary then led through northern France and spaces marked by the nation's struggles for national unity. Passing to the north of the once-enemy Burgundy,[29] Montaigne crossed through Brie and Champagne, stopping in Meaux, Charly, Dormans, Épernay, and Châlons before entering Bar and Lorraine, separate duchies belonging to the House of Lorraine with a feudal allegiance divided between France and the empire.[30]

During this crossing, Montaigne pays particular attention to France's recent history, commenting on signs of the wars that had contributed to creating a sense of national identity. Reading historical anecdote as he had done his recently published *Essais*,[31] Montaigne begins a process of historical interrogation that will continue throughout his journey. The trip from Paris to the Swiss border was marked by reminders of the Wars of Religion and France's decades of struggle with the Habsburg empire. Meaux was "une petite ville, belle, assise sur la riviere de Marne" (3) (a small town, beautiful, sitting on the Marne River). "Ce lieu," he writes, "estoit autrefois très-bien fortifié de grandes et fortes murailles et tours; mais en nos secondes troubles Huguenots, parce la pluspart des habitans de ce lieu estoit de ce party, on fit demolir toutes ces fortifications" (ibid.) (This place was formerly very well fortified with great strong walls and towers; but in our second Huguenot troubles, because most of the inhabitants were of that party, all the fortifications were demolished [ibid.]). This subdued reference to the famous "surprise de Meaux," when Louis I de Bourbon-Condé had attempted to kidnap the French King Charles IX, illustrates the degree to which these recent events had become markers of the French political landscape, a reading continued in Vitry, known as Vitry-le-François and "Vitry-le-Brûlé" (the burned), and in the borderlands around Plombières situated "aux confins de la Lorraine et l'Allemaigne, dans une fondriere, entre plusieurs collines hautes et coupées qui le serrent de tous costés" (9) (on the confines of Lorraine and Germany in a deep valley between several high, steep hills which close it in on all sides [872]). In Épernay, Montaigne seems overcome by the death of France's great general Piero Strozzi, the Florentine condottiero and marshal of France, who had been buried without ceremony in the Épernay cathedral. Montaigne conducts his own investigation:

> Il s'enquist de sa sepulture, et trouva qu'il y estoit enterré sans aucune montre ny de pierre, ny d'armoirie, ny d'epitaphe, vis à vis du grand autel; et nous fut dit que la Reine l'avoit ainsi fait enterrer sans pompe et ceremonie, parce que c'estoit la volonté dudit Mareschal. (5)

> (He inquired about his sepulture and found that he was buried there, without any indication in the form of a stone, or coat of arms, or epitaph, opposite the high altar. And when we were told that the queen had had him buried thus without pomp or ceremony because that was the will of the said marshal.) (868)

Read in context with later visits to tombs and battlefields this burial conveys the soldierly idealism that will underscore much of Montaigne's historical reading of the Italian peninsula. A figure Montaigne describes as one of the "plus notables hommes que j'aye jugé par les apparences externes" (most notable men I have judged by outward appearances) in the art of war,[32] Strozzi's presence anticipates the historical and political connections between France and Italy and the tensions between Montaigne's romanticized view of a military past and his less enthusiastic vision of political courtship that will continue to occupy his journey through Italy.

ITALY OF THE MIND

Concetta Cavallini describes Montaigne's idea of Italy, before his departure in 1580, as a combination of literary and personal memory associated with the image of his father, who had fought in the Italian wars.³³ In the first edition of his *Essais*, Montaigne had cited a number of Italian authors that included Ariosto, Machiavelli, and Petrarch, whom the essayist had "riletto assai volta."³⁴ While these cultural references were in keeping with the fashion of his day, the memory of an Italy Montaigne had never seen was also related to his father's participation in the Italian wars and Montaigne's nostalgic view of everything related to his father.³⁵

Montaigne carries an image of Italy that is both anachronistic and literary in character. Having been raised to speak Latin for the first years of his life, his particular education—received thanks to "la prudence et l'affection d'un si bon pere" (*Essais* I, 26, 174) (the prudence and example of so good a father [129])—allows him to substitute his original homeland with the topographical locations of the Tiber and the capitol:

> Or j'ay esté nourry dés mon enfance avec ceux icy; j'ay eu connoissance des affaires de Romme, long temps avant que je l'aye eue de ceux de ma maison; je sçavois le Capitole et son plant avant que je sceusse le Louvre, et le Tibre avant la Seine. J'ay eu plus en teste les conditions et fortunes de Lucullus, Metellus et Scipion, que je n'ay d'aucuns hommes des nostres. (III, 9, 996)

> (Now, I have been brought up from childhood with these dead. I was familiar with the affairs of Rome long before I was with those of my own house. I knew the Capitol and its location before I knew the Louvre, and the Tiber before the Seine. I have the abilities and fortunes of Lucullus, Metellus, and Scipio more in my head than those of any of our men.) (762)

These dead people are one of the main reasons, as we shall see, for Montaigne's contentious relationship with the real Rome as he moves through Italy, coming closer to a city where he would seek out and claim an honorary citizenship. Montaigne's purely written vision of Rome will be supplemented, moreover, by further reading by authors who attempt to reconstruct ancient Rome, inciting a sense of inner conflict that leads to abstraction and contemplation.³⁶

The association between these readings and his father, moreover, mixes with a sentiment of a moral perfection whose achievements modernity can never live up to:

Feu mon pere, ayant fait toutes les recherches qu'homme peut faire, parmy les gens sçavans et d'entendement, d'une forme d'institution exquise, fut advisé de cet inconvenient qui estoit en usage; et luy disoit-on que cette longueur que nous mettions à apprendre les langues, qui ne leur coustoient rien est la seule cause pourquoy nous ne pouvions arriver à la grandeur d'ame et de cognoissance des anciens Grecs et Romains. Je ne croy pas que ce en soit la seule cause. Tant y a que l'expedient que mon pere y trouva, ce fut que, en nourrice et avant le premier desnouement de ma langue, il me donna en charge à un Allemand, qui depuis est mort fameux médecin en France, du tout ignorant de nostre langue, et tresbien versé en la Latine. (173)

(My late father, having made all the inquiries a man can make, among men of learning and understanding, about a superlative system of education, became aware of the drawbacks that were prevalent; and he was told that the long time we put into learning languages which cost the ancient Greeks and Romans nothing was the only reason we could not attain their greatness in soul and in knowledge. I do not think that is the only reason. At all events, the expedient my father hit upon was this, that while I was nursing and before the first loosening of my tongue, he put me in the care of a German, who has since died a famous doctor in France, wholly ignorant of our language and very well versed in Latin.) (128)

Montaigne's own imperfection is proof of the disconnect between linguistic proficiency and "grandeur d'ame." Rome thus becomes a locus of anxiety, waiting at the end of his itinerary, charged with the myths and legends of a childhood he seems loath to debunk.

THE NONLINEAR VOYAGE

These tensions between imagination and reality, desire and regret, come to a head during Montaigne's crossing of the political and cultural patchwork of the Alps. His passage through independent cantons of the Swiss Republic, cities and provinces subject to the Habsburg Empire, and subsidiaries of the Duke of Austria challenge his ability to read political and cultural space, causing a sense of disorientation characteristic of borderland spaces as described by Homi Bhabha, inciting "an exploratory, restless movement caught so well in the French rendition of the words *au-delà*—here and there, on all side, *fort/da*, hither and thither, back and forth."[37] This interstitial perspective relates, moreover, to both Montaigne's personal restlessness and his acute understanding of the contradictions and conflicts implicit in an emerging discourse of politics and national identity, inciting him to bring together these contradictory impulses in conclusions reminiscent of his famous essay *On Cannibals*.[38]

As Montaigne continues over the Alps, the Alpine scenery serves as a prelude to discourse, provoking comments on how pleasant and beautiful the scenery is, how the mountains move in dizzying succession, and how plots of land and castles seem to float overhead. Montaigne imagines flattening the land out like a blanket in an attempt to comprehend its complex morphology and feels the need as he moves closer to the end of Germany to sum up and rationalize the meaning of his trip, writing to his friend, the exiled Huguenot François Hotman, whom he had met in Basel:

> De ce lieu (Bolzano) M. de Montaigne escrivit à François Hottoman, qu'il avoit veu à Basle, qu'il avoit pris si grand plaisir à la visitation d'Allemaigne, qu'il l'abandonnoit à grand regret, quoy que ce fust en Italie qu'il alloit [. . .] Tout le demeurant luy sembloit plein de commodité et de courtoisie, et surtout de justice et seureté. (57–58)

> (From this place [Bolzano] Monsieur de Montaigne wrote to François Hotman, whom he had seen at Basel, that he had taken such great pleasure in visiting Germany that he left it with great regret, although it was Italy he was going to . . . All the rest seemed to him full of comfort and courtesy, and especially of justice and security.) (912)

The philosopher's regret at abandoning Germany lends a strong, subconscious power to the key moment in his journey. Always a glutton for "nouveauté," Montaigne had enjoyed the food, company, and novelty of the Germanic nations he had visited. More particularly, he had explored the political spaces of the Alpine communities, where he sensed a concept of "justice and security" that was lacking in war-torn France. On a subconscious level, then, his unexpected, paradoxical ("though it was Italy he was going to") resistance to leaving what he calls "l'entre-deux des Alpes" (55) (this in-between space of the Alps [translation mine]) relates to more pressing philosophical and personal concerns regarding the imaginary side of his seventeen-month journey.[39] Germany—where, by pure chance (or some psychosomatic miracle) Montaigne suffers not one attack of his dreaded renal "colick"—becomes the subject of a utopic elaboration that conceals anxiety over both his own sickness and the "troubles" affecting the nation he had left behind. The Brenner Pass, the highest geographical point on a journey covering some five thousand kilometers, not only marks Montaigne's long-awaited entry into Italian linguistic and cultural space but also signals his return to reality, to the work of Franco-Italian politics and cohabitation with his dread disease and ideas of having gone "too far down this road" toward an unfortunate ending.[40]

Montaigne's attempts to sum up his German experience thus underline an important aspect of how the travel narrative works. Despite the sequential format of the *voyage*, composed of linear lists of cities, provinces, rivers, border crossings, and experiences, the narrative of space eschews linear representation. Backtracking and summarizing, conflating and comparing, the spatialized text anticipates and moves inside and out in a circular loop between exterior stimuli and subjective internalization.[41] Recording the here and now of travel incorporates and externalizes flights of fancy, movements of the "cheval débridé" of the mind, in a reading of symbolic space that combines geographical reality with a personal elaboration of the mind.

ALPINE PASSAGES

The enunciative situation of Montaigne's *Journal, composed in collaboration with an unidentified secretary*, further complicates and explains the ways in which landscape is produced through the interaction between the Renaissance subject's inner and outer selves. François Rigolot identifies a complex dialogue between not just Montaigne and his secretary but also Montaigne the writer and Montaigne the reader of his own work.[42] The secretary often appears to write the *Journal* on his own, while at other times his voice clearly overlaps that of his master in a complex mixing of the *nous* of the troop, the *je* of narration, and the *il* of Monsieur de Montaigne.[43] The subjective power of the landscape also plays an important role in the creation of this triangular dialogue, as Montaigne, initially a distant, third-person entity, steps out of the travel narrative and into the discourse of constructing space.[44]

As the travelers make their way across the Inn valley and over the Brenner Pass, Montaigne's personality emerges in reaction to the changing landscape as a series of exclamations, comments, and observations inspired by the changing landscape lead to an assessment of his time in Germany and a more general consideration of cultural difference. The secretary's skill at representing these interventions makes the separation of these two voices almost impossible. At the same time, the existence of both voices is important because, while Montaigne expresses himself, his secretary actively recreates the topographical context from and through which his lord is heard. The secretary becomes a supportive voice whose observational sympathy allows the figure of "M. de Montaigne" to emerge.

The first sign of Montaigne's voice occurs outside Seefeld, between Munich and Innsbruck, where the slopes of the Inn valley offer a marvelous example of Alpine variety:

> De là nous trouvasmes un vallon d'une grande longueur, au travers duquel passe la riviere d'Inn, qui va se rendre à Vienne dans le Danube. [. . .] Ce vallon *sembloit à M. de Montaigne* representer le plus agreable paysage qu'il eust jamais veu; tantost se reserrant, les montaignes venant à se presser, et puis s'eslargissant asteure de nostre costé, qui estions à main gauche de la riviere, et gaignant du pays à cultiver et à labourer dans la pente mesme des monts qui n'estoient pas si droits, tantost de l'autre part, et puis descouvrant des plaines à deux ou trois estages l'une sur l'autre, et tout plein de belles maisons de gentilshommes et des eglises; et tout cela enfermé et emmuré de tous costés de monts d'une hauteur infinie. (50, emphasis mine)

> (Beyond we found a valley of great length, through which passes the river Inn, which flows into the Danube at Vienna. . . . This valley seemed to Monsieur de Montaigne to present the most agreeable landscape he had ever seen: now contracting as the mountains pressed close, then widening, now on the side we were on, which was the left side of the river, and creating new land for plowing and cultivating in the very slopes of the less steep

mountains; now on the other side; and then revealing plains on two or three levels, one above the other; and all full of beautiful noblemen's houses and of churches; and all this closed and walled in on all sides by mountains of measureless height.) (906–7)

This seemingly casual observation goes further than earlier passages in the *Journal* where Montaigne's activities are the subject of a third-person narrative. Here it is less Montaigne's movements and activities than his thoughts and engagement with the landscape that become the subject of the secretary's mediation. The discovery of the valley is once again communal (*nous trouvasmes*), but the aesthetic judgment of the scene belongs to Montaigne. Even more interesting is how space itself informs, justifies, and mixes with other forms of discourse. The secretary follows his quotation of Montaigne with an accurate description of the landscape that inspired his master's thoughts, attaching it as if it were an addendum to his lord's thoughts and actions. The secretary confirms and explains, making Montaigne's observation more effective and credible, tracking the land and subject that move along *se resserrant (contracting)*, *s'eslargissant (widening)*, *gaignant du pays (creating new land)*, and *decouvrant (revealing)*, creating a "representation" of a contact with the "paysage."

Leaving Innsbruck, the travelers again find a spectacular view:

A main gauche nous avions la veue de plusieurs autres montaignes, qui, pour avoir l'inclination plus étendue et plus molle, sont remplies de villages, d'eglises, et la pluspart cultivées jusques à la cime, tres-plaisantes à voir pour la diversité et variété des sites (53).

(On our left hand we had a view of several other mountains, which, having a more extended and gentler incline, are covered with villages and churches, and for the most part cultivated right to the top, very pleasant to see for the diversity and variety of sites.) (908)

The mountains on their right are uninhabited and "a little more savage" as they cross many streams "ayant les cours divers" (with various courses) and pass several large towns and villages, castles, and the homes of noblemen. Montaigne gleams with contentment at the "diversité des objets qui se presentoient" (ibid.) (diversity of objects to be seen [ibid.]). They see several beautiful inns, whose location the secretary records as a matter of discipline (and perhaps because he was hungry), as Montaigne forces the troop onward to make a near record of fifty-four kilometers (seven leagues) in a ten-hour leg that leads over the Brenner Pass. Arriving in Sterzing, Montaigne announces his satisfaction at his accomplishment, boasting that "c'estoit là l'une de ses traites" (54) (that was the distance he liked to cover in a day [translation mine]).[45] The secretary again follows Montaigne's declaration with comments on his master's habits, confirming how he prefers to skip lunch and feed the horses early in the morning so as to make good time: the secretary explains and verifies Montaigne's behavior to Montaigne.

In the secretary's depiction, Montaigne comes off as the intellectual and moral leader of his "troop," pushing the others to make good time and enjoy the countryside.[46] Preferring the glory of masculine adventure to the comfort of a noon meal, he sets an example for the others in his passion for the road. It is only the next day that we learn of the contrast between Montaigne's outward appearance and what is going on inside him:

> M. de Montaigne eut cette nuit la colique deux ou trois heures, bien serré, à ce qu'il dit le lendemain; et ce lendemain, à son lever, fit une pierre de moyenne grosseur, qui se brisa aisement. Elle estoit jaunastre par le dehors, et brisée au dedans plus blanchastre. Il s'estoit morfondu le jour auparavant et se trouvoit mal. Il n'avoit eu la colicque depuis celles de Plommieres. (54)

> (Monsieur de Montaigne had the colic this night for two or three hours and was very hard pressed, from what he said in the morning; and in the morning on rising he passed a stone of medium size, which broke easily. It was yellowish on the outside, and, when broken, more whitish on the inside. He had caught a cold the day before and felt bad. He had not had an attack of the colic since the one at Plombières.) (909)

Montaigne's final push occurs while he is coming down with a cold and perhaps even feels another attack of his dread disease, the first he had felt since before entering Germany.

The correspondence between Montaigne's inner and outer experiences does not end there. As the essayist begins to digest the fact that this important section of his journey is coming to an end, the expression of his observations and moods begins to take on a sense of urgency. The secretary's description of the land also implicitly recalls the characteristics of Montaigne's disease in a strange coincidence between geography and suffering as breaking stones and raging waters accompany the travelers through narrow passages, squeezing them in with a violence the secretary tracks in detail:

> Au partir de là, le chemin *nous serra* un peu, et aucuns rochiers *nous pressoient* de façon que, le chemin se trouvant *estroit pour nous* et la rivière ensemble, nous estions en dangier de *nous choquer* si on n'avoit mis entre elle et les passans une barriere de muraille, qui dure en divers endroits plus d'une lieu d'Allemaigne (56).

> (As we left there the road *narrowed on us* a bit and some *rocks pressed in on us*, so that, since the defile was *narrow for both us* and the river together, we would have been in danger of *colliding*, if they had not placed between it and the travelers a wall as a barrier, which in various places extends for more than a German league.) (911)

Firs are "arrachés de leur pied" (57) (torn up from their footing [ibid.]) and carry small mountains along with them. Savage crags "touch" the travelers and obstruct their path. Raging waters break huge rocks—"les uns massifs, les autres crevassés et entrerompus" (ibid.) (some massive, others split and broken up [ibid.])—into pieces of "a strange size." The secretary worries how dangerous it would be to pass there during times of "tourmente." Montaigne's imagination shifts, however, to the vistas above, where he can make out lands "plus hautes cultivées et logées" and "learns" of great fertile plains, where they "discover" a castle perched on a high peak and are told of a baron living "up there" surrounded by beautiful hunting grounds, "toutes ces montagnes" (all these mountains), and "une bordure des Alpes" (57) (a top fringe of Alps [911]). Rather than to a succession of pleasant hills and lakes, the travelers' view is drawn in two directions at once: on the one hand, savage, almost frightening scenes dominated by the themes of breaking stones and water and, on the other, glimpses of the civilization and order of a quickly fading "Germany."

Montaigne is further reminded of this transition in the towns of Brixen/Bressanone and Colman/Colma, where the secretary pens this vivid description of German order and variety:

> Sa pleine n'est guiere large; mais les montaignes d'autour, mesmes sur nostre main gauche, s'estendent si mollement qu'elles se laissent testonner et peigner jusques aux oreilles. Tout se voit rempli de clochiers et de villages bien haut dans la montagne, et près de la ville, plusieurs belles maisons très-plaisamment basties et assises. (55)

> (The surrounding plain is not very wide; but the mountains round about, especially on our left hand, stretch out so gently that they allow themselves to be combed and primped right up to the ears. Everything seems to be filled with steeples and villages well up into the mountainside, and near the town are many beautiful houses very pleasantly built and situated.) (910)

Montaigne's anthropomorphic vision of the landscape captures his affection for his German experience, the last glimpses of which call him to reflect on the meaning of his trip. His affectionate descriptions encapsulate a sense of longing and loss.

Rather than confirm the writings of Pliny, Ptolemy, or even Sebastian Münster, moreover, Montaigne challenges the status quo and engages the larger issues of human civilization and barbarism.[47] Launching into a diatribe against bigotry and chauvinism, his praise of the Alps is also a castigation of the discourse of "autruy":

> M. de Montaigne disoit: "Qu'il s'estoit toute sa vie mefié du jugement d'autruy sur le discours des commodités des pays estrangiers, chacun ne sçachant gouster que selon l'ordonnance de sa coustume et de l'usage de son village, et avoit fait fort peu d'estat des avertissemens que les voyageurs luy donnoient; mais en ce lieu, il s'esmerveilloit encore plus de leur bestise, ayant, et notamment en ce voyage, ouï dire que l'entredeux des Alpes en cet endroit estoit plein de difficultés, les moeurs des hommes estranges, chemins inaccessibles, logis sauvages, l'air insupportable. Quant à l'air, il remercioit Dieu de l'avoir trouvé si doux,

car il inclinoit plutost sur trop de chaud que de froid; et en tout ce voyage, jusques lors, n'avions eu que trois jours de froid, et de pluie environ une heure, mais que du demeurant s'il avoit à proumener sa fille, qui n'a que huict ans, il l'aimeroit autant en ce chemin qu'en une allée de son jardin, et quant aus logis, il ne vit jamais contrée où ils fussent si drus semés et si beaux, ayant tousjours logé dans belles villes fournies de vivres, de vins, et à meilleure raison qu'ailleurs" (55–56)

(Monsieur de Montaigne said that all his life he had distrusted other people's judgment on the matter of the conveniences of foreign countries, since every man's taste is governed by the ordering of his habit and the usage of his village; and he had taken very little account of the information that travelers gave him; but in this spot he wondered even more at their stupidity, for he had heard, and especially on this trip, that the passes of the Alps of this region were full of difficulties, the manners of the people uncouth, roads inaccessible, lodgings primitive, the air insufferable. As for the air, he thanked God that he had found it so mild, all this trip up to that time we had had only three days of cold and about an hour of rain. But that for the rest, if he had to take his daughter, who is only eight, for a walk, he would as soon do so on this road as on any path in his garden. And as for the inns, he had never seen a country where they were so plentifully distributed and so handsome, for he had always lodged in handsome towns well furnished with victuals and wine, and more reasonably than elsewhere.) (910)

Montaigne's reproach of preconceived notions emerges as a reaction to the beauty and hospitality of the landscape around a domesticated "Brixe." Topography sheds light on the fallacy of the difficulties and strangeness of "l'entredeux des Alpes," leading him to make a more general reproval of stereotypes used to depict the savagery of the other. Comparing the landscape to a gentle giant allowing itself to be "combed and primped" and the safety of its "savageness" to the walkway in his garden, he also seems to suggest the false sense of security people felt in their homes and the real insecurity in which he had in fact left his daughter during his journey to Italy.

Montaigne's enthusiastic defense of German civilization is as paradoxical as his first negative reactions to Italy, standing the usual French desire for Italy and scorn for Germany on its head. Bolzano is the first town he criticizes since Königsdorf. Tellingly, this negative assessment also reminds him of home, as he compares Bolzano to Libourne, the medium-sized town nearest his home in Guyenne. Montaigne also notes it as "assez mal plaisante au prix des autres d'Allemaigne" (57) (rather unattractive compared with others in Germany [911]). It is here that Montaigne emotes and interjects emphatically into his secretary's narrative: "M. de Montaigne s'ecria 'qu'il connoissoit bien qu'il commançoit à quiter l'Allemaigne': les rues plus estroites, et point de belle place publicque" (Querlon edition, I, 183) (Monsieur de Montaigne exclaimed that he clearly recognized that he was beginning to leave Germany: the streets narrower, and no handsome public square [911]).

As strange as it may seem to modern editors, Meusnier de Querlon's placement of the colon announcing the secretary's explanation of Montaigne's words replicates the cooperation we have seen between the servant and his master. Read literally, it shows Montaigne inviting his secretary to complete his thoughts, illustrating the blurriness of the boundaries between these two authors. In a remarkable symbiosis of authorial intent, Montaigne expects his secretary to stage his own utterances.

STAGING MONTAIGNE

Understanding the role of the secretary in the composition of the *Journal* thus goes to the heart of what Montaigne's journey was all about. For if Montaigne's entrance into Italy shows signs of self-fashioning and performative behavior, the theatricalization of travel depends on the professional secretary's ability to assist in painting this spectacle onto the spatial backdrop of the voyage. Other questions, of course, arise out of this form of cooperation. How, for example, with such an intermediary, can psychological readings of Montaigne's comments be read, if they are mediated through this other voice? To what degree, moreover, is the inner dialogue with space a truly existential experience, and to what extent is it a performance? The passages leading up to Montaigne's entry into Italy establish a compositional and emotional collusion between Montaigne and his servant that suggests an implicit theatricalization of behavior characteristic of the sixteenth-century gentleman.[48] The secretary writes in a way that facilitates this self-representation. Not just the *Journal* but Montaigne's actions as represented in the *Journal*, in other words, portray Montaigne's sense of belonging to a specific social class. By emphasizing his intellectual approach to travel and possession of a certain political acumen and interest, they tacitly represent or reperform Montaigne's performed behavior. The secretary's narrative and description may depict Montaigne's actual behavior, but they do so in a way that participates in Montaigne's spatial discourse and contributes to its enunciation.[49] Viewed in this context, the secretary's famous description of Montaigne's "humeur vagabonde" (vagabond humor)[50] seems less an isolated flash of brilliance than a rhetorical conclusion to the passages that preceded it. The secretary's depiction of Montaigne *en voyage*—proof, according to Querlon, that Montaigne traveled as he wrote[51]—is the culmination of thirty days of observation and increasingly symbiotic composition, a period in which Montaigne slowly but surely acquired a psychological space within the discourse of his servant.

This arrival into Italy thus marks a symbolic passage that is at once professional and personal, a celebratory arrival in which Montaigne, as is his custom, takes the countercultural stance of wanting to go somewhere else:

> Je croy à la vérité que, s'il eust esté seul avec les siens, il fust allé plutost à Cracovie ou vers la Grece par terre, que de prendre le tour vers l'Italie; mais le plaisir qu'il prenoit à visiter des pays incognus, lequel il trouvoit si doux que d'en oublier la foiblesse de son aage et de sa santé, il ne le pouvoit imprimer à nul de la troupe, chacun ne demandant que la retraite. Là où il avoit accoustumé de dire qu'après avoir passé une nuit inquiete, quand au matin il venoit à se souvenir qu'il avoit à voir ou une ville ou une nouvelle contrée, il se levoit avec desir et allegresse. Je ne le vis jamais moins las ni moins se plaignant de ses douleurs, ayant l'esprit, et par chemin et en logis, si tendu à ce qu'il rencontroit et recherchant toutes occasions d'entretenir les estrangiers, que je croy que cela amusoit son mal.
>
> Quand on se plaignoit à luy de ce qu'il conduisoit souvent la troupe par chemins divers et contrées, revenant souvent bien près d'où il estoit parti (ce qu'il faisoit ou recevant l'avertissement

de quelque chose digne de voir, ou changeant d'avis selon les occasions), il respondoit qu'il n'alloit, quant à luy, en nul lieu que là où il se trouvoit, et qu'il ne pouvoit faillir di tordre sa voye, n'ayant nul project que de se proumener par des lieux incognus; et pourveu qu'on ne le vist pas retomber sur mesme voie et revoir deux fois mesme lieu, qu'il ne faisoit nulle faute à son dessein. Et quant à Rome, que les autres visoient, il la désiroit d'autant moins voir que les autres lieux, qu'elle estoit connue d'un chacun et qu'il n'avoit laquais qui ne leur peust dire nouvelles de Florence et de Ferrare. (61)

(I truly believe that if Monsieur de Montaigne had been alone with his own attendants he would rather have gone to Cracow or toward Greece by land than to make the turn toward Italy; but the pleasure he took in visiting unknown countries, which he found so sweet as to make him forget the weakness of his age and of his health, he could not impress on any of his party, and everyone asked only to return home. Whereas he was accustomed to say that after spending a restless night, he would get up with desire and alacrity in the morning when he remembered that he had a new town or region to see. I never saw him less tired or complaining less of his pains; for his mind was so intent on what he encountered, both on the road and at his lodgings, and he was eager on all occasions to talk to strangers, that I think this took his mind off his ailment.

If someone complained to him that he often led his party, by various roads and regions, back very close to where he had started [which he was likely to do, either because he had been told about something worth seeing, or because he had changed his mind according to the occasions], he would answer that as for him, he was not going anywhere except where he happened to be, and that he could not miss or go off his path, since he had no plan but to travel in unknown places; and that provided he did not fall back upon the same route or see the same place twice, he was not failing to carry out his plan. And as for Rome, which was the goal of the others, he desired less to see it than the other places, since it was known to every man, and there was not a lackey who could not tell them news of Florence or Ferrara.) (915)

Montaigne abandons himself to the pleasures of travel, wandering along unknown paths, exploring the whims of his avid curiosity. We see his "tense spirit" following "various paths and lands" as the "commerce" of "rubbing his brain against those of others" is replaced by the diversionary pleasure of wandering.[52] The alterity of place lures him along, causing him to dream of universes that lie beyond, of Krakow "or" Greece and other unknown places.[53] Montaigne the dreamer, always suspicious of group mentalities, resists the normative behavior of his "troop" and longs to go far away, "alone."

One question we might ask, however, is the degree to which Montaigne's presentation is part of a performance. Just as important as the veracity of his travel method is the presented image of Montaigne traveling. Traces of Montaigne within the secretary's discourse raise suspicion, not to the veracity of the portrait, but to the degree the secretary's representation creates an image of Montaigne for the pleasure of his lord. The well-constructed description, with its measured periods and colorful verbs, seems almost too precise, too similar in style to the *Essays*, creating a favorable version of "Monsieur de Montaigne." Montaigne's wanderlust and his viatic insouciance or *sprezzatura* of the road are both true and constructed. Perhaps Montaigne does truly desire to light out to distant climes. At the same time, it is important that, in this crucial moment, when he finally arrives in the region of his expressed geographical desire, his emotion is not one of having arrived at a longed-for destination but of a continued, insatiable desire for space. Montaigne, the constantly "in between" participant in the "commerces" of life, politics, and society, feels more at home in the liminal region of Switzerland than in either France or Italy.

In this period of endless war and growing bureaucracy, the complexity of the underlying sociopolitical systems that inform such activities as the journey to Italy, the aesthetic appreciation of antiquities and newly constructed cityscapes is at once an experienced and staged performance. The secretary's official duties meld with the private experience of the "gentilhomme ordinaire de la chambre du roy," placing pressure on the concepts of individual identity and group experience. At the same time, the secretary's representation of *his* lord may be read as an extension of identity itself contributing to the creation of the individual through the prism of experienced space, as the following chapters will explore.

Chapter 2

TEXTUALITY, SEXUALITY, AND POLITICAL GEOGRAPHY

André de la Vigne and the French Conquest of Naples

In his influential study of the fabric of Montaigne's *Essais*, Robert Cottrell analyzes the relationship between sexual desire and the production and consumption of text.[1] The same dynamics that signal a linking of opposites implicit in Montaigne's use of the word *accouplage* are discernible in the discourse of textual production.[2] Reading, likewise, extends this erotic commerce through technology, transferring the author's desire in altered form to a reader who then enters in direct experience of text.[3] Cottrell's idea is helpful in understanding how Italy, a space in which French kings and noblemen exercised their profession as men at arms for a period of more than sixty years, became a locus of written desire in the French imagination, a textualized space essential to the French identity due to its intermediate and oppositional nature.

This chapter interprets the writings of an author whose work lies at the margins of the Middle Ages and Renaissance and at the intersection between historiography and literary creation. André de La Vigne, secretary and court poet, organizer and poetic translator of royal and civic spectacles, made his fame writing for King Charles VIII, the young monarch whose "entreprise de Naples" opened the French imagination to the new culture and technology of the Italian Renaissance and the French nation to a period of military engagement that would last more than sixty years. In his works written for King Charles, published around 1500 in a collection titled *Le Vergier d'honneur*, La Vigne applies the literary practices of the *grands rhétoriqueurs* to justify and recount an invasion. In the first of these, titled *La Ressource de la Chrestienté*, written before the 1494 expedition, La Vigne eroticizes the topography of conquest as a feminized object of sexual desire. In the *Voyage de Naples*, written during and after the war, La Vigne illustrates the king's prowess in the conquest of territory. In both cases, the aesthetic use of topographical space, used in a political argumentation for the honor, justice, and efficacy of Charles's controversial, and ultimately futile, *entreprise*, shows how writing, desire, and the emerging image of the French nation anticipate and prepare for later emanations of the French experience in Italy. The secretary and the travel narrative, both instruments of the emerging French state, use the discourse of spatial seduction to second collective impulses of an international scale.

THE SPATIAL ARGUMENT FOR WAR: ANDRÉ DE LA VIGNE'S
RESSOURCE DE LA CHRESTIENTÉ

In 1494, as Charles VIII held court in Lyon in preparation for his Italian "entreprise," La Vigne was one of a number of aspiring court poets who came forth, eager to gain recognition and future employment. His work was sure to impress. Alternating between a phantasmagorical prose and verse forms that showed off all the tricks of a would-be *rhétoriqueur*, La Vigne describes "la plus estrange vision du monde" (the strangest vision in the world).[4] He recounts falling asleep after a night spent worrying over something he does not want to tell us and envisioning, in the guise of the allegorical "Acteur," awaking amid a horrifying landscape covered with "ronces, espines, chardons, genests et jonc-marins" (brambles, thorns, thistle, juniper and sea thrifts) that grow wildly—"sans art et sans mesure" (without art or proportion). A dark forest bodes menacingly on one side; on the other, dirt-filled waters of a "grant, enorme, terrible et accreuse riviere" (large, immense, terrible, gouged-out river) crash against frightful rocks. He searches desperately for a way out and sees, far in the distance, a lady of "refulgent arroy" (splendid appearance) but tattered and reduced to a state of desolation: "Moitié de sa robe [...] luy avoient osté, decipé, gasté, desrompu et emporté [...] que la peau ou du mains la chemise lui paroissoient quasi de toutes parts" (They had ripped off, torn up, ruined, broken, and removed half her dress so that her skin, or at least her underclothes, were showing all over). As tears well up from the "divine essence" of her "delectable" and "loveable" face, she gives forth a piteous lament and falls amid tears, "pale, deffaicte, morte, morne, froide, roide, fade et mate, triste, desconfortee, persuadee, foulee, troublee et de tous points vilipendee" (pale, defeated, dead, gloomy, cold, stiff, dull and maddened, sad, inconsolable, crushed, troubled and reviled). The name of this forlorn damsel, as we find out in her lengthy soliloquy that follows, is *Dame Chrestienté*, the allegorical embodiment of Christianity, who has come to plead her case for waging war against the "mametus heretiques" (heretical Muslims).

André de la Vigne uses medieval allegory to justify Charles VIII's invasion of Italy, or "Entreprise de Naples,"[5] presenting the moral and legal reasons for his claim to the Neapolitan throne,[6] and addressing the controversy of his precipitous march to war.[7] The work also has a diplomatic and propagandistic role, working as a message to Italian diplomats who would have heard the work read at Charles' court.[8] Its ambiguous allegorical language also asserts the importance of French cultural, historical, and literary prerogatives.[9] Staging a debate between allegorical figures that represent the various forces in the French political system, as Alain Chartier had done in his *Quadrilogue invectif*, La Vigne presents arguments for and against the war.[10] More importantly, he stages a French vision of power that draws on martial, literary, and historical traditions emphasizing the Crown's role as *tres-Chrestien*, leader of *Chrestienté*.

At first view, the allegorical debate of the *Ressource de la Chrestienté* is quite simple. *Dame Chrestienté* enters in her forlorn state to lament how Christians have abandoned her. She bemoans the distant day when the "loy judaique retrograde et matte" (A ii) (outdated and somber Judaic Law) had been displaced by Christianity, whose followers have now allowed her to be captured by a hostile, barbaric people:

> Depuis ce temps je suis tumbee es mains
> D'un tas de turcs et de chiens inhumains
> Qui m'ont de maulx cent milliers faict souffrir
> Et qui pis vault les crestiens humains
> D'autre coste n'en font gueres mains (i.e. moins)

(Since this time I have fallen in the hands of a bunch of Turks and inhuman dogs that have made me suffer a hundred thousand ills, and what is worse, the human Christians have done no less.)

Christian apathy and neglect have allowed "dogs" to rule the earth, leaving Chrestienté a pale, violated image of her former self. Acteur then sets the scene for other allegorical speeches, accompanying Dame Chrestienté over the Alps to a resplendent *"vergier"* (garden) located in the "clymat francigene" (French clime) where Dame Noblesse (Lady Nobility) holds court surrounded by aromatic plants and allegorical symbols representing the French court. Dame Noblesse promises to help find knights "pour leurs paÿs et contrees conquerre" (A v) (to conquer their lands and countries) and advises Chrestienté to seek the counsel of Majesté Royalle (Royal Majesty). Dame Chrestienté addresses a third moving speech to Majesté Royalle, promising the reward of eternal bliss and fame to all "good subjects" who come to her aid. Majesté Royalle and Prince are moved to ask Dame Noblesse's opinion but are cut off by the dissenting voice of Je ne sçay qui ("I don't know who"), who praises peace, warns of the costs and risks of war, and advises caution, an opinion quickly dismissed by the voice of Bon Conseil (Good Advice) and the heckling of the court.

While this lightly veiled allegory seems straightforward enough, La Vigne uses several rhetorical and logical distortions that relate to the issues of travel, national identity, military invasion, and the representation of geographical and political space. The most apparent of these is the argument proposed in favor of a crusade. Even as King Charles prepares to invade the Christian Kingdom of Naples, La Vigne argues for a holy war against Muslims. Je ne sçay qui openly derides these larger plans, attacking the king's intention "D'aller a Napples pour faire du Rolant" (135, v. 1163) (to go to Naples to play Roland), a reference that would not have been lost on members of the French and Italian aristocracy familiar with the depiction of Roland's vainglory in the popular epic of Matteo Maria Boiardo.[11] La Vigne's suppression of the wise voice of Olivier and the true motive for Charles's action thus introduces in a subtle, if not subversive, way the importance of literary and historical models of behavior in the lead-up to war. King Charles follows the models of Charlemagne, Clovis, and Saint Louis, while La Vigne follows historiographical and literary models of nobiliary representation in which reasoned discourse and debate are suppressed and derided.

La Vigne links literary and historical models of chivalric behavior to veiled references of the cultural and political differences between the French kingdom and the spaces he plans to invade to convince a larger audience of the justice of the war. If historians today downplay whether or not Charles's plans to conduct a crusade were realistic, there is little doubt that fighting an ideologically defined enemy weighed heavily in the argument for going to war.[12] In addition to a desire to increase his territory and place France in a position to become a Mediterranean power, the king was known and even ridiculed for his desire to conduct heroic endeavors and lead a major campaign into battle.[13] Charles's taste for chivalric romances and Arthurian legend and the example of Saint Louis contributed to his sense of justice and desire to save Christianity from its enemies.[14] Historiographers of the period describe Charles variously as naïve but good hearted (Commynes), steeped in a religious faith resembling superstition, and above all, absorbed by models of chivalric behavior that had little relation with the *realpolitik* of the Italian peninsula.[15] The Florentine Guicciardini portrays the king as virtually illiterate (his knowledge of Latin was evidently limited) and completely misinformed but fiercely determined and avid for power. Charles's plans for war, conceived around the beginning of 1490, thus involved the cultivation of his image as a Christian knight following in the footsteps of Charlemagne and Saint Louis.[16] During the celebrations and triumphs the king received as he traversed Italy, prepared in cooperation between French and Italian artists, references to Clovis and Charlemagne abounded, and Charles's ambassadors were instructed to remind the Italians—in particular, the Florentines—of these links.[17] Dame Chrestienté specifically mentions Charlemagne, Roland, Oliver, and the great Saint Louis, "le noble roy, roy des roys terrifique" (121, v. 568) (the noble king, terrifying king of kings), in the presence of Majesté Royalle (the allegorical embodiment of the king). Je ne sçay qui's cowardly proposal also pokes at the nobleman's sense of honor. Speaking in a contorted "ryme retrograde" that highlights the specious nature of his logic, he lists the many reasons the French should mind their own business, noting the expense of war and the risk to the monarchy—all reasons that are quickly put down as "plaisans motz et (les) doulces epistres" (136, v. 1205) (nice words and sweet letters) motivated by the placing of "syen proffit" above *prouesse*.

The promise to defend Christendom can be read as a way of sidestepping the controversy that surrounded the king's plans.[18] The erasure of the identity and opinion of Je ne sçay qui in the *Ressource de la Chrestienté* shows the king's deafness to opposition and his redefinition of the mission as a clash of civilizations.[19] The strategy to win Christendom back from the Turk is to take Naples "par belle main armee." Even in the more realistic account of the *Voyage de Naples*, La Vigne will emphasize Alfonso's abuse of power as the *casus belli* and not King Charles's claim to the throne or desire to expand French power into the Mediterranean. Read together, the *Ressource de la Chrestienté* and the *Voyage de Naples* thus suggest that while proprietary dynastic rights motivated Charles's taking his country to war, literary, historical, and moral arguments were needed to present and accomplish the war project.[20] The call to a crusade thus sells the French *entreprise* as a response to the menace of Turkish expansion, covering up the more obvious reasons for the invasion.[21]

NATION, RELIGION, AND RACE

If chivalry is called upon to defend Christendom from its enemies, the depiction of a barbarous, subhuman enemy is also part of the rhetoric of war. Dame Chrestienté invites the dreaming narrator to help fight "un tas de Turcs et de chiens inhumains" (a mass of Turks and inhuman dogs) (109, v. 47) that were mistreating her, appealing to the chivalrous nobleman to take up arms and rescue her: "Me lairrez vous ainsi vilipender? / Voyez, oyez [. . .]" (ibid., vv. 75–76) (Will you allow me to be tortured in this manner? / Look, listen . . .). All good Christians have "hung up their armor" (v. 79) and are content to waste their time in pleasure and amusements while the "mescreans sont si avant conquerans" (112, vv. 228–32) (the unbelievers have advanced so far in their conquest) that it seems that "Chrestienté dort" (ibid., v. 225) (all Christendom sleeps).

Midway through his presentation of arguments for war, La Vigne shifts his focus from the Turkish "dogs" to a more generalized enemy whose geographical location is less explicit. Dame Chrestienté refers to these "mastins [. . .] / Qui sur nous veullent dessus terre regner" (109, vv. 80–81) (dogs who want to rule over us on earth) as "*estrangiers* pis qu'es mains d'Atropos" (A ii v) (foreigners worse than [being] in the hands of Atropos) that work alongside "ses turcs mausdiz desloyaulx chiens mastins" (ibid.) (these damned Turks, disloyal dogs). She complains of having fallen

> Entre les mains d'une cepte paÿenne
> Qui desnuer veullent mon povre cueur
> Du tout en tout de divine liqueur
> Pour adorer *l'ydolle turquïenne*
> Leur synagogue et loy barbarïenne (112 vv. 201–5)

(in[to] the hands of a pagan sect that wants to strip my poor heart completely and in every way of its divine essence and force it to worship a Turkish idol, their synagogue and barbaric law.)

Before this point, La Vigne's only reference to Jews had been his praise of the replacement of their "outdated" law (109, vv. 40–41). Here Jewish religious practice is mixed in with that of the Turks as pagan idolatry, or rather, the Turks are accused of Jew worship and of following a barbarous law. In her second speech, Dame Chrestienté again calls Muslims non-human dogs but recalls Jeremiah's prophesy that "une cité seroit un jour deffaicte [...] que de nully ne seroit habitee / Fors de Juïfz, par leur offence vile" (119, vv. 473, 477–78) (a city would one day be destroyed... and be inhabited by no one but Jews, for their vile offence). So while Turks are not people, Jews manage to eke out a sort of semihumanity somewhere between Christianity and pagan barbarism.

Further on, Dame Chrestienté praises Charlemagne for defending Christianity from "Les dyvers tours, les oppressions dures / Que me faisoyent les dampnables Juïfz" (the various tricks and rude offences the damnable Jews did to me). Dame Noblesse, the allegorical voice of the French nobility, chimes in that Jews already control and "possess" the entire country and, even worse, "marchent sur nous et viennent / Nous courir sus" (126, vv. 763–64) (march upon us and come to run us over). Her most ironic statement (considering the true objective of Charles's enterprise) comes when she invites all good Christians to wage war against "ces mastins et chiens, / Maulditz Juïfz" (127, vv. 800–801) (these mastifs and dogs, damned Jews), rather than spilling the blood of Christian neighbors, for "qui est chose inhumayne" (v. 804) (that is an inhuman act)! These conflations of Turks, Jews, barbarians, foreigners, and enemies that already possess us might explain the enigmatic reasoning of Bon Conseil, who, in response to Je ne sçay qui's reasoned remarks, protests,

> Et qui la chose a ung chascun notoire
> Veult denÿer tant par dit que par faict
> ung chascun dit que c'est a luy mal faict. (135, vv. 1190–92)

(He who denies the thing everyone knows is by everyone said to have acted in bad faith.)

He never goes on to explain what that thing everyone knows is, but he uses it again in his concluding remarks, noting that it is apparent to everyone "a Naples et Venise, / en Angleterre, en Espaigne et Boësme, / En Turquië et en Sarrazinesme" (139, vv. 1352–54) (in Naples, Venice, England, and Spain, in Bohemia, Turkey, and in the land of the Saracen).

The melding of chivalric ideals conveyed using literary models and the antisemitic message of the French propaganda suggests that the contrast of national identities centered less on questions of faith (Christian versus non-Christian) than on a fundamental difference between the agrarian, feudal nations of the north and the urban, trading culture of the Mediterranean, as David Abulafia has suggested.[22] Accusations of harboring Jews and the blurring of distinctions between Naples and the Arab world underline the more cosmopolitan bases of the Neapolitan court, illustrated by King Ferrante's proposed alliance with the Turks' and his hosting of Jewish refugees fleeing from Spain in 1492.[23] France's first attempts to establish itself as a Mediterranean power were thus, ironically, based in Germanic ideals of racial purity and an antagonism toward the religious and ethnic diversity that characterized Mediterranean culture.

SEXUAL TOPOGRAPHY

The most original aspect of La Vigne's spatial allegory is its openly eroticized nature. The spatial allegory of Dame Chrestienté sets her "facunde" beauty against a "sterile" topography that both justifies French territorial expansion and translates it into a sexualized aesthetic space. The succubus-like appearance of Lady Christianity, or Lady Christendom, as her territorial embodiment would imply, bubbles up from a linguistic landscape that communicates the aesthetic blurring of an erotic dream. Her presence "coagulates" amid the "boursouffleuse oisiveté" (bloated idleness) of an afternoon slumber, while the delicate innocence of a "povre berbis esgaree" (poor lost sheep) magnifies her "doulce et sumptueuse" (sweet and sumptuous) physique and "delictable, doulx, amyable" (delectable, sweet, and loveable) face. Her torn clothing exposes bits of flesh, her underclothes show her mistreatment at the hand of Christianity's enemies but also mark her as the embodiment of male desire as she falls to the ground in "debille sensualité" (weak sensuality).

As La Vigne reworked early versions of the *Ressource* for the printing of *Le Vergier d'honneur*, he concentrated further on these aspects of his description of Dame Chrestienté, adding details that allow us to "see" the "virginalle essence de la facundissime dame" (167) (virginal essence of the extremely fecund lady).[24] He adds the senses of taste and smell to his vision, describing her as a "tresaffable nourriture celique [...] de souefve odeur" (most wonderful celestial food... of most exquisite odor) (ibid.). The feeble lament of the lost sheep who "doulousoit et lamentoit" (108) (is pained and lamented) is reinforced in the enumeration of "exclamations merveilleuses, cris douloureux langoureuses complaintes et doleances ameres" (167) (marvelous exclamations, painful cries, languorous sighs, and bitter pains); "lugubres imploractions rengorgees de sanglotz ignomineux" (168) (gloomy half-choked implorations of ignominious sobbing); and "exclamations doleances complainctes piteuses" (ibid.) (cries, pains, and piteous whining) emitted "soubz le sexe femenin" (167) (in the form of the feminine sex). Acteur, in this eyewitness account of "refulgente plasmation" (168) (splendid creation), becomes a spectator who anticipates his intended reader's reaction to this "paranymphe" (meganymph) whose pained beauty makes her "tresdesiree tresaffable et debonnaire" (169) (extremely desirable, oh so delectable, and noble).

The framing of Dame Chrestienté's sexualized figure in a topographical wasteland thus links French territorial interests to male pastimes such as hunting, jousts, chivalry, military endeavors, land acquisition, and sexual conquest. Dame Chrestienté is despoiled and abused like the landscape that surrounds her. The surrounding "desert" marks her abandonment by civilized peoples, while the lack of *mesure* in her overgrown vegetation illustrates the cultural barbarity of the Turks, Jews, and "marchants" (merchants, or marchers) who have come to steal her "propre heritage" (ibid., v. 110) (proper heritage) misuse her "grans biens" (110, v. 91) (fantastic goods), and "march" on her "tail."

The relationship between these topographical metaphors and French national identity is made clear when Dame Chrestienté is magically transported across the Alps to the "clymat francigene" (113) (French climate). She arrives in the *vergier* or "pourpris" (garden), bringing her "grans biens" into the controlled space of French domination.[25] La Vigne even seems to suggest a sort of mythical transport of the places of the Orient into the French national space, associating the French border of Mont Cenis with Sinai through an unetymological spelling of "Mont Synys." France's fertility is a sign of its divine calling as a protector of Christianity and sacred "valeurs" and is decorated with "fleurs d'esbaulpins, eglantiers, loriers, grenadiers, guygners, serisiers, poriers, prunyers, et pommyers fleuris, frutiffiez et maturez selon l'exercice de Dame Nature" (114) (hawthorn flowers, eglantines, laurels, pomegranates, cherries, pears, plumbs, and apple trees all flowering and full of fruit and matured by the arts of Mother Nature), cultivated plants that underline the fertility of France and order of the French state.

Specific references also identify Dame Chrestienté with geographical locations in the Middle East that shift from Jerusalem (vv. 469–79) and Constantinople (vv. 856–63) to a more ambiguously marked Holy Land that must be reconquered.[26] She embodies these places, remarking, in reference to the destruction of Israel recounted by the prophet Jeremiah, "je suis cete ville" (119, v. 479) (I am that city). The message of the *Ressource* is thus a call to retake Jerusalem, or Constantinople, or perhaps even a vaguely defined Christendom that covers any territory held by other enemies of Dame Chrestienté.

All these elements—Christianity's association with territory and the use of female sexuality as a call to male action—reflect the personal interests of the young King Charles and the mass of young soldiers that will be called to avenge the violation of Christian territory:

Car desja sont si avant conquerans
Que de mes terres tant mauvaises que bonnes
Ont transgressé les lymites et bonnes (i.e., "bornes," 112–13, vv. 232–34)

(They are so far advanced in their conquest that of my lands, good or bad, they have transgressed their limits and borders.)

The fecund Dame Chrestienté finds herself, like the land of the allegorized state, unable to produce neither "fueille ne fruit" (leaf nor fruit). Like a "terre pour le sens" (land for the census/senses), whose products have been divided between lord and tenant (111, vv. 195–98), she has nothing left and becomes sterile. They run over "me" (v. 190), she notes:

Dont je deviens brehaigne et sterille
Pour leur soubdars qui par ville et par champs
A leur soubhait vont tousjours esparchans
Sans contredit ne deffence virille (113, vv. 237–40)

(I become barren and sterile, because of their soldiers that go around pillaging as they like in the city and fields without any opposition or virile defense.)

This transgression of a delicate, fecund damsel whose weeping had so moved us clearly requires rectification from the knights of the *vergier*. Dame Chrestienté even begs for it, asking the French to reclaim her "tresor," mixing hope with a renewed lamenting whose invitation needs no explanation:

Si pour me plaindre, pour gemyr, pour plourer
Je me pouoye de lÿesse implorer
Ou de tourment aulcunement estraindre
De pleurs piteux me vouldroye *deflorer* (117, vv. 370–74)

(If, in order to make my complaint, weep, and cry, I could in happiness beg or in torment embrace myself, I would want, with piteous pleas, to deflower myself.)

STAGING CHARLES VIII

La Vigne's account of the Italian expedition of 1494–95 contrasts with the florid allegory of the *Ressource de la Chrestienté*. The *Voyage de Naples*, published in 1500 along with the *Ressource* in a collection titled *Le Vergier d'honneur*, is a linear, day-by-day account of the expedition based on La Vigne's eyewitness testimony. Alternating journalistic realism with the epic glorification of his patron, La Vigne creates a document that is at once didactic, propagandistic, and commemorative. Like other historiographers of this period, he records events and glorifies the exploits of France's heroes, mixing heroic exploit and quotidian detail in a way that accentuates the confusion between the epic and the historiographical chronicle.[27]

This hybrid form allows him to punctuate a narrated, journalistic account with epic amplifications of heroic exploit. In the first section of his work (vv. 1–941),[28] La Vigne recounts the preparations for war in weighty stanzas that replicate the might of the forming French army. Short prose paragraphs help the reader understand what is going on, situating verse sections that then paint the scene more vividly. This first section ends with a ballade dedicated to the "Prince" and a rondeau solemnizing his march to war. The second section captures the troops' movement from Grenoble to Naples in expeditious quatrains interspersed with lengthy descriptions of the king's entrances and stays in various Italian cities. The final section, written primarily in prose, covers the return to France and includes Charles's important encounter at Fornovo. La Vigne generally uses verse to replicate ceremony and movement, the two essential elements of his diplomatic and military *Voyage*, in passages that both record and celebrate historic action.

Both of these rhetorical functions, however, are directed toward a positive, openly propagandistic representation of the king's actions. As can be seen in the poem's opening verses, the king is the subject of the *Voyage* as well as the prime mover of the war's activities:

> Mil quatre cens et quatre vings et treze,
> le roy Charles huytiesme de ce nom,
> pour repulser l'iniquité maulvaise
> du roy Alphons qui tenoit a malaise
> en son pays plusieurs nobles de nom
> aussi pour los, gloire, bruyt et renom
> a main armee en brief temps conquester
> il entreprist de Napples conquester. (vv. 1–8)

> (One thousand four hundred and thirteen, King Charles, eighth of this name, in order to push back the evil iniquity of King Alfonso who held in bad conditions several men noble in name, and also to conquer quickly by force of arms praise, glory, applause, and renown, made plans to conquer Naples.)

La Vigne presents the premises for war from the king's point of view, and while the basic facts are correct, he gives them a journalistic spin that favors the French enterprise. La Vigne also emphasizes the young king's motivation for "los, gloire, bruyt et renom" (praise, glory, attention and renown), combined with the moral imperative to suppress the "iniquité maulvaise" (horrible iniquity) of his Neapolitan counterpart. The Neapolitan expedition is at once a humanitarian enterprise and a praiseworthy feat that illustrates the king's noble constitution, which is the inverse of that of his Neapolitan rival, who

> estoit tres mal par tous lieux renommé
> et tant avoit le peuple diverty,
> gasté, seduyt, destruyt, aneanty,
> que la contree de Napples bien aymee
> *voulut* ravoir par belle main armee. (emphasis added; 131 vv. 47–51)

> (was very ill-reputed everywhere and had so misled, spoiled, seduced, destroyed, annihilated the people, that [King Charles] decided [voulut] to take beloved Naples back by military force).

Alfonso has "spoiled" and "seduced" the people by fighting his (pro-French) land-owning barons, upsetting the natural hierarchy of the three estates and providing a legal argument for Charles's controversial invasion.[29]

The king's presence and decisiveness, his ability to observe, take counsel, and move to action, are embodied in the structure of the *Voyage*. Occupying the entire second stanza, the king acts, in effect, as the grammatical subject of the entire narrative of the preparations and march to war as Charles conducts business, musters the troops from Flanders and Germany, contracts with arms dealers, hires mercenaries, and commissions the French fleet.[30] The king's name often goes without saying and is often replaced with the third-person pronoun "il," a characteristic shared with Montaigne's secretary's *Journal*. In La Vigne's *Voyage*, the king thus appears in grammatical and stylistic structures that imitate the order and force of the military formations heading off to war, while factitive constructions emphasize the force and efficacy of the king's will.[31] Rather, the king names, orders, directs, and delegates, causing the actions of *son armee* or *son lieutenant*.

Once the action is set in motion, events occur of their own accord, as if to demonstrate the engendering power of the royal will. La Vigne represents this action in a concatenation of events and stanzas that emanate from one another in succession. After Charles orders the assembly of noblemen and foot soldiers in stanza 8 (vv. 52–59), rows of weapons and troops headed by "him" appear in martial order. Stanza ten then picks up with a nominal phrase (having no express subject) that mimics the forces' spatial order and mass:

> D'autre costé, Lancequenetz, Suÿsses
> et leurs complices a tous leurs escrevisses

picques propices, albardes, espees,
grans cranequins, chaulces, brayes coulysses
(vv. 68–71)

(On the other side, Lansquenets, Swiss soldiers
And their accomplices with their armor
Propitious pikes, halberds, swords,
Great crossbows, underarmor, and well-oiled breeches)

The effect of this sequence is to place the king at the head of marching lists of soldiers and swords that continue for a full ten stanzas. A matrix of objects mimics the twenty-five thousand troops that departed from Vienne on August 22, 1494, and made their way into Italy.

Further on in the narrative, La Vigne uses ceremonial entries to focalize his glorification of the king, developing a skill that will earn him a successful career as a secretary to nobility and orchestrator of royal ceremonies.[32] The *Voyage de Naples* contains detailed reproductions of the festivities in Chieri (vv. 1277–1614), Pavia (2139–2226), Piacenza (2227–2376), Lucca (2497–2568), Pisa (2569–2721), Florence (2860–3331), Siena (3372–3497), and Rome (3688–4029). These expressions of power, charged with military, propagandistic, and logistical meaning, allowed the monarch to establish his ascendancy over the towns in spectacles that his allies and enemies would then hear or read about.[33] Through each successive triumph in Savoy, Piedmont, Lombardy, and northern Tuscany, Charles affirmed his ability to wage a campaign and acquire support, placing pressure on Alfonso's forces and the indecisive Pope Alexander VI.[34] La Vigne recreates the spectacle and emotion of these encounters using a spatial painting of the king's relation to his new subjects and allied cityscapes.[35]

Charles's reception in Chieri offers a good example of how these ceremonies were conducted. After his welcome in Turin by Bianca di Monferrato, he received his first grand triumph, featuring music, dance, and theatrical performances and culminating in his "couronnement d'un chapelet de violettes" (163) (crowning in a necklace of violets) as "vray roy et vertueux Champion de l'onneur des dames" (true king and virtuous champion of the honor of women). The city officials meet the monarch outside the city in order to escort him through the gates as a guest of honor. A procession of the town's civil, commercial, and religious notables passes in review: "les gros rabs, pincemailles, milors" (164, v. 1287) (rabbis, money-lenders, rich lords), "changeurs, banquiers, grossiers, riches marchans" (1290–91) (money-changers, bankers, wholesale salesmen, rich merchants), and "les gens de l'église" (1296) (church officials), followed by other secular and religious orders, trade guilds, apprentices, columns of horsemen, bankers in gold cloaks of Venetian satin, and even the town's children (165, vv. 1335–39). Accompanied through the city, the king meets *bergeronnettes* playing *pastoureaux* and performing "invencions entieres / de grans sentences et parfondes matieres" (new inventions of great discourse and deep subjects) (166, 1386–87). The streets, houses, doorways, and windows are decorated in gold and silk, and perfumed incense wafts through the crowded pavilions. Finally, an allegory of "le triumphe et celeste victoire" (the triumph and celestial victory) of King Clovis (166, 1393–1401) brought the king to the grand finale of a fastuously decorated "acouchee" (birth) featuring a charming damsel lying in an embroidered bed holding an infant for all to see (167–69, 1402–91), leading to the king's crowning by three beautiful young ladies reciting poetry.

The town emphasizes the king's presence, with La Vigne writing from the viewpoint of a reporter in the king's party, leading the reader from outside the city through the streets, where the inhabitants exalt and crown the young monarch. All the ceremonies focus on the king, from his *recueil . . . sur les champs* (greeting in the fields), where the townspeople give "leurs salutacions . . . au roy" (1340–41) (salutes to the king), to the pastoureaux and mysteries recited "pour publier la vertu de ses faitz" (1392) (to publicize his great deeds). The king's lodging is decorated with scaffolding draped in white and violet satin decorated with the letters *C* and *A* for Charles and his wife Anne of Brittany, and young damsels recite poems "a la louenge et exaltacion de sa magnificence" (169) (to the praise and exaltation of his magnificence).

The staging of an elaborate "accouchee" and the hordes of young women arranged outside the king's bedchamber is yet another allusion to the king's youth and sexual appetite:

> De leurs habitz, de leurs façons et gestes,
> de leurs mignons et propres corps faistiz
> elles estoyent tant propres et honnestes
> que plusieurs gens aux amoureux bicextes
> se convoloyent par frianz appetiz.
> Une bouchette, ungs rïans yeulx petiz,

ung cler vïaire pour roynes ou princesses,
ungs blancs testins, ungs longs bras et traictifz:
je ne croy point qu'il soit d'autres deesses. (170, vv. 1500–1518)

(Of their clothes, their manners, and movements, of their dainty and well-proportioned bodies, they were so elegant and attractive that several people fought over them in amorous disputes. A mouth, small smiling eyes, a radiant face for queens or princesses, white breasts, and long, slender arms: I do not believe there are any other goddesses [more beautiful].)

The festive, sensual theatrical performance of Chieri is, as Sandra Provini points out,[36] to be contrasted with Charles's entry into Florence, where the political tensions of this somewhat reluctant ally are seen in La Vigne's depiction of the king "en grant triumphe et parfaicte excellence, en bruyt, en los d'onneur victorïeux" (208 vv. 2860–61) (in grand triumph and perfect excellence, in resounding display of victorious honor). The king enters as conqueror to receive the keys to the city, benignly accepting the city's submission. Florentines look on from scaffolding with "angelic faces" as Venetians and Romans come to witness "le roy des hardiz" (2923) (the king of the audacious). The procession begins with Florentine officials, followed by French companies of cannoneers, pikemen, halberdiers, captains, archers, soldiers, crossbowmen, and then by the king's gentlemen, pages, and servants. The king rides his jewel-bedecked stallion at the center of the parade "de pondereux arroy" (3122) (in ponderous display).

THE KING ON TOUR

The king's activities are always performative, fusing the military, political, religious, and private aspects of his multiple roles. The touring of towns and cities as performed leisure thus becomes a function of the royal projection of power. La Vigne's emphasis of the details of the road highlights this ongoing relationship between military and political endeavors and the nascent leisured activities of the French nobility in Italy.[37] His work, arguably linked to the medieval epic tradition, also reads like a personal travel narrative tracing the young Charles's path from Grenoble to Gap through Briançon and over the pass of Montgenèvre through Cesana,

Susa, and Turin, punctuated by official visits of Chieri, Asti, Pavia, Piacenza, Lucca, Pisa, Florence, Siena, and Rome.

La Vigne even provides documentation of the types of lodging his royal traveler used: castles in Turin, Casale, Mortara, Vigevano, Pavia, Massa di Carrara, Pietrasanta, Pisa, and Capua and the bishops' palaces in Gap, Embrun and Lucca. His visit to Ludovico il Moro's Villa della Sforzesca, Battista Pandolfini's villa in Lastra a Signa, an unidentified "maison plantureuse" (luxurious home) in Piacenza,[38] and the villa and gardens of Poggioreale in Naples anticipate the tourism of luxury homes that fills the narratives of late sixteenth-century travelers.

Food is another ethnographic theme that La Vigne inserts into his military narrative. Within the context of the *Voyage*, meals provide a record of the type of reception provided to the monarch and illustrate the type of relationship the young king establishes with the various political entities of Italy. In Dauphiné, the troops consume "force vïandes, . . . force bons vins" (lots of food, . . . lots of good wine). Allied Piedmont and Lombardy were also particularly eager to show the king and the troops a good time. Vigevano provided noteworthy bread, wine and cooked meat, while Casale served pheasants, ostriches, swans, peacocks, hares, partridges, rabbits, chickens, pigeons, and capons and "vins de toutes nacions" (1994) (wines of all nations). In Piacenza, tables were filled with wines spiced with corianders and accompanied by other "nouveaulx metz" (191, v. 2272) (new foods), such as the famous cheeses, "si grans, si espes et si larges / que peullent estre grans meulles de moulins" (193, vv. 2372–73) (so big, so thick and large that they could be large millstones) that the king had sent back to France.

The description of geographical space itself becomes a function of the king's interaction with the towns, as the passage "par tous les lieux, rivieres, pors, passages, / de forteresses, de villes, de villaiges" (vv. 710–11) (through all the places, rivers, ports, passages, of fortresses, cities, and villages) marks the king's ceremonial procession toward Naples.[39]

ANDRÉ DE LA VIGNE

The various roles played by La Vigne and his literary persona *acteur* highlight relationships between literary, political, and geographical spaces. Within the literary world of the *Ressource*, La Vigne performs like a professional lawyer and administrator of Dame Chrestienté to seek reparation of her "biens" (property).⁴⁰ As secretary of the expedition, a similar figure acts as the witness of and participant in the king's political and military action.⁴¹ Finally, at the conclusion of the *Voyage*, the metaphor of the garden/vergier, home to the literary production of "La Vigne" (the vine), creates additional linkages between the idealized spaces of the French national ethos and the real topography of political and military conquest.

La Vigne exerts a strong sense of ownership over his texts and their content in a way that challenges the forced anonymity of the court secretary's role.⁴² In the continuation of the *Vergier d'honneur*, the acteur who opened the *Ressource de la Chrestienté* returns, penning a series of political dedications that anticipate Du Bellay's famous *sonnets courtisans*. La Vigne, moreover, identifies himself as "l'acteur qui est au vergier" (the actor who is in the garden) and sends his friends other works signed by "Maistre Andry de la Vigne."⁴³ La Vigne also weaves his name into the text at the exact point in which the king's activities come to a climax, marking the codependency between the king's status performance and La Vigne's literary production:

> Dedans Lÿon en tres puissant seigneur
> Et en triumphe de bruyt chevalereux,
> Le per sans per, de vertus enseigneur
> Alors se tient comme victorieux,
> Vray pocesseur de renom glorïeux,
> Incomparable en decoration,
> Grave empereur, roy sans exception,
> Noble et inclit, portant double couronne
> En son royaulme ou digne lis floronne. (521–22, vv. 5018–26)

> (Into Lyon, as powerful lord and in a triumph of chivalrous flare, the unequaled father, teacher of virtues, now holds himself, victorious, true owner of glorious fame, incomparable in decoration, grave emperor, king without exception, noble and illustrious, wearing a double crown in his kingdom where the fleur de lys flourishes.)

It is easy to see, therefore, how La Vigne's skills would be needed in the increasingly bureaucratic political life of the French court. Representing the performed activities of courtly politics, the author-actor is at once a promoter and progenitor of cultural identity. His assertion of self from within a dynamics of self-effacing servitude illustrates the tensions created by the increasing importance of literary representation to the nobleman's identity. It also anticipates the secretary's resistance to oppression that will reach a point of rebellion in Joachim Du Bellay's *Regrets*, as my next chapter will explore.

Chapter 3

SPACE, TRAVEL, AND WORK

Joachim Du Bellay's experience in Rome takes the question of geographical contextualization of personal aesthetics to its extreme limits. Confronting idealism with reality, transforming his quest for idealized space into a mystery that is never resolved, the poet articulates a complex sociopsychological problem without proposing a solution.[1] The *Regrets* leaves as many questions unanswered, exploring the "fundamental ambivalences that torture the poet" through a process of refusal and indirection.[2] The *Regrets*, in sum, reads as a sort of mirror of the poet's tortured soul and sense of self, projecting a conflicted sense of national and social identity onto an ambiguous, metaphorical space that roughly corresponds to the place he lived in for four years.[3] This creation of a "versified journal,"[4] which plays with the idea of work while eschewing a concrete engagement of reality,[5] pits the poet's idealistic goals against the poems' political and social context.[6] The poetic importance of this sociopolitical context, as Marc Bizer has shown, is sometimes ignored due to the conflicting value quotidian references have on the poetics of the work, depoeticizing the poems even as they create a new poetic world.[7] Rome, this pit of filth, in effect becomes Du Bellay's alter ego, reflecting the various facets of his conflicted identity.

This chapter concentrates on the personal and spatial aspects of this struggle as expressed in the poet's conflicted sense of work. In the most basic way, Du Bellay's *Regrets* can be read as a prolonged complaint about the poet's job—or rather, jobs. Du Bellay hated the duties he was called to do as secretary of his uncle, Cardinal Jean Du Bellay. He despised sycophants, adulators, prostitutes, and the entire pompous parade of papal Rome and was appalled by the corruption that led to France's failure in the international struggle to gain control in Italy.⁸ More importantly, the images Du Bellay uses to describe the toxic work environment in mid-sixteenth-century Rome show that a conflicted sense of the value of work influenced his social identity. As a member of a secondary branch of one of France's most illustrious families, Du Bellay gravitates to idealistic models of human action. His vision of poetic creation points to a world separated from the debasement of transactional relationships even as the persona who speaks in the *Regrets* is forced to perform the most debasing and valueless chores. At the same time, the collection's implicit narrative can also be read as a defense of this work, whose value is constructed around the poet's dualistic sense of self. The spatial reality of the backdrop of Rome thus comes to reflect both the inner ideals of the poet and their debasement in a world ruled by economic necessity.

THE *REGRETS* AS *VOYAGE D'ITALIE*

The *Regrets* has traditionally been read as a narrative of disillusionment.⁹ While serving in Rome as Cardinal Du Bellay's adviser and personal secretary from June 1553 to August 1557, the poet observed the moral dissolution of the papal court and the machinations that went into the selection of two popes, which eventually lead to the obliteration of French hopes for an ultramontane empire.¹⁰ Du Bellay's moral judgment of these political events contributes to the satirical tone, content, and even the form of the *Regrets*.¹¹ Richard Katz's analysis of the order of the collection, along with the readings of Jerome Schwartz, interprets Du Bellay's narrative as a vehicle for the poet's desire for transcendence.¹² This order also builds a work narrative similar to those presented in letters written by later French travelers engaged on diplomatic missions. The satirical tone of the *Regrets* skews this underlying message, which can also be read as a poetic vindication of practical experience and work. While critics have long noted that the collection's order and progression present an impression of narrative, there is little consensus as to what the overall message of this narrative might be.

Roughly told, the story of the *Regrets* is as follows. After introducing his subject, stating his location (Rome), and explaining how his new writing style (spoken and simple) fits his new social and existential situation (exiled and depressed; S 1–11), Du Bellay gives an ironically pessimistic depiction of his duties in Rome. He describes himself variously as a slave, a prisoner, or a frazzled manager occupied with a thousand appointments and fastidious, humiliating tasks. His natural character, by contrast, is that of an honest, direct individual forced to go against his own nature by the need to "courtiser" (court) and navigate the "dangereux escueils" (dangerous shoals) of "ceste mer Romaine" (this Roman sea) (S 12–26).

After this initial lament, however, Du Bellay begins to gain perspective and contemplates the reasons for his journey. He resigns himself to poverty and the absence from friends in the name of service to his lord and ridicules the superficial reasons that had inspired his trip (S 27–33). He compares his awful state to that of his friends Morel and Ronsard, as well as to his former self, praying the gods will help him through his suffering. Finally, he arrives at a fork in the road (S 45) and begins to develop strategies appropriate to his new social environment, considering hypocrisy and dissemblance and remaining firm in the service of his lord despite any lack of recognition. He submits and gives up his fight against "l'orage" (the storm) (S 56).

These philosophical observations prepare Du Bellay's most direct attacks on Roman society. He takes Le Breton to task; denounces hypocrites, unfaithful friends, and pedants; and trains himself to funnel his bitterness into a "riz Sardonien" (sardonic laugh), laughing at his own condition as a ridiculous, aging traveler. In the court, he sees ambition, pride, hatred, and hypocrisy, with Rome depicted as a mound of ruins surrounded by a mass of human corruption. The intrigue of the conclave and empty ceremony have transformed the former home of love and music into a barracks for debauched soldiers and courtiers (80–86), leading the poet into the trap of the "doulce force" (sweet force) of sexual temptation (87–89). Decrepit prostitutes, lecherous priests conducting exorcisms, honest women locked up in their homes, and the infamous example of Lucretia Borgia complete a series centered around the woman as a symbol of the city's vice and corruption.[13] Finally, specific current events begin to seep into this moralistic description of vice; the machinations of the court, surprise appointments of cardinals and popes, the death of a tyrannical Jules III and his affair with an unnamed Ganymede, imprisonments, poisonings, carnivals, and bullfights precede the unleashing of chaos, with Mars representing Rome's imminent invasion by imperial forces.

The poet's return home continues in this satirical vein and, more importantly, completes the travel narrative of the *Regrets*.[14] Du Bellay returns to France, recounting his itinerary and describing the stereotypical vices of the inhabitants of Urbino, Ferrara, and Venice before crossing Graubünden into Switzerland to arrive in Lyon and Paris. In France, Du Bellay, like Ulysses, finds trouble in his home but manages to reestablish contact with his social network. He even begins to offer political advice to some of his friends—Dilliers (Oudart d'Illiers), Ronsard, an unidentified friend, Baïf (Jean-Antoine de Baïf), and Thiard (Pontus de Thiard)—before concluding with a series of *louanges* (to Diane of Poitiers, Jean Bertrand, François Olivier [Chancellor of France], and d'Avanson) that concludes with "ceste belle fleur" (this beautiful flower) Marguerite of France, Du Bellay's patron and muse. The collection's final poems deplore the decline of the arts in France before asking the king directly to "eslargir" (spread) his power in Du Bellay's direction.

HEROIC MODELS (REVERSED): SUFFERING AND WORK

Robert Estienne's 1539 *Dictionnaire Françoyslatin* provides valuable information on the changing status of work in sixteenth-century France. More than a dictionary of words, the *Dictionnaire* provides numerous examples of French phrases translated into Latin, making it a useful tool for the writing of correspondence conducted by secretaries.[15] His entries of words referring to work—*ouvrage/oeuvre*, *labeur*, and *travail*—show connotations and usages ranging from work as artistic production to the kind of pointless toil and suffering described in the *Regrets*. *Labeur*, translated as "opera" or "labor," is the more neutral term and is used in expressions relating to work productivity and the relative difficulty and quality of work, as well as its distribution in society.[16] *Travail* carries many of these same meanings but is the only term used in a negative context, referring to productive work (*industria*) and painstaking effort but also struggle, suffering, difficulty, and worry.[17] These negative connotations make *travail* the exact opposite of *repos* (*otium*), a word whose positive values for humanist culture are well known.[18] *Ouvrage* and *oeuvre*, on the other hand, are the terms most closely related to emerging technologies, artistic production, the mechanical arts, and, of course, writing.[19] The *ouvrier*, translated variously as *faber, fabricator, opifex, operarius*, or *artifex*, falls into a category distinct from that of the *laboureur* associated with agricultural work and covers a range of technical and artistic vocations not covered in the medieval tripartite social division of society into *aratores, bellatores*, and *oratores*. The social and theological importance of this distinction can be seen in the fact that nature (*artificiosa natura*) is referred to as *la bonne ouvriere*.[20] Du Bellay's use of these terms in reference to his own situation as a secretary, poet, exile, traveler, friend, and public servant thus presents a complex range of feelings and social perspectives relating to his dual identity as poet and political secretary, as well as those of a nobleman forced to work.

Du Bellay makes much of his suffering and exile in a foreign land. Pushed by economic necessity, he lives far from his prince even as his friends relax in the arms of their mistresses or reap the advantages of political appointments in the French court. The poet's flight from poverty leads him to a world of suffering and pain, described in a characteristically redundant use of related synonyms that occupy all of verse 12 of sonnet 24:

> Je vieillis malheureux en estrange province,
> Fuyant la pauvreté: mais las ne fuyant pas
> Les regrets, les ennuys, le travail, et la peine. (S 24, vv. 10–12)

> (I am growing old, unhappy, in a foreign land, fleeing poverty, but not, alas, fleeing the longings, the troubles, the torment, and the suffering.)[21]

The various meanings of these words (*regrets*, *ennuys*, *travail*, *peine*) would seem only to amplify the negative aspects of suffering and work, wrapping *ennuys* and *travail* in *regrets* and *peine*. Estienne's translations thus open the possibility of a more positive reading, as the negative terms of *regrets* and *ennuys* are followed by expressions that underline his effort and diligence, implicit in the expression "la peine et travail qu'on prend a faire quelque chose."[22]

Further on, the exile falls into a state of despair, envying the *repos* of the ox retired to the field or the horse let out to pasture after serving in the "work of war," abandoned by God and men on Ausonian shores:

> Mais moy, qui jusqu'icy n'ay prouvé que la peine,
> La peine & le malheur d'une esperance vaine,
> La douleur, le souci, les regrets, les ennuis,
> Je vieillis peu à peu sur l'onde Ausonienne,

Et si n'espere point, quelque bien qui m'advienne,
De sortir jamais hors des travaux ou je suis. (S 35, vv. 9–14)

(But I, who until now have known only suffering, suffering and the misery of a vain hope, pain, care, regrets, troubles, I grow old little by little on the Ausonian shore and have no hope, whatever good may come my way, that I will ever escape these travails.)

Here pain (*peine, douleur*), misfortune (*malheur*) and worry (*souci, ennui*), all synonyms of his work's title, present an image of Du Bellay as a prisoner without the hope of redemptive work, "condamné à perpetuel travail" (*damnatus longi laboris*) (condemned to hard labor),[23] and growing old before his time due to living in "peine sugette" (servile suffering) (S 48).

This version of work as suffering clearly applies, however, only to his duties as secretary to Cardinal Du Bellay and not to his work as poet, as Du Bellay defends writing poetry as "plaisant labeur" (pleasant work) (S 13 and 18) and, near the end of his collection, chides his friend Jodelle for expecting payment for a vocation that should be its own compensation (S 153). If the legislative and theological models of sovereignty create a space exempt from the economics of exchange,[24] Du Bellay, like the failed poet Montaigne, seeks out a more deeply engaged form of social discourse. Like Montaigne, too, the separation between the literary persona, engaged in a self-reflexive quest for ideal form,[25] and the political actor is constructed through the opposition between refusal and engagement, a spatial localization that creates narrative and self-situation in an "other" space.[26]

Despite his complete refusal of the ethics of his workplace and his depiction of his work in Rome as a form of slavery, Du Bellay strategically demonstrates his worth in the field of political action. In his dedication to the French ambassador in Rome, Jean d'Avançon, he juxtaposes this image of servitude with the heroic figure of Achilles, underlining the nature of his heroic sacrifice that violates his true nature as a poet:

Ainsi voit-on celuy qui sur la plaine
Picque le boeuf, ou travaille au rampart,
Se resjouir, & d'un vers fait sans art
S'esvertuer au travail de sa peine.
Celuy aussi qui dessus la galere
Fait escumer les flots à l'environ,

Ses tristes chants accorde à l'aviron,
Pour esprouver la rame plus legere.
On dit qu'Achille en remaschant son ire
De tels plaisirs souloit s'entretenir,
Pour addoulcir le triste souvenir
De sa maistresse, aux fredons de sa lyre.
(À Monsieur d'Avanson, conseiller du Roy en son privé conseil, vv. 11–20)

(So the man who on the plain herds cattle or toils on the ramparts rejoices and with an artless poem he has made relieves the burden of his labor. Likewise he, who on the galley makes the sea around him foam, accords his sad songs to his rowing, so that his oar will seem lighter. They say that Achilles, brooding on his anger, with pleasures of this sort used to converse with himself, easing the sad remembrance of his mistress with the humming of his lyre.)

The poetry of the *Regrets* could not be more different from the ethereal model of purity proposed in Du Bellay's previous collection, *L'Olive*. A plowman plowing in the field, a mason or soldier working on the ramparts, a galley slave tied to his oar, all these become poets composing simple tunes to ease their pain and suffering. Oddly enough, Achilles is the only figure that does not represent a sort of work/suffering even as he anticipates a possible heroic intention in the composition of verse. Toward the end of his collection, Du Bellay will exhort the dauphin to pursue "la penible montee / Qui par le seul travail veult estre surmontee" (the arduous path of virtue that painful effort alone can climb), recognizing in the future king a heroic model that he himself is unable to achieve:

Je m'adresse ou je voy le chemin plus batu:
Ne me bastant le coeur, la force, ny l'haleine
De suivre, comme luy, par sueur and par peine
Ce penible sentier qui meine à la vertu. (S 3, vv. 11–14)

(I turn to the path that I see more beaten: For neither my heart, nor my strength, nor my breath suffices to follow, as he does, in sweat and pain, that arduous trail that leads to virtue.)

After describing his situation as a form of forced labor, Du Bellay claims to have given up on following Apollo on the "painful path" of heroic "labor." Du Bellay's interior dialogue of subjective experience, in effect, presents two opposing models of work: one that the poet develops in redundant laments tinged with irony and the other denied but pointing toward a possible transcendence.[27] Du Bellay writes himself both in and out of the spaces of an idealized poetic space caught between purely symbolic representation and references to the harsh reality of economic production and need.

At the same time, many passages in the *Regrets* move toward a definition of work less rooted in the traditional opposition between servitude and nobility, suggesting that Du Bellay perceived himself as belonging to a "fourth estate" of working intellectuals or artisans whose work deserves remuneration.[28] If his suffering is tinged with a sense of hopelessness and futility, Du Bellay also underlines the injustice of this situation, reaching out to friends for assistance and lobbying for his salvation with fellow artists and other strategically positioned noblemen. Du Bellay travels, not out of vainglory or ambition, but in the pursuit of "honest service" of his patron:

> Ce n'est l'ambition, ny le soing d'acuerir,
> Qui m'a fait delaisser ma rive paternelle,
> Pour voir ces monts couvers d'une neige eternelle,
> Et par mille dangers ma fortune querir
> [. . .]
> L'honneste servitude, où mon devoir me lie,
> M'a fait passer les monts de France en Italie,
> Et demourer trois ans sur ce bord estranger,
> Où je vy languissant. (27, vv. 1–4, 9–12)

> (Neither ambition nor greed made me leave my paternal shore to see those peaks covered with everlasting snow and to seek my fortune in the midst of a thousand dangers. . . . The honorable service to which duty binds me made me cross the mountains from France to Italy and abide three years on this foreign shore where languishing I live.)

He depicts his sacrifice in the service of country in a heroic and touching light, denying, once again, the interests of personal gain. The rhyme between *acuerir* (acquiring) and *querir* (seeking) is particularly well chosen, as it underlines the direct opposition of spiritualized, idealistic action and work for pay, a theme that distinctly connects him to the Petrarchan theme of poetic struggle in a corrupt, indifferent world.[29] Hannibal's "opening" of the Alps, moreover, amplifies the importance of Du Bellay's crossing, during which he evidently fell gravely ill, and underlines heroic models of transalpine engagement.[30] The rapprochement between his abandoned "rive paternelle" (paternal shore) and the "neige eternelle" (eternal snow) also adds a physical and emotive barrier to his sense of abandonment. More importantly, Du Bellay's ever-present irony seems to disappear here, as his touching enjambment of "où je vy languissant" (I lie languishing) describes the sacrifice he would gladly continue in far greater journeys to India or regions inhabited by the Moor.

Du Bellay increasingly places examples of work worthy of compensation alongside emphatic descriptions of his own personal sacrifice and denied references to heroic action. This "peine ou travail qu'on prend à parvenir" (pains or work done to get ahead, or to get "some place")[31] prepares his eventual return to France, where his sonnets of praise to a plethora of potential noble supporters works as a plea for help getting back on his feet.

Writing to Jean de Morel, the frustrated laborer asks whether he should continue to waste his time in Italy or return to France as the snows melt:

> Mais fault-il vivre ainsi d'une esperance vaine?
> Mais fault-il perdre ainsi bien trois ans de ma peine?
> Je ne bougeray donc. Non, non, je m'en iray.
> Je demourray pourtant, si tu le me conseilles.
> Helas (mon cher Morel) dy moy que je feray,
> Car je tiens, comme on dit, le loup par les oreilles. (33, vv. 9–14)

(But must I live thus on a vain hope? But must I lose thus a good three years of my toil? I will not budge then. No, no, I will leave. Still, I will stay, if that is what you advise. Alas, my dear Morel, tell me what I should do, for I have, as they say, the wolf by the ears.)

He decides, however, that his investment is too great and, despite his not receiving the slightest hint of gratitude on the part of his uncle the cardinal, leaving would mean losing three years of service. This very practical observation makes good on Du Bellay's promise to write in a way that imitates the style of everyday correspondence. It hints at the logistical and economic reality of the French situation in Rome, where ambassadors were often left unfunded for long periods of time despite their obligation to keep up ambassadorial appearances.[32] In sonnet 47, Du Bellay hopes his friend Vineus (Girolamo della Rovere) never has to suffer the indignity of "une vertu / qui se void defrauder du loyer de sa peine" (a virtue that sees itself robbed of the reward for its trouble):

> Si par peine, & sueur, & par fidelité,
> Par humble servitude, & longue patience,
> Employer corps, & biens, esprit, & conscience,
> Et du tout mespriser sa propre utilité,
> Si pour n'avoir jamais par importunité
> Demandé benefice, ou autre recompense,
> On se doit enrichir, j'auray (comme je pense)
> Quelque bien à la fin, car je l'ay merité. (46)

(If by hard work and sweat and by loyalty, by humble service and long patience, expending body and goods, wit and conscience, and utterly neglecting my own interests, if by never wheedling for a benefice or other compensation, one should get rich, I will [as I think] have some reward in the end, for I have earned it.)

The poet's return proves less fruitful than this optimistic prediction.

LESSONS LEARNED

The *Regrets*' most explicit reference to travel comes through the repeated mention of Ulysses, who provides a countermodel for Du Bellay's inability to adapt and conquer. Du Bellay's voyage is an inverted version of the wandering of the "grand Dulichien":

> Fertile est mon sejour, sterile estoit le sien,
> Je ne suis des plus fins, sa finesse est cogneue,
> Les siens gardans son bien attendoient sa venue,
> Mais nul en m'attendant ne me garde le mien:

Pallas sa guide estoit, je vays à l'aventure,
Il fut dur au travail, moy tendre de nature,
A la fin il ancra sa navire à son port,
Je ne suis asseuré de retourner en France,
Il feit de ses haineux une belle vengeance,
Pour me venger des miens je ne suis assez fort. (S 40)

(My home is fertile; his was barren. I am not very clever; his cleverness is famous. His people, watching over his estate, awaited his coming, but no one, waiting for me, watches over mine. Pallas was his guide; I go haphazardly. He was hardened to his task; I am tender by nature. In the end he anchored his ship in his home port; I am not assured of my return to France. He achieved a great revenge over his enemies; I am not strong enough to avenge myself on mine.)

In his dedication to d'Avançon, Du Bellay had compared his enchantment with poetry to Ulysses's tying himself to the mast to hear the sirens' song while coasting along the shore of Italy. Du Bellay entertains himself with thoughts of Ulysses's tribulations and ten years' wandering, reminding himself of the hero's happy return. The most famous sonnet of the collection, "Heureux qui, comme Ulysse, a fait un beau voyage" (Happy the man who, like Ulysses, has traveled well) (S31) describes the poet's exasperation at being far from home. The poet falls for a "Circe" in sonnet 88 and, finally, when he returns to his beloved *patrie*, it is only logical that, like Ulysses, he finds his home invaded by "mille souciz mordants ... en (sa) maison" (a thousand biting worries ... in his house). Do these multiple references imply that Du Bellay has returned, like the hero of Ithaca, "sage et plein de raison"?

The answer to this question, as to others, is made problematic by Du Bellay's tortuous progress through the emotional shoals of his education. His poetics of negation, in which he affirms through denial, creates an image of a desperate soul incapable of progressing due to his lack of contact with friends and the corrosive environment he is forced to inhabit. Early on in the collection, Du Bellay thus denies the possibility of achieving any specific pedagogical goals during his stay in Italy:

Je me feray sçavant en la philosophie,
En la mathématique, et medicine aussi,

> Je me feray legiste, et d'un plus hault souci
> Apprendray les secrets de la theologie:
> Du lut et du pinceau j'ebateray ma vie,
> De l'escrime et du bal. Je discourois ainsi,
> Et me vantois en moy d'apprendre tout cecy,
> Quand je changeay la France au sejour d'Italie.
> O beaux discours humains! Je suis venu si loing,
> Pour m'enrichir d'ennuy, de vieillesse, et de soing,
> Et de perdre en voyageant le meilleur de mon aage.
> Ainsi le marinier souvent pour tout tresor
> Rapporte des harencs en lieu de lingots d'or,
> Aiant fait, comme moy, un malheureux voyage. (32)

("I will become learned in philosophy, in mathematics, and medicine, too. I will become a jurist, and with a still higher ambition, I will learn the secrets of theology. I will brighten my life with the lute and the paintbrush, with fencing and dancing." Such were my thoughts, boasting to myself that I would learn all this, when I left France for a stay in Italy. O fine reasonings of men! I came all this way to enrich myself with trouble, age, and care and to waste in travel the best years of my life. Thus the seaman often brings back, as his only treasure, a load of herring instead of bars of gold, having made, like me, an unlucky trip.)

On the one hand, this negation recalls Du Bellay's earlier denial of the poetical models of the Greeks, Horace and Petrarch, an "extremely authoritative" denial, in the words of Floyd Gray, which relates the parameters of Du Bellay's new "pedestrian" style.[33] Du Bellay's stylistic denials thus find a parallel in the poet's simultaneous refusal of affirmative models of pedagogical travel. As Rabelais had done in his introduction to Sebastiano Marliani's *Topographia antiquae Romae*,[34] Du Bellay cites reasons for which travel to Italy had become popular among the sixteenth-century French elite, portraying himself as an optimistic and enthusiastic youngster ready to be disillusioned.[35] His denial is also a fatalistic recognition of the Horatian commonplace that "Caelum non animum mutant qui trans mare currunt" (they change their clime, not their mind, who rush across the sea),[36] which underlines the futility of his grandiose intellectual plans when traveling abroad. Just as Du Bellay denies one model of poetic creation in order to assert another more honest and directly linked to the tribulations of his struggling soul, the dismissal of these models of learning does not necessarily exclude his adherence to a more general objective of gaining an understanding of the workings of politics and humanity. A number of sonnets show how Du Bellay learns the art of political maneuvering, deception, and intrigue. Through his suffering and work, Du Bellay grows increasingly aware of how things work in the papal court. After sonnet 45, he already begins to exhibit some of the lessons he learned in Rome, underlining the importance of maintaining false appearances and good relations with his colleagues even as he continues to pursue a higher model of virtue:

> Allons où la vertu et le sort nous convie,
> Deussions nous voir le Scythe et la source du Nil
> Et nous donnons plus-tost un eternel exil,
> Que tacher d'un seul poinct l'honneur de nostre vie. (50, vv. 5–8)

> (Let us go where virtue and destiny invite us, even if we have to see Scythia or the source of the Nile, and let us rather give ourselves over to everlasting exile than stain with a single spot the honor of our life.)

The interplay of virtue and honor places tension on Du Bellay's cynical take on courtly life. More than empty gestures, they reflect a desire to serve and achieve that he sees as out of reach. Indeed, his understanding of how politics really works places his political idealism and desire to serve on the same level as his poetic aspirations. Despite his growing understanding of these dangers, he opts to sail on through the stormy sea of political service:

> Le sage nocher craint la faveur de Neptune,
> Sachant que le beau temps ne peult durer:
> Et ne vault-il pas mieux quelque orage endurer,
> Que d'avoir tousjours peur de la mer importune? (51, vv, 5–8)

> (The wise sailor fears the favor of Neptune, knowing that good weather cannot last for long. And is it not better to endure an occasional storm than to be always afraid of the importunate sea?)

Du Bellay passes into a period of introspection and apprenticeship, learning to manage money, speak kindly to people, and define the purpose of his satirical writing as a study of himself, "comme en un miroir." Acting and observing like an "homme sage," he observes "tout ce qui est en luy de laid ou de beau" (62, v. 11) (all that in him is ugly or beautiful). The advantage of living in Italy, he remarks, is not found in "les doctes escripts" (learned writings) but "pour l'air plus subtil qui doucement nous amble / Ce qui est plus terrestre, et lourd en noz esprits" (72, vv.) (because of the subtler air [that] gradually steals away what is most earthy and heavy in our minds). The "air" of Rome allows Du Bellay to become a perfect courtesan, but at the expense of effacing his sense of personal identity:

> Je ne sçay comme il fault entretenir son maistre,
> Comme il fault courtiser, et moins quel il fault estre
> Pour vivre entre les grands, comme on vid aujourdhuy.
> J'honnore tout le monde, et ne fasche personne,
> Qui me donne un salut, quatre je luy en donne,
> Qui ne fait cas de moy je ne fais cas de luy. (74, vv. 9–14)

(I do not know how to converse with a master, how to act like a courtier, and still less how to live among the great, as they live today. I am polite to everyone and annoy no one. If someone gives me a greeting, I give him four in return. If someone pays no attention to me, I pay no attention to him.)

The dreamy poet also learns to "mesdire" (76, v. 1) (speak ill), giving himself over to the "riz Sardonien" (77, v. 14) (Sardonic laugh) and transforming his travel narrative into an open criticism of the running of the church:

> Je ne conteray de Boulongne, et Venise,
> De Padoue, et Ferrare, et de Milan encor',
> De Naples, de Florence, et lesquelles sont or'
> Meilleures pour la guerre, ou pour la marchandise:
> Je te raconteray du siege de l'eglise,
> Qui fait d'oysiveté son plus riche tresor,
> Et qui dessous l'orgueil de trois couronnes d'or
> Couve l'ambition, la haine, et la feintise. (78, vv. 1–8)

(I will not tell you about Bologna and Venice, about Padua and Ferrara, or about Milan either, about Naples, about Florence, and which are the best for war or trade. I will tell you about the Holy See, which makes idleness its richest treasure and which, under the pride of the triple crown of gold, breeds ambition, hate, and dissimulation.)

Du Bellay condemns the debauched idleness of his social superiors in contrast to his own secretarial and poetic work.[37] His shift to the future tense halfway through his collection shows too that the poet has discovered the true subject of his collection. Like the explorers of the New World, Du Bellay discovers something truly "new"—that is, the truth about Rome, whose vice (80), corruption (81), and dissimulation (82) he then exposes with merciless honesty. His description of the vices of Italy's major cities also inverts the model of the Italian journey as an affirmation of the particular advantages of various cities. Describing all the major Italian cities except Turin, Du Bellay replaces topographical description with an assessment of the human vices that motivate a political system.

The poet of Parnasse thus returns to France with useful skills that include the art of servility (85–86), knowledge of the company of prostitutes (87–92), and the curse of knowledge acquired through discovery and travel:

> Maudict soit mille fois le Borgne de Libye,
> Qui le coeur des rochers persant de part en part,
> Des Alpes renversa le naturel rampart,
> Pour ouvrir le chemin de France en Italie.
> [. . .]
> Le François corrompu par le vice estranger
> Sa langue et son habit n'eust appris à changer,
> Il n'eust changé ses moeurs en une autre nature.
> Il n'eust point esprouvé le mal qui fait peler,
> Il n'eust fait de son nom la verole appeller,
> Et n'eust fait si souvent d'un bufle sa monture. (95, vv. 1–4, 11–14)[38]

(Cursed a thousand times over be the one-eyed Libyan, who, cutting through the heart of the mountains from one end to the

other, broke down the natural rampart of the Alps, to open the
road from France to Italy. . . . The Frenchman, corrupted by
foreign vice, would not have learned to alter his language and
his dress. He would not have exchanged customs for a second
nature. He would not have known the disease that makes your
hair fall out. He would not have given his name to the pox, and
would not so often have ridden the ox.)

Du Bellay arrives at a sort of wisdom, not due to his mastery of the technical intricacies of the court and his job as secretary, but due to his capacity to observe and learn how society works, pursuing honor, but acutely aware that his efforts may be in vain:

Qui dit que le sçavoir est le chemin d'honneur,
Qui dit que l'ignorance attire le bonheur,
Lequel des deux (Melin) est le plus veritable? (101, vv. 12–14)

(Some say that learning is the road to honor. Some say that ignorance attracts good fortune. Which of the two, Mellin, is truer?)

Du Bellay's advice to his friends Ronsard and Girolamo della Rovere (a.k.a. Vineus) illustrates the poet's acquired practical experience.

The narrative effect of the *Regrets* captures Du Bellay's experience in a series of poetic images. Read together with the *Antiquitez*, they transpose the alternation between chorographical description and the narrative of the journey that characterized the Italian travel journal in poetic form. By narrating his return after a journey through the debauchery of the Roman *Urbs*, Du Bellay also unwittingly anticipates the type of narrative that is increasingly common in the travel diary, in which the journey abroad brings a better understanding of politics and courtly etiquette.

TRAVEL AND WORK

Du Bellay was not the only one to note the potential negative effects of travel abroad and its relationship to work. Lionello Sozzi, in a nearly book-length article that has become a classic point of reference, describes an anti-Italian movement based on religious, political, and nationalistic themes that warned of the moral dangers of travel to Italy.[39] The last quarter of the sixteenth century takes to defending travel itself by providing a method by which the work of travel will be made useful. The authors of the so-called *Travel Methods* are called upon to confront the moral ambiguity implicit in the extralegal status of the traveler, as Jerome Turler writes in 1574:

> This worde Peregrinus which signifieth a straunger or traveiler, in the Latine tongue in sundrye ages hath had sundry significations. For as Varro, and Festus Pomponius doe report, ye auntient Romans called an enemie by the name Peregrinus a straunger: and an enemie whom they call now at this present Hostis.... But the worde grewe out of the signification of a straunger, and continued so long in signifying one that was our adversarie, or tooke armes against us, untill it fell to a more gentle use, the Romanes calling all suche by the name of Straungers as were not free of the Citie of Rome, as being perhaps Latines borne, or altogether Aliens: and in this signification it is used at this present. So that this worde Peregrinatio to traveile, descendeth from the worde Peragrare to wander, which signifieth to traveyle in straunge and forreine Cuntry or Citie. (1–2)[40]

The negative connotations of the words *peregrinus, stranger, adversarie, alien,* and *enemy* portray travel as an immoral and dangerous activity. Turler makes a philological point, however, showing how words' meanings change over time, allowing him to propose a new definition. Asking whether travel does good or harm, he reasons that men do not "commit themselves to straunge and foreyne Cuntryes to the entent to consume their time in idlenesse, to be subject as a mocking stocke unto Fortune: but they sometimes have just causes that move them, and some proposed ende in respect whereof they take in hande theyr travel."[41] The negation of idleness redefines travel as "painestaking to see and search forreine landes ... to see, learne and diligently marke suche things in straunge countries, as they shall have neede to use in the common trade of lyfe, whereby they maye profite themselves, their friendes, and countrey if neede require."[42]

Justus Lipsius, in his famous letter "De ratione cum fructu peregrinandi" ("Of a system for traveling usefully"), emphasized the same investigative exploration described by Turler but underlined that "id fiat non cum voluptate solum, sed cum fructu. Vagari, lustrare, discurrere quivis potest: pauci indagare, discere; id est, vere peregrinari" (travel should be done not only for pleasure. Anyone can wander, gaze, or run to and fro; few can investigate, that is, to truly travel).[43] "True" travel is not a pure form of leisure, since, as John Stradling writes in his English adaptation of Lipsius's letter, "to stand here to dilate how your Lordship may receive pleasure by travailing, is to teach your eyes to see, and your ears to heare, a thing both needlesse and follishe."[44] Spatial aimlessness and diligent exploration become visual and mental exercises in which the "accidentes and motions of the mind"—gazing, wondering, and wandering—trace a path to qualities as elusive as "profite," "wisedome," and "pollicie."[45] Rather than an alien, the *peregrinus* becomes an exalted being whose superiority and imagination play out in the reading of spaces around him. The desire to move in "imitation of the heavens" becomes proof of the "heroycall disposition" of men who "think it a great stain to be Cosmopolites, that is Cytizens of the whole world and yet to bee restrained within the narrow precincts of a little countie, as poore prisoners kept in a close place, or sillie birds cooped up in a narrow pen."[46] The arguments used to reform the status of travel at the close of the sixteenth century join philosophical precepts to very practical advice on how to travel and observe, but their principal contribution is the transformation of wandering into work.

POLITICAL CAREERS

The period that followed Du Bellay's return was marked by the political turmoil of the Wars of Religion. Much happened during those troubled times to complicate the political and social structures of France and their relations with Italy. Struggles between noble clans, Huguenots and the Crown, the Catholic League, royalists, "politiques," and Protestants under Henri de Navarre strengthened the culture of political affiliation and patronage even as the lines of these connections became increasingly harder to trace. The career paths of French travelers who have left documents describing their journeys show that the Italian journey had become a way to both broaden one's knowledge through spatial rambling and solidify political connections in Italy.

Many of the travelers examined in the following chapters were in fact linked together in a common web of political alliance.[47] Most, if not all, were involved with the law and politics.[48] Most were Catholic but identify themselves more through their relationship to the monarchy and have every appearance of belonging to the party of the "politiques" whose triumph came with the ascension to the throne (1589) and eventual victory of Henri IV.[49] This political rootedness and the need to bring back the proof of one's experience provide the impetus for writing, description, and narration, allowing space to become a stage of intellectual exploration and political staging, as the following chapter will show.

Chapter 4

THE TOPOGRAPHICAL NARRATIVE

Il nous faudroit des topographes qui nous fissent narration particuliere des endroits où ils ont esté.

—Montaigne, *Essais*, I, 31 ("Des Cannibales")

François Rabelais uses characteristic irony to recount the dashing of his intellectual hopes during his first trip to Italy. Writing to Cardinal Jean Du Bellay in his dedication of Bartolomeo Marliani's *Topography of Ancient Rome*, he thanks his patron for allowing him to achieve his lifelong dream, conceived during his first initiation into the study of letters, of "traveling to Italy and visiting Rome, capital of the World."[1] He had set himself lofty intellectual goals. First, he would consult learned men living between Lyon and Rome in order to ask their advice on "certain difficult questions" that had long vexed him. As a physician, he would seek out any "plants, animals and medications not known in France,"[2] a reference not only to differences of climate but also to the fashion of horticultural collecting among Italy's nobility and intelligentsia. His third goal touched on his conception of the Eternal City and its relationship to his identity as a man of letters. Rabelais wanted to map his readings of classical literature and history onto the Roman landscape and to "describe the City using a pen and pencil, so that upon returning, there would be nothing (he) could not take out of books and explain to the people of (his) hometown."[3]

In a manner that resembles Du Bellay's satirized intentions of "becoming an expert in philosophy,"[4] Rabelais lays out a plan of intellectual conquest and exploration that is destined for failure. He achieves only mediocre results in resolving his intellectual quandaries. Finding "a single plain tree we saw at the Speculum Aricinae"[5] and obtaining no answers to any of his unnamed questions, he seems poised to recount the futility of searching for wisdom abroad.[6] So too with his plans to draw an image of Rome. After months of research, conducted so "diligently that no one . . . knows their own home as well as (he) knew the alleys of Rome,"[7] he begins to realize that connecting the topography of Rome to questionable passages of ancient literary texts would be harder than he had thought. The owner of a "shapeless mass" of notes taken from "Greek and Latin authors," Rabelais is unable to give birth to his work and suffers like a woman in labor.[8]

Rabelais describes his scientific dabblings as a move upward to the summit of the city. Climbing a hill accompanied by two assistants, Nicolas Leroy and Claude Chappuis, whom he describes as "extremely worthy young men, extremely dedicated to the study of antiquity," he uses a *sciotherum* to draw a survey of the city:[9] "I went about, following the invention of Thales of Miletus, setting up a *sciotherum* and then divided the city into quarters by means of a transversal line cutting through a circular from east to west and north to south; and I drew with my own eyes."[10] His approach is scientific and precise and is described as an architectural survey. By marking off a circle into quadrants, we can only imagine he intended to measure various points at a distance, triangulating the location of Rome's various monuments and mapping them in his quadrants as Leonbattista Alberti had done some eighty years earlier.[11] This method allowed for an individual to draw an image of Rome using a series of angles and distances, an innovative approach useful to an architect or intellectual who wants to visualize the city, but somewhat paradoxical for someone who claims, like Rabelais, to seek answers to his questions on reading.

Rabelais's introduction thus seems to play a double game, justifying his publication of Marliani's text[12] while humorously depicting his own scientific misadventures. His self-comparison to Thales of Miletus—known less for any contribution to the geometry or surveying than as the father of abstract, speculative philosophy—reinforces the image of the mad scientist traipsing up the Janiculum, papers under his arm and some obscure technical device in hand, on a futile search to answer all his questions.[13] This image of feckless enthusiasm appears to be as important as any possible obtained results, even as Marliani's "graphic view" offers the real possibility of viewing space from a new perspective.

FROM MYTH TO PHILOLOGY TO NARRATED SPACE

The sixteenth century witnessed a revolution in the way geographical and topographical space was imagined and experienced.[14] It is easy to see this progress as a positivistic advance toward increasingly detailed and complete representations of space, but a more accurate description would be that of a number of competing representations in which the descriptive and rhetorical abilities of language adapt to various spatial techniques.[15] Near the time Montaigne penned his famous call for "topographers," the movement to envision the world from the perspective of Ptolemaic cosmography also appears to have reached a point of crisis.[16] If the topographer represents a smaller and thus more reliable piece of reality,[17] equally important is how Montaigne's topographer contextualizes knowledge. Montaigne calls for topographers "qui nous fissent **NARRATION PARTICULIERE** des lieux où ils ont esté" (who would give us a **PERSONAL NARRATIVE** of the places they have been).[18] Emphasizing the importance of context and experience, he inserts the individual traveler's viewpoint, a viewpoint that is then "owned" by its narrator.[19] It is not only a question of scale, in other words, but also the "narration" that allows sequencing, focalization, and the construction of narrative voice.[20] By calling for a narrative approach to topography, Montaigne asks not for the repression of cosmographical error but for the proper documentation of the traveler's relativistic viewpoint along with a description of the conditions under which observations are made. The technical question of representing an experienced space thus comes to have moral consequences, blurring the lines between cognitive and moral relativism.[21]

Rabelais's praise of Marliani hints at the changes in topographical representation that began with the description of Rome and its environs. As the first world capital, Rome became the subject of early and insistent study, inspiring representations that paved the way for the description of other cities and territorial spaces. Building on a tradition of writing that began with the twelfth-century *Mirabilia Romae*, these writers and mapmakers were constantly debating and changing the way Roman space was viewed and organized.[22] According to Rabelais, the originality of Marliani's *Antiquae Romae Topographia* was its spatial approach that gave a "graphic view from the hills" using the various neighborhoods to orient the reader's viewing of the city. More precisely, Marliani is the first to use a roving viewpoint to describe Rome. He does, in fact, cite Pausanias, author of the second-century *Periegesis*, whose title literally means a "walking around."[23] Marliani is the first of the Roman antiquarians to abandon the topical, nonspatial format of dividing Rome's monuments into categories (walls, temples, baths, etc.) used in previous descriptions of Rome, such as the twelfth-century *Mirabilia Urbis Romae*, Flavio Biondo's *Roma instaurata* (1443–46), and Andrea Fulvio's *Antiquaria Urbis* (1513) and *Antiquitates Urbis* (1527).[24] He is also the first to use the word *topography* as the title of his book.[25] Marliani follows the landscape on foot, reading space in a movement future travelers could imitate and use to recount their own experiences with Roman space.

Another aspect linking Marliani's topography to narrative has to do with the literary nature of the Renaissance guidebook itself.[26] Like his predecessors, and in accordance with the wishes of Rabelais, Marliani relates archaeological data accumulated during the progressive excavation, survey, and pillaging of Roman antiquities to a body of authoritative references on Roman geography, history, and literature.[27] He is extremely literary—excessively so in the opinion of his critics Pirro Ligorio and Benedetto Egio[28]—adapting spatial surveys conducted by "very learned men" working amid Rome's "altissimis ruinis" (very great ruins)[29] to a literary corpus that tells the story of Rome. Literary models and the philologist's love of words ultimately determine Marliani's conception, depiction, and narration of space.[30]

Compared to his predecessor, Andrea Fulvio, however, Marliani's narrated space can indeed be seen as a significant disruption of previous efforts to "restore" Rome. Fulvio's two descriptions had in fact used a rhetorical approach that blurred the lines between past and present, mixing images of the Rome of the popes with those of the ancient city. The first of Fulvio's works, published in 1513, in fact, envisioned the papacy of Leo X as the beginning of a new golden age, conflating past and present to rhetorical and political purpose.[31] Fulvio admits that "difficile est adeo confusa ruinis scire loca" (it is difficult to know the locations of [Rome's] confused ruins), but he also uses this confusion to build a picture of a Rome that is an image of its past, present, and future.[32] A few years later, when Fulvio took to "pounding the mass" of his earlier work to create the *Antiquitates Urbis* (1527), the need for a more "free" and "logical" order to his "literary monument" was evident.[33] Both works continued, however, to view Rome as a semantic field rather than a topographical space, as Fulvio collected and described the "memoratu digna" (things worth remembering) not as a geographer or architect but "etymologice... historice" (as a philologist and historian) in order to "refarcire" (restuff) Rome's memory markers with their original contents.[34]

Marliani, on the other hand, follows the topography of the modern city and identifies the remains of the past, navigating through history as he reconstructs it. His seven books lead the reader around the city's seven hills, beginning in its temporal and spatial beginning at the capitol and spiraling out in a spatial sequence that follows Rome's expansion through history.[35] Unlike Francesco Albertini, Pomponio Leto, Antonio Ponte, Fabio Calvo, and Andrea Fulvio, in other words, Marliani writes from within the city rather than from above it, an approach that recognizes the vastness of his material and the incomplete, contradictory evidence of ancient Rome's structure.[36] Marliani writes a topographical narrative that allows individual moments rooted and focalized within a specific spatial and historical context.

In the opinion of Marliani's translator, Ercole Barbarasa, it is precisely this "new order" that allows for a renewed comprehension of Roman grandeur. Marliani collects what had previously been "sparso per infiniti Scrittori latini, con molta diligenza, et nuovo ordine" (dispersed among infinite Latin writers, with great diligence, and a new order), and "narra distintamente a Monte per Monte tutte le cose, che sono state, et sono ancor' hoggi in ciascuno d'essi, seguitando il medesimo ordine, ne le Valli, et tutti gli altri luoghi di Roma" (distinctly narrates from hill to hill all the things that have been or still are located on each of these, following the same order in the valleys and other places of Rome).[37]

This topographical and historicized narrative thus offers a new way to read Roman greatness, one in which the symbolic message of antiquity is redirected toward the observer, who can then relate the "high ruins" of Rome to a personalized experience of place, as Barbarasa writes in his dedication to Giovanbattista Grimaldi:

> Convienvisi, per molte cagioni [...] massimamente, havendo voi l'animo (per propria natura) tutto volto a quelle operationi, le quali, con l'ardor de la gloria, v'infiammano a seguitare la grandezza, et Magnificenza de gli antichi, de la quale, niuna cosa è al mondo, che ne possa fare, ne più vero, ne più vivo testimoniano, che la maravigliosa Città di Roma, e per le cose, che vi sono hoggi, et maggiormente per quelle ne le miracolose ruine,

scampate da l'ingiuria del Tempo, con estremo stupore di tutto il mondo vi si contemplano.[38]

(It is worthwhile, for many reasons . . . and especially, since you have a soul [by its very nature] completely dedicated to those acts, which, with ardor and glory, inspire you to follow the greatness and magnificence of the ancients, of which there is nothing in the world that can provide a more truthful and living testimony than the marvelous city of Rome, for both the things that are there today and especially for those in the miraculous ruins, escaping the injury of time, evoking the great stupor of everyone who contemplates them.)

Narrating Rome's ruins transforms the spaces of antiquity into a speculum of the observer, whose soul assumes, as if by symbiosis, a reflection of their greatness. The traveler's "particular" narrative appropriates Roman space and assimilates it as an expression of self.

THE RE-MEMBERED TEXT: JOSEPH CATIN'S *DE L'ANTIQUITÉ DE PEZOLES*

Thanks to the efforts of Marliani and his predecessors, antiquarian symbols, embedded with the values of heroic action and philosophical introspection, are transformed into a spatial experience that humanists, noblemen, and aspiring servants of the state can weave into their own narratives of spatial experience. The intersection between land and text implicit in antiquarian discourse allows the traveler to use the tools of philology and rhetoric to cultivate the symbolic capital of contact with antiquity. This desire to appropriate space is evident in the *voyage d'Italie* in its various generic and stylistic manifestations. The question of authority and authorship is also a major concern as topographical references and classical *auctores* are deployed to narrate an individual's experience. Reflecting a construction of self, through a personalization of spatial contact, the mode of deployment of literary authority reflects on questions of social and political identity as well.

An early example of a late humanist creation of a rhetorical and narrative antiquarian space can be seen in the work of Joseph Catin, a French traveler who visited Naples and the Campi Flegrei in 1569, as recounted in the narrative he titled *De l'Antiquité de Pezoles*. This cosmographically inspired title belies the fact that what Catin actually presents is a narrative, which Luigi Monga appropriately retitled *Voyage de Pezoles*.[39] Catin borrows an image from the ritualized language of epic travel, describing a sailor caught in a storm at sea, battling the elements at the helm of a ship.[40] Protected only by his deity, he offers up "prayers and invocations." Returning to his homeland, he sacrifices to his god, bringing a gift of gratitude for the assistance he receives:

> Quemadmodum qui exteram navigationem agressi, ventis ac procellis diu longeque agitati, aliquod numen acclamitare eique vota vovere solent (peregrinatio enim huiusmodi vera est orationis votorumque disciplina, quia qui nescit orare discat navigare, ut ait D. Augustinus), salutis autem litus, portumque tandem advecti cum fuerint eidem numini non libare, non vota persolvere, non denique summam habere gratiam, impii nedum ingrate penitus esse(n)t animi. Sic ego . . .
>
> (Those who, engaged in a long journey by sea, tossed about for a long time by the wind and storms, offer up prayers and invocations to a divinity [this type of journey is indeed a discipline of prayer and devotion, since, as Augustine says, he who knows not how to pray must at least know how to navigate], would be truly ungrateful if, having at last reached the shore and port, pretended to no longer sacrifice to the same deity nor pray to it and, finally, to properly thank it. Thus I . . .)[41]

By writing his quid pro quo repayment in Latin, Catin affirms a double relationship with authority based on letters and commercial models of transactional exchange.[42] Offering his book as payment, he seeks the protection of his "illustrious and reverend lord, Lord Jacques Hugon" to protect his "small work" ("parvul[um] argument[um]") from the "envy of naysayers" ("a invidia maledicorum").[43] At the same time, Catin's figure of the sailor asserts his authorial independence,[44] discovering "lieux admirables tant en nature qu'en artifice" (admirable places both natural and manmade), "choses excellentes, dignes de merveilles" (excellent things worthy of marvel), and other things "peu cogneues" (little known) to the world at large, offering himself as the director of both his spatial discourse and his itinerary.[45]

Catin also undercuts traditional authority in a subtle and more erudite way, citing an invented proverb he attributes to Saint Augustine.[46] Calling for divine assistance, Catin insists on the dangers of traveling abroad and uses the authoritative words of the pseudo-Augustine to elevate the importance of navigating on one's own, as Pantragruel had done when he invited the frightened Panurge to "incessamment implorer, invocquer, prier, requerir, supplier (Dieu)" (incessantly implore, invoke, pray, search for and beg [God]) but to also stand on deck and "estre cooperateurs avecques luy" (cooperate with Him).[47] By calling the "exteram navigationis" (journey abroad) an "*orationis votorumque disciplina*" (discipline of oratory/prayer and devotion), moreover, Catin equates travel to a verbal performance. Travel is not only a substitute for discourse but also a form of it.[48]

THE RE-CITED TEXT

Joseph Catin was a lawyer from the city of Tonnerre, near Dijon. He traveled to Italy for unknown reasons on or before 1569, visiting Rome and Naples and making the tour of the Campi Flegrei and seaside city of Pozzuoli following the route described by Benedetto di Falco in *Descrittione dei luoghi antichi di Napoli e del suo amenissimo distretto*,[49] a work first published in 1549 that Benedetto Croce called the first description of Naples.[50] The tour began in the famous tunnel leading under the Posillipo to the lake and baths of Agnano, Pozzuoli, Cuma, Baiaie, and the surrounding regions marked by ancient ruins, marvelous geological phenomena, and historical sites that made this region fertile territory for a reading of space poised between myth and reality.

Catin uses this landscape to stage a personalized reading of his journey, appropriating the structure and title of Di Falco's description of Pozzuoli.[51] At the same time, Catin uses a method, common among humanist antiquarians, of following his guidebook as if it were a guide through texts. Giving preference to the pieces of text found in Di Falco and other sources, Catin constructs a new textual version of reality in a creative imitation of his source. He reconstructs, or re-members, antiquarian space, "rimembrando anzi cogliendo le sparse miche della nostra nobiltà, la memoria della quale, per la poco cura anzi per l'avaritia de purgati inchiostri se va di giorno un giorno tuffando nell'onde de l'oscuro oblio" (unnumbered)[52] (remembering, rather, collecting the spare crumbs of our nobility, the memory of which, due to the lack of care, worse, the stinginess of purged pens, goes everyday diving into the waves of obscure oblivion). Catin's restructuring of experience vacillates between textual servility and an absolute freedom to use text as he sees fit.

Signs of performance can be seen in the way Catin manipulates verbal authority. Besides its linear format, the most notable trait of *De l'Antiquité de Pezoles* is Catin's conspicuous display of authoritative references that threaten to take over his text. Listing his sources at the beginning and marking their use in the margins, he highlights the relationship between authority and his personal journey.[53] These practices, borrowed from geographical writing,[54] are further reinforced by his work's chosen title, which gives his work the appearance of a technical treatise. Catin's three-day excursion through the Campi Flegrei thus reads much like a meticulous combing through a the library, a reading from one text to another in a linking that makes sense only when viewed through his topographical itinerary.

At the same time, Catin avoids a straightforward dependence on literary authority, limiting this use to the opening presentation of his famous subject matter:

> Et est la part de ceste campagne que l'on appelle Terre de Labeur, pour la grande peine qu'on a à la cultiver, laquelle toutefoys est si fertile que le mesmes Pline en rend tel tesmoignage: *Quantum universas terras campus (Campanus) antecedit, tantum ipsum pars eiusque Leboriae vocantur,* "d'aultant que surmonte le champ de Campagne toutes les aultres terres d'aultant aussi la surpasse la partye d'icelle que l'on nomme Terre de Labeur." Et Polibe, autheur grec, maistre de Scipion l'Africain: *Est enim Campanus Ager copia rerum et fertilitate regionis ace amoenitate et pulchritudine loci excellentissimus, nam in littore maris positus est, et ex eo universo terrarum orbe venientes in Italiam innumerae gentes confluunt,* c'est à dire, "Le champ de la Campagne est en abondance et fertilité de sa region plaisant, et beaulté du lieu tresexcellent,

car il est situé sur le rivage de la mer et pour ce de toutes partz infinies nations du monde abordent l'Italye." (34)

(And this part of the country is called Terra di Lavoro, due to the great pains they take to cultivate it, which is nonetheless so fertile that Pliny himself gives testimony: *Quantum universas terras campus [Campanus] antecedit, tantum ipsum pars eiusque Leboriae vocantur*, "as much as the landscape of Campania surpasses that all the others of the world, so too the part called Terra di Lavoro surpasses it." And the Greek author Polybius, teacher of Scipio Africanus writes: *Est enim Campanus Ager copia rerum et fertilitate regionis ace amoenitate et pulchritudine loci excellentissimus, nam in littore maris positus est, et ex eo universo terrarum orbe venientes in Italiam innumerae gentes confluunt*, that is to say, "The land of Campania is pleasant in its abundance and fertility and beauty of its excellent location, as it is situated on the coast and for this reason infinite nations of the world come to see Italy.")

The hyperbolic praise of recognized authority provides the reader with a succinct reason for reading Catin's narrative. Catin speaks through the words of the ancients to establish the worth of his subject matter. His legal training shows in his conclusion that "on m'accordera donc facilement . . . , comme aussy c'est la vérité, qu'il n'y a paÿs au reste du monde qui se puisse égaler à ceste Terre de Labeur" (ibid.) (one will thus easily grant me that, as it is in fact truth, that there is no other country in the rest of the world equal to this Terra di Lavoro).[55]

In his "Prologue au lecteur," however, Catin bypasses what Deborah Losse calls the "chain of authority," entering directly into the narrative of events he experienced firsthand.[56] Explaining the genesis of his work, anchoring it in space-time, and assuring the reader of its truth, Catin steps into the role of an authorizing *auteur*:

L'an de grace mil cinq centz soixante et huict, le seiziesme jour du moys d'aoust ung jeune gentilhomme d'Auvergne et moy partismes de Naples pour aller veoir et, le plus diligemment qui seroit en nous, observer les lieux admirables tant en nature qu'en artifice d'une villette prés d'icelle Naples, nommée Pezoles, et ses circonvoisins. Ès environ de laquelle, en l'espace de huict milles du royaume, qui sont quatre lieues françoyses, *j'asseureray* librement que l'on peult veoir autant d'antiquitez et choses excellentes, dignes de merveilles, comme en tout le reste d'Italye. (31, emphasis mine)

(The year of our Lord, 1568, the sixteenth day of the month of August, a young gentleman from Auvergne and myself, left from Naples to go see the sites, admirable by nature and artifice, of a small city near the aforementioned Naples, named Pozzuoli, and its environs. In the vicinity of which, in the space of eight miles of the Kingdom, which are four French miles, *I will ensure* freely that one can see as many antiquities and excellent things, worthy of marvel, than in all the rest of Italy.)

By multiplying and overlapping the functions of the prologue in various prefatory sections, Catin highlights his creative use of authority.[57] Navigating a textual topography whose correspondence to the external world is not always stable or verifiable, Catin uses the stability of the written word to revive an estranged discourse, certifying the veracity of marvels that challenge the mind and senses.

Citation also has an aesthetic function, allowing for the pleasure of recognition and providing his reader "quelques relasches à leurs afaires" (some relaxation from their affairs) so that they "soulagent leurs espritz par la lecture de ce petit discours" (comfort their spirits by the reading of this small discourse). Familiar words, repeated like well-known images today, allow the reader to find her way "without taking the pain to go so far" (sans prendre peine de s'acheminer si loing) through imagined distant space.

Understanding the boundaries and functions of citation is one of the primary challenges to reading the *voyage d'Italie*. Is citation an ancillary, aesthetic tool used for the entertainment of the reader, a necessity for the traveling researcher, or part of the itinerary itself as readings of topographical "inventions poétiques" insert themselves into the traveler's narrative? The abundance of citations that come to play in Catin's first chapter illustrates the difficulty of assigning one role to each as a series of direct and indirect quotations by Petrarch, Giovanni Pontano, and Saint Jerome come in sequence, culminating in an almost liturgical citing of

Pontano's praise of the nymph Patulcis, which Catin translates into an affectionate and playful French:

> Tuque, o mihi culta Patulci, ...
> Prima adsis primosque mihi dea collige flores
> Impleat et socios tecum Antoniana quasillos,
> Sic tibi perpetuum est spiret rosa, floreat urna
> Scilicet urna tui qua conditur umbra Maronis
> Premiere icy, ma Patulque tresbelle,
> assiste moy, viens, ma dive, amasser
> les primes fleurs et qu'Antignane attelle
> les plains paniers, sans aucung en laisser,
> chez toy la rose au doux soufler respire
> et puisse aussi y fleurir le tumbeau
> ce tumbeau sainct lequel l'umbre retire
> de ton Maro en son sein cher et beau.

By highlighting the literary nature of the topography of the Campi Flegrei, Catin's narrative thus becomes, as promised, a performed *oration*, an example of performative narrative that creates and ascertains reality.[58] Citation provides information and generates new textual and spatial encounters, allowing the previously unvoiced Catin to express his own authority through contact with space and letters.

REWRITING GEOGRAPHY

Catin's Campi Flegrei is a space of mystery and philological depth.[59] But while this geographical area is real, it is also a chosen space, selected "out of all that (he) remarked and learned during his travels in Italy" ("inter ea quae peregre aliquando in Italia notaverim et didiscerim" [28]). In addition to having a wealth of ancient and natural wonders, the Campi Flegrei's man-made and volcanic morphology allow Catin to frame his narrative and reinforce the themes of philological and topographical digging. The most important of these literary and geographical topoi (places) is the tunnel that opens and closes his narrative and serves as a symbolic liminary marker between external reality and the created space of narration. Catin's narrative begins at the entrance to the "grotte obscure" (obscure cave) of Chalcidian origins that leads from the Mergellina to the

Campi Flegrei and ends with another cave of even greater mythological importance. Thus separated from the world of everyday existence, Catin's narrative between two caves leads the reader through a space dominated by mystery and driven by subterranean exploration.

Catin's quotation of Virgil, Strabo, or Pliny also works as a rhetorical manipulation whose consequences can become topographical. Using the land-text to make an argument, he transforms space into a discursive tool. Catin first does this as he traverses the tunnel leading from Naples to Pozzuoli and enters a topographical and narrative space characterized by the sympathetic resonance of text. Recounting an incident borrowed from Petrarch through a reading of Benedetto di Falco's *Descrittione dei luoghi antichi di Napoli* (25–27), he neglects to mention his source, Di Falco, transitioning directly into Petrarch's words in a way that blurs the borders between original and borrowed text. Petrarch's experience becomes a part of Catin's story, lending it an associative meaning connected to his position in space.

Catin describes his physical location in precise detail. Proceeding from "un bout de faulzbourg du quay près la marine" (35) (a bit of suburb near the port) (Mergellina) and passing "par dedans une montagne percée" (inside a pierced mountain named Posillipo), he focalizes his narrative onto a specific topographical point in space-text.[60] He describes the tunnel's dimensions as thirty feet wide and eight hundred long and describes its opening as well as "un soubzpireau ou larmier qui s'escoule et panche de ladicte montagne" (ibid.) (a small hole that flows down from the said mountain, giving air to this cave or grotto). His search for the right word to describe this "pertuys et ouverture appellé en italien *grota*" (35–36) (hole or opening called in Italian *grotta*) illustrates his amazement at the tunnel's size and ancient origins.[61] A faint light sifts down from above, not so much, however, that "qu'il ny face tresobscur" (ibid.) (it was not exceedingly dark). Coachmen race madly in the darkness, calling out "*Verso il mare* (or) *Alla montagna*" (ibid.), and Catin meets Petrarch, riding with King Robert of Anjou:

> Le Petrarche, lequel chevauchant avec le roy Robert, de Naples par ceste grote resolut ainsi ceste question, comme luy mesmes l'escript en ses oeuvres latines [. . .] entre le mont de Falerne (lequel est proche de la Roche Montdragon) et la mer y a une montagne persée par les mains des hommes, lequel oeuvre le

vulgaire ignorant pense avoir esté faict de Virgile par enchantemens magiques. (36)

(Petrarch, who riding with King Robert, of Naples through this tunnel resolved in this manner this question, as he himself writes in his Latin works: Between Falernum [which is near Mondragone] and the sea there is a mountain pierced by the hands of men, which the ignorant masses believe was made by Virgil through some magical spell.)

The king asks Petrarch "en presence de beaucoup" (in the presence of a lot of people) what he thinks of this belief, to which Petrarch answers, "Jamais je n'avoys leu Virgile avoir esté magicien" (ibid.) (I had never read that Virgil was a magician). The king, "Lors, approuvant ceste response d'ung visage remply de joyeuse auctorité et clinant la teste confessa n'y veoir vestiges quelconques de magie, mais bien plus clerement la trasse du burin, ciseau et aultres instrumens de fer" (36) (then, approving this answer with a face filled with joyous authority and nodding his head confessed that he had not seen any signs of magic, but rather clear traces of the chisel and other iron implements). Petrarch's encounter with King Robert occurs in the same spot where Catin begins his narrative. The textual *locus* also pertains to Catin's political situation, which, like that of the young Petrarch, is that of a secretary in search of employment, protection, and honor. Catin, like Petrarch, must entertain his lord through verbal interpretation linked to topographical space.

The mythical topography highlighted by Petrarch's encounter with King Robert provides a key to reading Catin's text, justifying his subsequent indiscretions with the poet's ability to play with "fables et mensonges" (fables and lies) and "fictions poétiques" (poetic fictions) (75). The first of Catin's rhetorical modifications of the landscape occurs shortly after his meeting with Petrarch, as he exits the tunnel and finds, "si tost qu'on peult veoir l'air" (as soon as one can see the air), the tomb of Virgil, principal poet of the Campi Flegrei:

Illec se veoyent ancor les anciens characteres à demy effacez et rompuz par l'injure du temps de l'epitaphe en ce distique commung que Virgile feit soimesmes:

> Mantua me genuit, Calabri rapuere, tenet nunc
> Parthenae, cecini pascua, rura, duces (37–38)

> (There can still be seen the ancient letters, half-erased and broken by the injurious hand of time the epitaph in this common couplet that Virgil himself wrote:
> Mantua gave birth to me, Calabria carried me off, now Parthenope holds my bones, I sang of pastures, fields, leaders)

Di Falco's description is correct, since the traveler going to Naples (from Pozzuoli and into the Mergellina) can indeed find the tomb of Virgil memorialized in Pontano's paganizing verses. Catin is heading in the opposite direction, reversing the location, allowing him to insert a key literary locus on the inside of his perfectly framed narrative.

FOLLOWING PLINY

Catin rewrites space more openly the next day as he attempts to prove, against all physical, written, and oral evidence, that the flaming caldera of the Solfatara is in fact Mount Vesuvius, where the Elder Pliny died in pursuit of his excessive curiosity. It is a curious staging, certainly, and one that can be explained by Catin's ardent need to work colorful literary passages into his narrative and associate himself with famous authors. He cites Robert Estienne, Pliny, Livy, Suetonius, and Sebastian Münster and culminates with the poet Martial, concocting a literary *locus* of volcanic fury that sets the stage for his entry into the valley "in quo a gigantibus gesta fabulae divulgant" (where fables tell of the giants' feats).

Catin actually builds a plausible case that he is actually inside the mouth of Vesuvius, using literary passages that resemble the places he had just been:

> Car comme tresbien disct Sebastien Munster: *Potest (autem) condescendi (mons ille) et ubi superatus fuerit collis praeceps, pervenitur ad craterem qui amplus et profundus est, et potest in eum sine periculo descendi;* c'est à dire "On peult monter et sitost que l'on est parvenu au dessus, le dedans est en forme de precipice et parvient on à sa large couppe ou vallée, car telle est sa concavité; et peult on sans danger y descendre." (46)

(As Sebastien Münster says so well: One can go down into this mountain and once you have gone over the precipice, you come to a crater that is large and deep, and you can go down in without risk.)

This textual detail proves Catin's position, while the abundant descriptions of flames and smoke, eruptions and danger, help him make his case. Without this textual rapprochement, of course, Catin's mention of Pliny's "voulant recherche cest embrasement et degorgement de flamme, pierres ardentes et feu" (46) (desiring to research the causes of this burning and spitting of flame, burning stones and fire) would also be out of place, leading Catin into a geotextual void, a space with no resemblance to the textual world. Catin thus has to argue against Pandolfo Collenuccio and his translator Denis Sauvage de Fontenailles, who claim that Vesuvius is the "Monte de Somi or Soma" (Mount Soma) (which it is), objecting that "le Mont Soma est huict mil au delà de Naples, tirant vers le Calabre, et j'ay oncques ouy dire qu'il jettast feu ou flammes, ains seulement des vignes, dequelles j'ay mangé des raisins jaunastres et duretz" (46) (Monte Soma is eight miles away from Naples, heading toward Calabria, and I have never heard of it throwing out fire or flames as I have also been to the center and did not see any signs [of flames], on the contrary, only vines, from which I ate some yellowish, hard grapes).

Catin's proof depends on textual resemblance that is approximate and accumulative, illustrating what Foucault calls the Renaissance logic of similitude.[62] The fact that Robert Estienne writes of a mountain "vomiting great quantities of fire" ("qui jadis vomissoit beaucoup de feu" / *olim plurimum ignis evomebat* [47]) and Münster recounts that "le Veseve s'enflamba et jetta des caillous treshaut, puys dégorgea tant de flammes de feu que de l'air ardent deux villes furent bruslées" (48), presents an image that resembles Catin's geographical location much more than the "hard, yellowish grapes" of Monte Soma. This setup thus allows him to recite and translate Martial picturesquely:

Hic pampineis viridis Vesuvius umbris
Cuncta jacent flammis et tristi mersa favilla; c'est à dire:
Voicy le verd Vesuve, à son umbre pamprée
Où tout est soubz le feu et soubz cendre eschauffée. (ibid.)

(Here verdant vines cover Vesuvius' slopes
Where all is burnt by fire and flames)

The *topos* of Vesuvian activity illustrates the danger Catin faces, painting a picture of a "grotte mortelle" (deadly cave) crossed in order to establish a literary connection to the elder Pliny, the emblem of excessive curiosity:

> Non contens encor, fusmes advertis de nostre guide de ne passer oultre, et si le voulions faire, nous menaçoyt de nous laisser; toutesfoys, après qu'il eut congneu que la curiosité me rendoit opinastre, aprochant toujours de plus près, me suyvant volontiers ce bon gentilhomme mien compagnon, le cueur saultelant d'aise tremblante, la guide demeuroyt derriere nous cria que si quelque vapeurs ou espesse fumée se levoyent, nous ne bougeassions d'un lieu et que nous eussions à diligemment boucher nostre nez tant de peur d'estre surpris d'icelle que aussy nous remuans en son obscurité cheoir en quelques de ces trous et chaudieres bouillantes, lesquelles encor qu'elles ne fussent creuses beaucoup, leur chaleur grande nous eust peu toutesfoys arrester et brusler. (49–50)

> (Still not satisfied, our guide entreated us to stop, threatening to leave if we went any further, but after seeing that curiosity had pushed me and this nice gentleman my companion to go closer our guide stayed back with trembling heart and warned us to diligently plug our noses lest some vapor or dense smoke overtake us and to avoid wandering in the fog and falling into one of these holes or boiling cauldrons, which, though they were hollowed out, could nonetheless burn us with their intense heat.)

Faced with this navigational hazard, Catin's companion falls, like Panurge, to "pensant à sa conscience" (50) (thinking of his conscience [praying]), while our author touches and tests the hollow sulfurous cavities and pushes on toward the shore, acknowledging with a note of self-approval his suffering from a "petite peur d'estre le second à Pline au mesme gendre de mourir" (50) (small fear of following Pliny in the same type of death).

Catin shows himself to be both a diligent researcher and a creative reappropriator of textual authority, two skills essential to his future career as a lawyer and royal secretary.

POLITICS, THE COSMOS, AND THE INDIVIDUAL: THE SUCCESS OF THE *VOYAGES DE JACQUES DE VILLAMONT*

Catin's unpublished work fits into a world in which literature and politics were linked through the writer's service to a wealthy patron.[63] Like Du Bellay's *sonnets courtisans*, they insert the writer into a social and political network by addressing specific powerful individuals. By publishing his *Voyages* with the Royal Press of Claude de Monstroeil and Jean Richer, the Breton gentleman Jacques de Villamont addresses a larger political, social, and ethical context. Like Montaigne had done in his *Essais*, Villamont downplays his desire to go public, composing a work for himself that he then contemplates in idleness:

> De moy (Amy lecteur) je confesse avoir esté des ma jeunesse fort curieux de voir pour apprendre, à quoy j'ay employé un fort long temps tant en l'Europe qu'en l'Asie, apportant tant ce que j'ay peu de diligence et d'exacte recherche, pour m'en retourner avec un esprit plus poly et propre aux affaires, je ne sçay si mon labeur m'a succedé selon mon desir. Quoy que soit, je me suis tant pleu en mes voyages, et en la souvenance des choses rares que j'y avois veues avec tres grande peine et frais presque insupportables, qu'estant en fin retourné sain et dispos en mon pais, j'ay voulu contenter plus longuement mon esprit et contempler la mer fracassée des vents et tempestes en mes perilleuses rencontres, me representant ceux qui sont encore en leurs peregrinations, et ay mis par escrit ce que j'ay veu et cogneu de singulier et rare par tout où j'ay esté, dont un autre qui sera employé en meilleurs affaires que je ne suis, pourra faire son profit.[64]

> (On my part, [my dear reader], I confess having been since my earliest youth very curious to see in order to learn, activity I have conducted for a very long time in Europe and in Asia, bringing what diligence and exacting research I could, in order to return with a spirit more refined and proper for affairs. I do not know if my work has been as successful as I had hoped. Nonetheless, I enjoyed my travels very much and also the memory of rare things I saw with great effort and nearly unbearable expenses, that, having finally returned in my country, I decided to take

pleasure a little longer and contemplate the wind-beaten sea and tempests of my dangerous encounters, representing to myself those that are still on their journeys, and I wrote down everything I saw and learned that is singular and rare everywhere I went, of which someone else, who might be better employed in affairs than me, might take proper advantage.)

This image of the noble traveler, retired in the harbor of his home, recalling his past adventures and imagining others still caught in storms at sea, accomplishes two goals. On the one hand, it introduces the reader to Villamont's accomplishments, alluding to the "perillous encounters" that form the content of the *Voyages*. Villamont presents himself as an inquisitive researcher who invests his own time and money in search of rare and interesting things. He also highlights his current inactivity in the world of "affaires," offering his research for others' use while he rests in leisured contemplation. Like Montaigne had done in the *Essais*, Villamont represents himself and, more importantly, studies his past in a way that allows him to highlight his formed judgment and ability.

Like Montaigne too, Villamont is forced to pass from his inner self, through a circle of friends, to the larger public, remarking that "Je m'estois resolu de garder cela comme un memoire pour moy seul, si beaucoup de gens d'honneur (mes amis) qu'en ont eu communication, ne m'eussent poussé, importuné et contraint de le communiquer à tout le monde" (ibid.) (I had resolved to keep it as a memoir for myself, if many honorable people [my friends] who had heard about it, had not pushed, importuned and constrained me to communicate it to the entire world). This circle of friendship forces him to offer private memory in the service of a larger political purpose, transforming private treasure into a public good: "Ainsi faut-il rendre à nostre patrie ce devoir, si nous ne sommes employez à le servir, pour le moins ne receler ingratement à ceux qu'on y employe les thresors qui sont cachez en nous" (ibid.) (Thus we must perform this duty for our nation, if we are not employed in her service, at least to not ungratefully hide to those that do work for her the treasure that are hidden within us).

The image of the inactive nobleman reminds the reader of Villamont's ability, punctuated, at least twice, by the remark that he has not yet been called upon to serve. The narrative of his journey thus substitutes for bodily service while at the same time underlining the injustice of his unemployment. Villamont thus portrays himself as conducting the useful work of exploration and discovery and reminds his reader that travel is the primary means by which political experience is obtained:

> Entre les moyens que les anciens ont recherché pour acquerir la science de regir et gouverner les grands estats et republiques, celuy semble avoir esté le principal et plus certain que l'experience des gouvernements estrangers apporte, pour ce que sur leur modelle on bastit telle forme qu'on veut, prenant des uns et des autres ce qui est bon, et delaissant le contraire: Comme à la vérité c'est la vraye science politique que l'experience, et n'y a aucunes regles de philosophie, ou maxime de police si certaines, que celles que nous apprenons par l'exemple d'autruy: Cela se void és livres des plus advisez et sages qui ayent onques escrit. Et certainement l'experience nous a faict cognoistre que ceux qui avoyent beaucoup voyagé, et remarqué avec jugement les façons de vivre des provinces les plus esloignees, estoient beaucoup plus propres au maniement des affaires, que ceux qui s'estoient contentez de vivre en leurs maisons et fueilleter leurs livres, qui ne peuvent si exactement representer les costumes gardees és pays estranges, que la practique qu'un chacun qui y a esté en apprend. A ceste cause Ulisses est recommandé de ce qu'il avoit veu plusieurs et divers pays, et retenu les mœurs des uns et des autres: car ce n'est rien de voir qui ne juge et qui ne retient ce qu'il a veu pour en faire profit: Et aussi changer d'air, non pas esprit, c'est pourmener sans profit. (a iii)

> (Among the means that the ancients researched to acquire the science of ruling and governing large states and republics, the primary and most certain appears to have been that brought by the experience of foreign governments, since on this model one builds the state one wants, taking from one or the other what is good and leaving the opposite: Since in truth experience is the true political science and there are no rules of philosophy or maxims of government more certain that those we learn by the example of others. This can be seen in the books of the wisest and most informed people who have ever written. And certainly experience has taught us that those who have traveled

extensively and taken judicious note of the ways of life of the most far away provinces were much more adept at managing things than those who were happy to live in their homes leafing through their books, which cannot represent so accurately represent the customs of strange countries as well as the practice that each individual who has been there learns. For this reason, Ulysses is praised for having seen many different lands, and retains their customs: for seeing is nothing without judgment and retaining of what one has seen and, also, changing air and not one's mind is to wander without profit.)

Travel brings knowledge of foreign governments and prepares the individual to govern "large states and republics." This "true political science" is a personally acquired good that can only be learned by going to a place ("qu'un chacun qui Y a esté apprend"). Villamont distinguishes himself from the sedentary humanist, whose book learning does not qualify him for public service, representing his "premieres actions" (first actions), conducted in the prime of youth. He apologizes for the inelegant presentation of his work, which is again a way of underlining his social status as a nobleman and soldier, "attendu que je n'ay employé mon temps à suivre la trouppe des muses, mais plustost me suis addonné, voyageant par diverses provinces, à l'exercitation des armes, comme propres à ma condition" (since I have not spent my time following the troop of the muses, but rather gave myself, travelling around various provinces, to the practice of arms, as is fitting to my condition). The publication of Villamont's "dangereuses rencontres" (dangerous encounters/meetings) thus underlines the injustice of the traveler writing a book and contemplating his own image even as books and contemplation are attacked as insufficient tools for learning.

COSMOGRAPHICAL FRAMING

First published in 1595, Villamont's *Voyages* became the most successful travel narrative of the close of the sixteenth century. At least a part of this success can be attributed to Villamont's extensive itinerary that covered a route from Paris through Italy, where he visited all the major cities that were fast becoming part of a standardized tour. Sailing from Venice, he followed the coast of Dalmatia and Greece and crossed the southern

Mediterranean to Haifa and Jerusalem. Villamont thus expands the "voyage de Jérusalem" into something much larger and more dispersive, visiting Italy, Syria, Phoenicia, and Egypt and offering "ample descriptions" of "la Sclavonie, Grece, Turquie, Moree, Cephalonie, Chypre, Hierusalem et de tous les Saincts lieux où nostre seigneur a faict des miracles" (n.p. [a i]) (Slavonia, Greece, Turkey, Morea, Cephalonia, Cyprus, Jerusalem, and all the Holy places where our Lord performed miracles). As an anthropologist, he also describes the social customs and practices of the peoples he encounters, the "croyance des Chrestiens Grecs, Armeniens, Syriens, Georgiens, Alyssins, et autres Chrestiens de l'Asie et l'Affrique" (beliefs of Greek, Armenian, Georgian, Alyssin, and other Christians of Asia and Africa); Turkish practices of childhood education, death rites, and beliefs in resurrection and punishment in the afterlife; the pyramids and mummies; information on an "herbe nommee opium" (207v) (herb called opium); and so on. By dedicating an entire book to his time in Italy, moreover, this rambling, dispersive journey becomes the first published *voyage d'Italie*, offering a narrated tour through the "villes et forteresses de l'Italie, et des antiquitez et choses sainctes et modernes qui s'y voyent" (n.p. [a 1v]) (cities and fortresses of Italy, the antiquities and holy and modern things that are seen there).

A second, no less important, reason for Villamont's success is the liveliness and readability of his work, which abandons the descriptive method of "cosmographers" in order to focus on the personal details of his adventures. Villamont provides details found in Leandro Alberti's *Descrittione di Tutta Italia* (1550) and Belleforest's version of Münster's *Cosmographia*, contextualized within the narrative of a personal journey. Like Marliani's move toward topographical narrative, this seemingly simple choice requires some theorization, which Villamont supplies in the opening pages of his work. Whereas his preface had highlighted the importance of developing political experience, the traveler who left Paris in June 1588 is a divinely inspired explorer of the excellent painting of the cosmos:

> Comme un excellent peintre, lequel voulant representer en son tableau, la description de plusieurs celebres regions et provinces, n'est content d'y avoir naïvement pourtraict les beaux paysages verdoyants, entre-suivis des prairies esmaillees de diverses fleurs, les claires fontaines et ruisseaux environnant de toutes parts: mais

tasche aussi par son industrie d'y effigier quelque belle figure d'homme pour le decorer et enrichir. Ainsi ce divin peintre et ouvrier de toute la nature, ayant une puissance infinie, basty ce beau temple et palais celeste, iceluy orné et embelly d'estincellans flambeaux, l'establissant le throsne et siege de sa Majesté divine, ne s'est contenté seulement de cela, ains a voulu ça bas, d'un divin pinceau peindre et tracer un autre monde terrestre, l'escabeau de ses pieds, auquel il a faict paroistre l'excellence de son ouvrage et labeur admirable de ses mains. Et afin qu'il ne manquast rien au comble de perfection de cest ouvrage, il a creé l'homme dedans le pourpris d'iceluy, auquel il a empraint et gravé l'idée et image de sa divine essence: le constituant Roy et Monarque de tout l'univers, pour s'esgayer et pourmener, par toutes les bornes et limites d'iceluy: afin qu'en telles peregrinations et voyages, il vint avec la raison et ratiocination dont il avoit esté doüé de Dieu à rechercher ce qui estoit de beau et rare sous la voulte des cieux. (1r–v)

(Like an excellent painter, who, desiring to represent in his painting the description of several famous regions and provinces, is not content to have naturally portrayed the beautiful green landscapes, interspersed with prairies enameled with various flowers, clear fountains and streams surrounding all around, but tries also in his work to affix some human figure to decorate and enrich his work. So too this Divine painter and craftsman of all nature, having infinite power, built this beautiful temple and celestial palace, decorated and beautified by shining torches, establishing it as the throne and seat of his divine Majesty, was not content only with this, but wanted to trace here below with a divine brush another, terrestrial world, the stool for his feet, to which he made the excellence of the admirable work of his hands appear. And so that nothing would be lacking from the ultimate perfection of this work, he created man within this enclosure, engraved with an idea and image of His divine essence, making him King and Monarch of all the universe, to enjoy and explore all its outer limits: so that in these wanderings and journeys, he arrives through the reason and logic God gave him to seek out what is rare and beautiful under the vault of the stars.)

The citation of painting gives another dimension to Villamont's self-framing as the image of a divine researcher exploring the cosmos supplants that of Villamont traveling to dangerous places. If the reader had been implicitly present in the figure of Villamont, sitting with his own book in a library among friends, this second description places him at the center of a Creation whose image is "imprinted and engraved" in his soul. This monarch is pushed to investigate the universe, learning and absorbing the wisdom embodied in rare and beautiful things, while God sits back, like the writer of the preface, to observe man observing His Creation. Man's observation thus gives perspective and meaning to what Villamont calls the "pourpris" (garden) of the universe.

Villamont's novel usage of the term *André de la Vigne*[65] reserved for the garden of France marks the opening of the traveler's horizon and affirms his editorial, spiritual, and perhaps even political independence. Rather than the closure of the Alps and France's shores, Villamont's "pourpris" reaches to the stars, making his traveler a seeker of a higher truth, unlimited by national barriers and viewpoints. Man's purpose on earth is to "rechercher . . . ce qui est(oit) rare et beau" (seek out what is rare and beautiful), and in this way the traveler becomes an allegorical embodiment of the human struggle for knowledge. The study of the universe in its infinite variety is man's greatest form of worship:

> Et à ceste fin Dieu a empraint en l'ame de l'homme un désir naturel d'apprendre, et de ne s'en lasser jamais jusques au tombeau, et ce qui plaist plus à l'homme sont les diversitez des choses qui s'opposent de jour à autre à ses sens, et entrent en son intellect, dont il fait son proffit, et petit à petit s'acquiert une science, laquelle il ne veut pas communiquer à lui seul, ains en veut rendre participans les autres, estimant son silence dommageable s'il se taisoit, ce qu'à peu pres il pense que les autres n'ont pas remarqué comme il a faict. (1v–2r)

> (And to this end God imprinted a natural desire to learn in the soul of man so that he never tires until he goes to his grave, and is most pleased by the diversities of things that come from day to day to his senses and enter his intellect, from which he takes his profit, and bit by bit acquires a science, which he cannot keep to himself, but rather wants to share it with others, considering

his silence damaging, since others will not have taken note of what he has done.)

The pleasure of research and the duty to communicate are means of realizing God's will. Rather than abstractly contemplating, man must investigate the "diversity of things" in order to gradually acquire "une science" (a science).

TOPOGRAPHICAL FRAMING

Villamont's narrative can thus be interpreted as an extended, self-centered depiction of personal action in which the surrounding spaces of the "divine" painting focus the reader's attention on the traveler. Just as Villamont will "voir pour apprendre" (see in order to learn), so too his reader will be "excitez et conviez" (excited and invited) by the "descriptions des belles villes, citez et provinces que je leur mettray devant les yeux comme en un tableau, en ce present discours" (2v) (descriptions of beautiful cities, fortresses, and provinces that I will place before their eyes as in a painting, in the present discourse). The spaces traversed are a painted decoration for the figure of the traveler.

A key moment in this moving picture occurs at the city of Lyon, where Villamont shifts from providing practical travel advice to the narrative of his departure from the "cité fort renommée" (3v) (the very renowned city) of Lyon. Having "rolled through" the familiar spaces of Champagne and Burgundy, Villamont embarks on the Saône River descending to the city famous for the "grand commerce que s'y fait de toutes parts" (3v) (great commerce that is practiced in all directions). After describing the city's location between two mountains and recalling the existence of a citadel that the Lyonais had dismantled, he describes the mixing of the Saône and Rhône in the center of the city:

> Par le milieu d'icelle passent le fleuve de la Saone, et de l'autre costé vers Savoye, le turbulent fleuve du Rosne, lequel baignant les murailles de la cité, vient courant et bruyant rencontrer la dormante Saone laquelle se sentant toucher d'un choc si violent, se retire à quartier, pour n'empescher son cours, la suivante toutefois jusqu'à la pointe d'un rocher, ou se va joignans ensemble courent baigner le bord des murailles de plusieurs belles villes

de Dauphiné de Languedoc, et Provence où ils entrent en la mer Mediterranee. (3v–4)

(In the middle of Lyon pass the river Saône and, from the other side, towards Savoy, the turbulent Rhône river, which, bathing the walls of the city, comes running and roaring to meet the sleeping Saône which, feeling itself touched by such a violent shock, pulls back so as not to block its course, following it nonetheless to the point of a shoal, where they go on joining together and flowing along the edge of the walls of several beautiful cities of Dauphiné, Languedoc and Provence where they enter into the Mediterranean Sea.)

The flow of these waters suggests the many possibilities offered to the traveler. Alluding to the many walled cities that grow up along the riverbanks, Villamont notes how the spaces pull him along, "inciting" him to explore new places. He is urged by the river's violence to hop a boat "pour aller veoir Vienne" (to go see Vienne), where he hoped to see "les antiquitez de Pilate" (4), but

y ayant navigé environ quatre lieuës, survint telle tourmente avec tonnerre et esclairs, que craignant faire un piteux naufrage au profond de ses ondes, priay le nocher me mettre à bord; ce qu'ayant fait avec grandissime difficulté, et me voyant hors du péril, où j'avois esté, je rendy graces à Dieu. (4)

(having navigated there for about four miles, such a storm came upon us with thunder and lightning that, fearing a pitiful shipwreck beneath the waves, I prayed my pilot leave me ashore, which, having done with great difficulty, and seeing myself out of danger where I had been, I gave thanks to God.)

As with Catin and Du Bellay, Villamont's near shipwreck is a thematic and spatial reminder of the dangers he will face in his upcoming journey. His risk of being left "beneath the waves" separates his narrative from the normalcy of what had preceded it and brings it into the magical space of the voyage. Later on, in the Adriatic, he braves the truly dangerous crossing of the Adriatic and southern Mediterranean. While

Villamont's foolhardiness appears to push him into this situation, his faith (his prayers first to the "nocher" and then giving thanks to God) guides him on the turbulent waters of his journey. This incident shows his determination, as the rivers that separate the familiar spaces of France from Savoy, the Alps, Italy, and the world become a barrier to be crossed, an obstacle surmounted using ingenuity and resolve.

From Lyon, Villamont, like most travelers, contracts with a "Maron" to take him to Turin. Traversing regions inhabited by bears, "autres bêtes sauvages" (other savage beasts), and thieves, he arrives in Chambéry, former capital of Savoy, whose position amid the hostile environment of the Alps Villamont paints in colorful detail:

> Son habitation est mal plaisante, à raison des grandes neiges et pluyes qui s'y font ordinairement: comme aussi par toute la Savoye, laquelle est composee de tres-hautes montaignes, les cimes desquelles se voyent peu souvent abandonnees de leur accoustumee blancheur: Mais celles que le clair Phoebus eschauffe de se plus ardens rayons, se reduisent incontinent en eau, laquelle on void descendre du haut des montagnes, menant un bruit fort impetueux. (6)

> (Living there is very unpleasant, because of the heavy snowfall and rains, which is true for all of Savoy, which is made up of very high mountains, the peaks of which are seldom seen without their accustomed whiteness, but those that shining Phoebus heats with his most ardent rays, are reduced immediately into water, which one sees flowing down from the tops of the mountains, making a most impetuous noise.)

Villamont's eyes follow the course of these streams that would lead him over the Alpine pass, viewing their formation on the mountains' peaks. The accumulative construction of his sentences imitates the concatenation of spaces that link the heating of snow, the formation of rivers, and the danger of inundations carried as far away as Grenoble. Movement and transformation are reflected in a multiplication of verbs in the present and present-progressive tenses similar to those used by Montaigne in his Alpine crossing ("se reduisant," "descendre," "menant," "s'engendre," "prenant," "murmurant," "s'augmentant," "descendent," "faict," "emporte").

If the principal characteristic appears to be the otherness and danger posed by these scenes, their picturesque beauty is not lost on the explorer:

(L'Isère) décore et embellit grandement la forteresse inexpugnable du château de Montmelian, qui est situé sur une montaigne, au pied de laquelle court ladite riviere, que nous passames sur un meschant pont de bois, qui est fort long comme de trois à quatre cents pas, et estroit, et sur lequel il faut necessairement prendre Bulettes des gardes qui y sont establis. (6)

(The Isère decorates and greatly beautifies the inexpungible castle of Montmélian, which is situated on a mountain, at the foot of which the said river flows, which we crossed over on a rickety wooden bridge, which is very long, like three or four hundred paces, and narrow, and on which you have to show your certificate of health to the guards standing there.)

The framing of the passage of Villamont (and his unmentioned companions) evokes the immensity of the mountain scenery. Violent rivers surround the travelers, who have been shrunk into tiny figures crossing a long, narrow, wooden bridge passing beneath the mighty fortress of Montmélian. The rolling hills and comfortable towns of France—all traces of the familiar—have disappeared, leaving Villamont to confront the bewildering otherness of the passage of the Alps.

BUREAUCRACY AND COURAGE

In the Piedmont town of Novalesa, Villamont has to confront another obstacle, having been subjected to the quarantine despite his meticulous preparation of his "bullettes" in Paris and Lyon. The health commissioner advises he send a messenger to Turin to seek permission to pass, but Villamont decides to listen to the local guides, who encourage him to climb the peak of the "treshaut mont de Roche-Melon" (very high Roche Melon).[66] In climbing this high mountain, Villamont abandons the standard path in favor of adventure. His display of audacity, moreover, reminds his reader of the purpose of his journey as an exploratory celebration of curiosity and pursuit of exceptional experiences.

The pages leading up to the summit of Roche Melon build up to a climactic scene at the mountain's peak. Passing over Mont Cenis, Villamont had described the inhospitable climate of the Alpine passes. He crossed a hostile landscape where the fluid elements threatened to carry him to an icy death, a place where whirlwinds "levent la neige en si grande quantité, qu'estant portée de violence, elle entraine avec soy quelques passans (qu'elle rencontre) et les ensevelit et accable tout à coup amoncelee sur eux" (7r) (pick up the snow in such great quantities that, carried with violence, whisks off any passers-by it happens to meet and entombs and overcomes them, piled all over them). Many travelers submit to the intense cold and "sont jettez en la chappelle des transis" (ibid.) (are thrown into the Chapel des Transis), where Villamont observed "grand nombre de corps morts" (7r) (a great number of dead bodies).[67] Villamont also describes the danger of hidden crevasses "lesquels estants comblez de neiges et le chemin pareillement, facilement on peut tomber dedans, et estre asseuré n'en relever jamais" (ibid.) (which, being covered by snow just like the road, one can easily fall in and be assured to never come back out).

The monstrosity of a landscape that threatens to devour the traveler is also reflected in the appearance of the Alpine residents, whose hypothyroidism is attributed to the melted snow, which is "fort pernicieuse à boire" and causes an "enfleure de gorge" that is "fort monstrueuse à voir" (6v) (very monstrous to look at).[68] Their desperation and poverty also cause a certain liquidity or amorphousness, since "ils sont tous pauvres, demandans l'aumosne importunement aux passans, *se laissant couler du haut des montaignes en bas pour avoir un pauvre quadrin*" (ibid., emphasis mine) (they are all poor, insistently begging for alms from travelers, letting themselves *flow* from the mountain heights down below in order to gain a miserable quattrino). Villamont nonetheless appears to be impressed by their determination, noting that they "labourent la terre à coups de main, à bien une lieuë de hauteur, sans craindre le danger de tomber és precipices" (6v) (work the land with their hands, at up to a mile up, with no fear of falling into the precipices). They are adapted to their environment and dig into it in order to save themselves.

Climbing Roche Melon, Villamont faces fatigue, a lack of decent food, and heights he had certainly never seen before. His initial ascent "duroit bien pres de quatre lieuës de hauteur" (lasted about four miles in height) and demanded "grand travail" (great work). Always ready for such situations, Villamont is quick to note the pleasantness of the Alpine valley, with "des prairies où le bestail paissoit," spotted with small houses and a spring with excellent water as proof of God's handiwork. He stops to rest in a chalet, where he dozes off, "le sommeil glissant peu à peu en mon cerveau" (sleep sliding bit by bit into my brain).

Like the dream recounted by the Acteur of La Vigne's *Ressource de la Chrestienté*, Villamont's slumber brings him into a new spatial dimension. He awakens to another world, where a perilous climb he describes as "beaucoup plus difficile" (much more difficult) disorients and confuses him. He pleads to turn back but is urged on by his guide, who keeps talking about bird traps just around the corner. After much struggling, they arrive at a spot some "three miles up," where "il fallut attacher aux mains et pieds des graffes de fer, pour grimper à mont et aussi de peur de glisser au bas des precipices, qui nous menaçoyent d'une horrible mort" (we had to attach iron spikes to our hands and feet in order to climb the mountain and also for fear of sliding into the precipices that menaced us with a horrible death). His guides are soon called to save his life as he approaches the mountain peak and "mesmement de la moyenne region de l'air" (even the median region of the air) and he is taken by "un froid insupportable" (unsupportable cold), falling to the ground, where the Marons give him some wine for the "courage de continuer notre chemin" (courage to continue our road). Despite his frightening description of this "perilleux passage" (perilous passage)—he climbs a ladder, scales the cliffs with his metal spikes and gazes into "abismes si profonds et effroiables qu'il ne convient attendre, fors la mort à ceux qui tant soit peu escoulent ou ne se tiennent fermement à leur graffe de fer" (abysses so deep and fearful that anyone who slips in the slightest and does not manage to hold on to their iron spike can expect nothing but death)—Villamont insists that his description comes nowhere near capturing the danger of this spectacle:

> Certainement la chose est beaucoup plus espouvantable et perilleuse, que je ne pourrois reciter, ce que je dy aux curieux, comme j'estoie, qui voudront parvenir à la cime de ceste montaigne au mois d'Aoust seulement, parce qu'és autres mois on ny peut aller aucunement.

> (Certainly the thing is much more fearful and dangerous than I am able to tell, which I say for the curious, as I was, who will want

to climb to the peak of this mountain, only in August, because in the other months you cannot go there at all.)

Villamont describes the dangerous fluidity of the Alpine environment, where unwary travelers "escoulent" (flow) off and wear spikes "de peur de *glisser* au bas des precipices" (for fear of sliding to the bottom of the precipices). This verb, used the day prior to describe Villamont's falling into semiconsciousness—"le sommeil peu peu glissant en mon cerveau" (8r) (sleep slowly slipping into my brain)—shows that the author has lapsed into a dreamlike world where spatial and temporal borders are unclear. It would seem that he has succumbed to the amorphous landscape in which the barriers between life and death, the solid elements and the fluid, are indistinct and formless. For a moment, Villamont even loses his steadfast will (perhaps for want of oxygen) and must submit to that of his acclimatized companions. His physical metamorphosis begins: "changeant de couleur, estant du tout recreu et affoibly" (changing color, being completely overcome and weakened), he melts into the hands of the marons, who carry him up the pass.

THE REWARDS OF CURIOSITY

It is tempting to read Villamont's climb as an answer to Petrarch's famous climb of Mont Ventoux, which is often cited as a first, hesitant expression of interest in landscape.[69] Though Villamont does not use allegory, his dreamlike climb into the "median region of the air" has an otherworldliness about it that gives it a heightened importance in the narrative and thematic message of his work. His fall into a dream effects a separation between reality and the world of Roche Melon that suggests a link with the long tradition of dream writing. Villamont's expression of faith and his depiction of the cosmos as a physical manifestation of divinity, in which God's feet rest on the earth while he watches overhead, also lend a spiritual value to the traveler's exploration of this angle of God's "pourpris." Villamont also slips, experiences hesitation and confusion, and contemplates death from an ethereal height. Rather than allegory, however, Villamont describes the physical details of his experience in a semimystical region in order to celebrate the visual reward of arriving at the mountain's peak.

After a short prayer in the chapel built by Bonifacio da Asti, Villamont gazes out in wonder across the glaciers and provinces of the surrounding

Alps. He describes the confusion evoked by a landscape that spreads 360 degrees around him: "Je sortis jettant ma veuë sur un grand lac glacé" (I came out throwing my vision onto a large frozen lake), "puis tournant ma veuë ... puis venant jetter les yeux" (then turning around and casting my eyes around.). His vision is dynamic, confused, and unhesitatingly enthusiastic as he alternates between vistas of Savoy and Dauphiné, Piedmont and Lombardy, provoking "une joye incredible" (an incredible joy). Rather than regret his past dangers or ruminate on the moral implications of his journey, as Petrarch had done, Villamont narrates the uninhibited pleasure of observing God's diverse creation. The reality of his description and narration does not, however, eliminate all metaphoric value from his climb. If anything, it diverts the metaphor of travel from a theological sphere to the real actions of an author traveling through a physical world, using topographical space as a narrative metaphor to underline the traveler's heroic call to action.[70] More importantly, the detour from his progress toward the Holy Land is not viewed as a distraction from his pilgrimage but as the central, dispersive focus of his voyage to Italy.

VILLAMONT'S PROMOTION

Villamont left France at the height of the tensions of the eighth outbreak of the Wars of Religion, visiting Paris less than a month after the Day of the Barricades. He visited Paris and organized the logistics of his journey in a city whose prince had been exiled and whose parliamentary president, Achille de Harlay, had been imprisoned in the Bastille.

Important events altered the kingdom's political situation while Villamont was off acquiring his political experience. While he was in Rome, Henri III had convened the Estates General at Blois, assassinating the Duke of Guise and executing his brother Louis de Lorraine, Cardinal of Guise. Villamont would have heard about this, at the latest, when he returned to Rome from Naples just before Lent in 1589. He left Rome on February 22, making his way up the Adriatic coast, visiting Loreto, Ancona, and Ravenna, and spending a month and a half in Venice as he prepared for his departure for Jerusalem on the "Nava Ferra." When he returned to Venice in 1591, he would have learned of Henri III's assassination, the Protestant Henri IV's accession to the throne, and the ongoing civil war that plagued the country. Not knowing where he stood in this political maelstrom, Villamont was forced to travel discreetly, dressing as a peasant and traveling in the company of a gentleman heading off to war:

> Adonc estans entrez dedans Lyon, eusmes plus de soucy de retourner en nos patries que n'avions eu (comme je croy) d'entreprendre si longs voyages: Car nous n'apprehendions pas tant de passer par les nations estranges, que nous faisions de passer par la nostre mesmes, par ce que generalement toute la France estoit en trouble et remplie de guerres civiles, toutesfois me mettant en hasard d'estre pris ou massacré par les chemins, partys seulet de Lyon, en habit de pauvre paysant . . . (319v–320)

> (Thus having arrived in Lyon, we were more worried about returning to our own homes than we had been [as I believe] to undertake such long journeys, because we were less apprehensive in passing through foreign nations than we were passing through our own because generally France was in a state of strife and filled with civil wars, nonetheless placing myself in danger of being taken or killed along the roads, I left all alone from Lyon, dressed as a poor peasant.)

With the king holding camp outside the walls of Paris,[71] Villamont crossed France without visiting the capital. From outside Lyon, he took a boat to Nevers, proceeded on horseback, crossed the Loire at La Charité into the Duchy of Berry, and traversed the "fascheuse" forest of Orléans to Corbeil. From there he went to Angers in the company of a gentleman going to serve in the army and arrived in his "patrie" (homeland) after a journey of thirty-nine months.

But what exactly does Villamont mean by "patrie," and which side of the fight was he on? In the passages cited above, Villamont uses this word as a synonym for his home in Brittany, and he and his companion return to their respective "patries." In the first edition of the *Voyages*, Villamont identified himself as a "gentilhomme du pays de Bretagne" (Gentleman of the Country of Brittany), a somewhat ambiguous expression that could either refer to the pays Nantais of southern Brittany or imply a certain nationalistic or separatist pride in Brittany's semi-independent status. The few details available regarding Villamont's career, moreover, further underline this hybrid of ambiguous identity.

Brittany was, in fact, the last great area of Catholic resistance to King Henri IV's rule over the French kingdom and the center of much of the fighting of the last of the Wars of Religion. After Henri III's death, the Duke of Mercoeur, leader of Catholic Brittany, had invited seven thousand Spanish forces, commanded by Don Juan del Aguila, to set up a fort in Port-Louis on the southern Breton coast. As Villamont returned to his home, important battles between royalist and Catholic-Spanish forces raged across Brittany.[72] Even after Henri converted to Catholicism in 1593 and was crowned at Chartres on February 27, 1594, and the other Catholic leaders capitulated, Mercoeur's Brittany fought on, surrendering only with the signing of the Treaty of Vervins in 1598. Villamont's declaration of service to his "patrie," expressed through the publication of his *Voyages* (1595), happens to occur in the same year Henri received papal absolution, a fact that would have reassured the Catholic knight.

The only archival traces of a Villamont prior to the publication of the *Voyages* suggest that he may have served in the resistance to the Protestant king. The accounts of the Spanish ambassador to Brittany Mendo de Ledesma record a payment dated April 3, 1592, of twelve écus to a "gentilhomme de Rosampoul, qui s'appelle Villamont" (gentleman of Rosampoul, named Villamont), who "se rendit de cette ville en Basse-Bretagne, pour traiter de ma part avec le même Rosampoul sur l'affaire de Brest" (came to from this city in lower Brittany to speak on my behalf with said Rosampoul). Villamont's service to an individual with such open Spanish sympathies and whose infamy was confirmed by his awful treatment of the inhabitants of Morlaix in 1594 would have required some sort of open declaration of fealty to the new king.

Inversely, it is also likely that such a declaration would have been useful to the monarch as well, since having a known Breton, manifestly Catholic, on his side would have helped him solidify control of the rebel province. Henri wanted his now famous edict of religious tolerance to carry the name of the seat of the Breton Parliament. The first drafts of the Edict of Nantes were written in 1597–98 in the royal stronghold of Angers and were signed April 30, 1598, in the Breton capital of Nantes.

Halfway between these two centers of power is the small village of Neuvy-en-Mauge, whose parish archives hold the only remaining documentation on Jacques de Villamont. These records show a series of promotions and political connections of a loyal servant of the king. Sometime between 1595 and 1600, Villamont was promoted to the rank of ordinary gentleman of the king's chamber, a job whose primary duty was to represent the king and carry diplomatic messages at home and abroad. In 1605, Achille de Harlay, the president of the Parliament of Paris who had languished in prison in 1588 as Villamont left for Italy and the Middle East, stood at the baptismal font in Neuvy, giving his surname to Villamont's second son. In 1611, Villamont became maître d'hôtel of the Prince of Condé. The key that opened the first of these promotions is clearly Villamont's *Voyages*, a narrative that joins entertainment, heroism, and the politics of self-promotion to present the figure of a nobleman the king needed on his side.

If the textual version of Villamont's journey is clearly political, the spaces that he and other French travelers encounter were also subject to a political viewpoint. Alongside an interest in the antiquities of Italy, an emerging spatial discourse relating to landscape, and a passion for new technology and the latest artistic accomplishments, the French also viewed Italian spaces through the lens of Franco-Italian affairs, creating a space of regret and desire, as the following chapter will show.

Chapter 5

SPACES AND PLACES OF THE *VOYAGE D'ITALIE*

While traveling through Italy in the period following the Italian Wars, French travelers shaped the practical circumstances of their visits around a personal and nationalized reading of space. Recording their experiences in notebooks, they preserved, rewrote, transformed, and monumentalized personal experiences in written form. Mémoires, narratives, and even poeticized journeys read geographical, topographical, and urban space using a growing body of mythology relating to national identity combined with the cumulative culture of collective experience of a repeated social practice, all of which were mapped out on itineraries whose names came to embody a series of repeated, confirmed, or contested ideas regarding French and Italian nationality. The itineraries followed on the journey to Italy ranged from point-to-point journeys, to lengthy stays enriched with excursions and trips to other locations, to genuine tours in which the itineraries' shape displayed a distinct interest in wandering, à la Montaigne, "par chemins divers et contrées" (various roads and regions).

Jacques Sirmond narrated the difficulties of a journey that followed the most common route into Italy, which crossed the Alps at Mont Cenis and descended through Turin, Milan, Piacenza, Parma, Reggio, Modena, Bologna, Florence, Siena, and Rome following the ancient Roman roads. Written in heroic Latin verse, the *Hodoeporicon* allowed the Jesuit priest to meld themes characteristic of the Catholic spiritual journey with details of a voyage to Rome more in keeping with the interests of the future geographer and political operative.[1] Sirmond concentrated on the symbolic aspects of his journey as well as a number of material aspects of the road, such as the dangers he faced from armed bandits in the Alps, his suffering from dysentery and hemorrhoids, and the insufferable quality of the inns in the mountainous regions of Italy. Years later, another prelate sent on a mission to the Vatican also ironized the mishaps of his journey. In the *Voyage de Paris à Rome* that appears as an appendix to his *Confessions*, Jean-Jacques Bouchard recounts a journey from Paris in 1630, following a route through Toulon and by ship to Civitavecchia via Genoa and Livorno. After braving a storm at sea and suffering a lengthy quarantine in Civitavecchia, he made his way to Rome, where his narrative ends.[2] Other examples of these short, utilitarian routes include the first journey of Jean Tarde (1593) from Avignon to Rome.[3] These journeys, like those of the first journey made by the anonymous author of the *Voyage de Provence et d'Italie*,[4] as well as the Paris-Marseille-Rome itinerary of François de Fontenay-Mareuil, who served as the royal ambassador to the pope in 1641, are all examples of mission-oriented journeys in which the political purpose of the journey is virtually absent from the narrative of exploration and sightseeing.[5]

Even in these linear accounts, travelers visited places far from their most direct route. Jean Tarde's group made stops in Nice and Genoa, disembarked in Portovenere, and then visited a number of points of interest in the Grand Duchy of Tuscany and the northern Papal States before arriving in Rome. They managed to visit Florence, Arezzo, Cortona, Perugia, Spoleto, Terni, and Narni on the way to Rome and Siena, Lucca, Genoa, and Savona on their return trip.[6,7] An anonymous traveler in 1606 followed Sirmond's route but added the trip to Naples and an excursion to the geological and archeological sites around Pozzuoli that were increasingly obligatory parts of the exploration of Italy's sites.[8] The author of the *Voyage de Provence et d'Italie* visited Turin, Asti, and Genoa before returning to Provence.[9]

Travelers who stayed in one location for an extended period of time include students at Italy's famous universities and semiofficial travelers to Rome. Nicolas Audebert, a native of Orléans, followed in his father's footsteps by studying law in Bologna from 1574 to 1578.[10] During his four-year residence, he visited Venice, Padua, Arquà, Abano, Mantua, and Ferrara after his first year of study; went to Genoa, Pisa, Lucca, Florence, Siena, and Rome after his second year; and made the voyage to Naples in March 1577 before returning to complete his doctorate in jurisprudence.

Claude-Énoch Virey studied law in Padua from 1592 to 1593, writing partially fictionalized verse accounts that combine descriptions of sites visited, personal experiences of the road, and a lightly veiled mapping of the political spaces leading from France into Italy and an amorous itinerary from Padua to Siena.[11]

Travelers used various strategies in order to work as many places as possible into their tours, often descending one side of Italy and returning on the other side. Florisel de Claveson sailed from Marseille, making his way to Rome down via Pisa and Florence, visiting Naples, and returning via Loreto, Ancona, Bologna, and Venice before following the Po basin to Milan and Turin and entering France over Mont Cenis.[12] Pierre Bergeron, who wrote a sort of idealized itinerary using information collected during two separate journeys, proposed a similar method, which was also followed by Montaigne on his journey of 1580–81.[13] The maximization of the tour can be seen in Henri de Bourbon, Prince of Condé's assiduous crisscrossing of the peninsula that left no sight unseen during his journey from Montpellier in 1622.[14] Such detailed itineraries suggest that even while conducting "affaires," travelers put considerable thought and effort into exploring all there was to see in Italy.

A few travelers managed to conduct larger journeys, like the one Montaigne secretly desired to conduct into Greece, incorporating Italy into a generalized wanderlust that included the Holy Land and lands controlled by the Ottoman Empire and other parts of Europe. Henri de Rohan replaced his desire to see the "l'empire des Turcs" (the empire of the Turks) with a long journey through Italy, Germany, Holland, England, and Scotland.[15] Villamont also worked in a complete *voyage d'Italie* crossing Mont Cenis to visit Turin, Milan, Bologna, Florence, Siena, Rome, and Naples before heading north to depart for the Holy Land from Venice. When he returned from the Middle East, he visited Padua, Mantua, Cremona, Pavia, Alessandria, Asti, and Turin before crossing back into France. Nicolas Bénard, while more of a pilgrim than a traveler of this same class, nonetheless managed to fit an extensive Italian itinerary into his journey to the Holy Sepulchre.

The common characteristics, the repeated locations and experiences, the channeling of travelers by guides and "marrons" toward specific hotels and routes, and the shape of the land itself all contribute to the creation of a shared cultural experience in which space is viewed through a collective lens. Published guidebooks of individual cities and geographical descriptions of Italy, such as Leandro Alberti's *Descrittione di Tutta Italia* (1550) or François de Belleforest's translation and rewriting of Sebastian Münster's *Cosmographia universalis* (1575), contributed to the textual representation of this journey, while the proliferation of maps and images of cities fed and stimulated the traveler's spatial imagination.

This chapter examines the material and imaginary aspects of the journey from France to Rome. Citing the comments of French travelers to Italy and relating them to the geographical sources used to conduct and write the Italian journey, it examines the material aspects of the journey, describing the things travelers saw and experienced on the itinerary from Paris to Rome. On the one hand, travelers are interested in the public works that mark Italy's cities and territories. From a more rhetorical standpoint, French noblemen view Italy as a Gallic space, citing ancient sources and recent history in the description of a French Italy. Many of the major cities on the route to Rome had deep roots in the French national story. Turin served as a city of transition; friendly and almost French from a cultural standpoint, its structure and political status were nonetheless a reminder of the French loss of the Italian Wars. Milan too was described as the great prize lost during the final phases of the war. The cities of central Italy were integral to France's self-image. Travelers along the Via Aemilia from Piacenza to Bologna and on the route from Siena to Rome recount a Gallic version of history centered on the Gauls and Franks, focused through the lens of the French actions in the Italian Wars. Before arriving in this Franco-Italia, however, the traveler had to cross the cultural borderland of the Alps.

THE ALPINE CROSSING

The *voyage d'Italie* officially began at the crossing of the Alps, an arduous journey that came to symbolize the traveler's departure from France's national space and entry into the "beyond" of travel. Accounts of the Alpine crossing use the sociological and historical tools of Renaissance humanism, cosmography, and the travelers' individual perceptions of national identity to create an "other" space, a border that compensates for France's lack of real borders in this period of changing national identity.[16] The barrier between cultures becomes a personal encounter with a dramatically varied space, where the physical and psychological challenges of the climb and the hostile, barbarous aspect of the mountain inhabitants reinforce the Alps' status in classical literature and Renaissance cosmography as *the* defining borderland of Western civilization. The Romans' protective wall from the *barbaria*, the Alps undergo a rewriting that emphasizes French cultural hegemony, in which the Alps are merely a border between versions of France's alter egos, connecting, in a tormented morphological way, the two Galliae—Transalpina and Cisalpina—which increasingly form into the ideas of France and Italy in the closing of the sixteenth century.[17]

The perceived dangers of the Alpine passage were based in reality. In a period when climbing mountains was viewed as an extraordinary, if not mystical, activity,[18] the Alpine crossing represented a mental and spiritual activity whose physical challenge was comparable to that of a military assault. The traveler had to choose the right time of year, hire the appropriate guides, and then "forcer" (force) the Alpine passage. The geographer Pierre Du Val lists eight routes connecting France to Italy, classifying them as "les uns aisez, les autres difficiles" (the ones easy, the others difficult).[19] The easiest pass followed the coast, while the road leading over the Col de Tende through the peaks of the *Alpes maritimes* was considered "bien penible" (very painful).[20] Provence and Dauphiné were connected to the Marquisate of Saluzzo, a principality heavily dependent on the French Crown, by the Col de l'Argentière and Col de Lagnes. Du Val notes that the passage of the Cottian Alps through the pass of Monviso was "merveilleux," having been opened "à force de fer et de feu l'espace d'un mille" (by force of iron and fire the width of a mile).[21] Another difficult route connected Quieras with Savoy via the Col de la Croix. There were two routes over Mongenèvre linking Grenoble to Susa and Turin, one of them difficult and "gueres practiqué si ce n'est par ceux du pays" (hardly used except by residents of the region) and the other, from Embrun, longer, but far more practicable "tant pour le Canon que pour les armées" (for cannon as well as for armies).[22] The most common route, however, was the crossing of Mont Cenis at Lanslebourg that passed the Piedmontese checkpoints of Novalesa and Susa, a passage that required two and a half days but was nonetheless far easier than the Val d'Aosta pass, classified as "tres mal aisé à forcer" (very hard to force).[23] Other possibilities could be opened, as we saw with Montaigne, by traveling through Switzerland, Bavaria, and Austria, leading to the important passes through the arduous Rhaetian Alps that descended through Valtellina past Chiavenna and Lake Garda to Milan, or through the Julian Alps at Brenner as described by Montaigne.

Crossing the Alps was dangerous and required the use of specialized equipment and the assistance of Alpine guides known as "Marrons." These stocky, goitered guides were famous for their rude behavior and exorbitant prices that left the traveler at their mercy as they entered Lanslebourg:

> L'ordinaire est que, quand l'on arrive à l'hostellerie, ils viennent au devant des personnes, cinquante et soixante à la foys, la teste nue et le bonnet au poing presentant leurs services, les uns pour estre Marrons, les aultres pour fournir des chevaux pour passer le mont, et soulager ceux que l'on menne; descendant de cheval, l'un tient l'estrier, l'aultre la bride du cheval, l'aultre soustient le corps, bref chascun scait trouver son office pour s'employer. Puis, ayant mis pied à terre, deux ou troys sont en querelle, prests à se battre, à qui menera le cheval en l'estable, un aultre d'aultre costé veult porter la valise en la chambre, dont il se fault donner garde, car telz valets sont quelques foys trop serviables, et mesmement en ce lieu ilz sont fort pauvres, et pour le peu de différence qu'il y a entre Marrons et Larrons.[24]

(The normal procedure is that, when one arrives at the inn, they come out fifty or sixty at a time to meet those arriving. Heads bare and hat in hand they present their services, some as guides [Marrons], others offering horses for the mountain pass. They offer assistance for those they lead off, helping them dismount, one holding the stirrup, the other the horse's bridle, the other helping you down, in brief, each one finds a way to be of service. Then, once you've set foot on the ground, two or three begin to argue and are near coming to blows over who will lead your horse to stable, another one wants to carry your suitcase to the room, of which one needs to be careful, because these servants sometimes help themselves a bit too much because this region is very poor and due to the little difference there is between Marrons and Thieves.)

The Marrons would slyly order wine when none was offered and lift food from guests' plates from under the table while looking the other way. Audebert notes the need to "les rudoyer de paroles" (treat them badly with words) in order to get them to do anything. They are nonetheless indispensable for their strength, knowledge, and technical expertise. They attach spikes to the shoes of their customers and the horses for passage over trails of rock and ice. They hold travelers up, push them over difficult areas, and carry them in litters over frightening passages as they "grimpent comme chats" (climb like cats) up vertical mountain walls despite their heavy features.[25] The author of the *Discours viatiques* recounts following the advice of his traveling companion, who had had the frightening experience of "la chaise" and determined to "s'aider du cheval" (make his own way by horse). He soon regretted "à chaque pas la chaise, à cause du mauvais chemin, et tout endiablé de pierres, qui nous fit, malgré nous et nous deulz, aller à pied" (not taking the chair at each step, because of the bad road, and all bedeviled by rocks that forced us, despite ourselves, to go by foot).[26] The last stretch before entering in Italy was known as *la Ramasse*, named for the use of

> une sorte de de traineau qui est conduit par un maron, lequel, se mettant au devant et au milieu de deux bastons qu'il empoigne de deux costez, se laisse glisser sur la neige, se tenant droit en pied, en une carrière de longtemps cavée en roche, et tire de ceste façon à bas celuy qui est sur ce traineau. Lequel doibt se tenir bien ferme et n'estre craintif, craindant l'eblouissement de la veue et la renverse dans les précipices que l'on void parfois à costez.
>
> (a sort of sled driven by a Marron, who, placing himself in front and between two poles that he holds on each side, allows himself to slide on the snow, holding himself upright, in a channel dug long ago in the rock, and pulls in this fashion the person sitting on the sled, who must remain calm and not be afraid, for fear of losing his sight or falling into the precipices that one sees at times at one's side.)[27]

In addition to falling to a "certain death," as Villamont writes, travelers experienced physical and psychological disorientation caused by the mountains' height and a harsh climate that could change at a moment's notice. Sudden storms could blind, cause the loss of a limb, or carry the traveler off into the abyss. Heat exhaustion was also common, though drinking water after such an effort was a sure way to die of pleurisy.

Travelers brought vinegar or strong wine in order to fight, as Pierre Du Gua explains, possible "defaillances et évanouïssemens, qui prennent, à cause d'un si soudain changement d'air, qui est subtil, qui attire les esprits à soy: le haut de la montagne est en la moyenne region de l'air" (failings and fainting, that occur because of such a sudden change of air, which is subtle, and attracts the spirits to it: the top of the mountain is in the middle region of the air.)[28]

Perhaps the most telling reminder of the dangers of this region, however, was the Chapelle des Transis (Chapel of the Dead), a small temple located at the crossing at La Tavernette where the frozen dead were stored. Villamont inserts a reference to this famous site in his description of the risks of inclement weather in the Alpine passes, where sudden storms could carry people away or freeze them, resulting in their bodies being "thrown" ("jettez") in the chapel. He notes that when he passed there in June 1588, "y avoit grand nombre de corps morts lors que j'y arrivay" (there were a large number of dead bodies when I arrived there) (I, 7).[29] While the chapel had a practical purpose, preserving the bodies until the weather allowed their transport down the mountain, it also served as a *memento mori* and happens to be located just beneath the large cross marking the border separating Savoy from Piedmont, where French travelers mark their entry into Italian territory. The author of the *Voyage d'Italie* of 1606 describes the scientific reasons that prevent the bodies from putrefying, noting how "les corps desquels estans morts roidissoient soudainement et estoient convertis en pierre, se servants eux mesmes de relief à leur sepulture" (the bodies of which, being dead, stiffen suddenly and are converted to stone, and serve as markers for their own graves).[30] The baroque nature of travelers' fascination recalls the tombs prepared by Capuchin monks in Rome, where bones and skulls are arranged to make altars, arches, and decorations for mass common graves. Here, however, the effect of horror is unintended, caused by the harshness of the environment and the difficulty of the landscape, reminding travelers of the transitory nature of human existence:

> Ceux ou qui, voulans passer en temps d'hyver sans guide, se trouvent precipités en des fonds totalement comblés de neige, ou bien qui, surpris de la nuit ou de la tourmente, sont demeurez morts, transis et engelés de froidure, engloutis dans les neiges jusque à tant que le soleil les ayant fondues et fait la descouverte,

ces pauvres cadavres paroissent noirs et garentis aucunement de pourriture, mais non pas comme les mumies d'Egipte; car combien que le froid, contraire à putrefaction aussy bien que le chaud, ayt vertu de reserrer l'humeur et durcir les corps (tesmoin le cristal et plusieurs fontaines qui petrifient le bois de leur froideur, tesmoings aussy les preuves des Hollandois en leurs navigations septentrionales, les corps desquels estans morts roidissoient soudainement et estoient convertis en pierre, se servants eux mesmes de relief à leur sepulture) [. . .] ces transis, non encore du tout degelés, sont portez joignant cette chapelle et jettés plustost que posés ou arrengés au sepulchre commun d'une voute, image de la mort et mirroir de nostre chetifvité humaine, où on les enterroit par une fenestre my pourris et exhalants une odeur la plus infecte qui se puisse imaginer.[31]

(Those who try to pass in winter without a guide find themselves thrown into the abyss and covered with snow, or else wind up dead, surprised by nightfall or by a storm, killed and frozen by the cold, gobbled up by the snow until the sun melts and uncovers them, leaving their poor corpses black and protected from rotting, but not like I imagined them, hard and dry like the mummies of Egypt, since the cold protects against putrefaction like heat, and has the property of concentrating liquid and hardening the bodies [proof of which can be seen in crystal and many fountains that petrify wood with their cold, as well as the experiences of the Dutch in their northern navigations, whose bodies stiffen and are converted to stone, serving as their own tombstone]. . . . These half-thawed dead people are then taken to a room at the side of the chapel and are thrown, half-rotten and emanating the worst odor imaginable, through a window into a common vaulted grave, forming an image of death and mirror of our human insignificance.)

The traveler's explanation of this horror demonstrates the degree to which the Alps were considered a hostile foreign region, located in the median region of the air and comparable to the upper regions of the north or the extreme deserts of Egypt. Nicolas Audebert, on the other hand, associates it with a tragic loss of French life that occurred during the Italian

Wars, when a Monsieur d'Anebault, "qui y pensa mourir, comme feirent aulcuns de sa maison; et de ceux qui n'y moururent point, aulcuns y perdirent la veue, et les aultres les pieds, du reste la plus grande part ne fut depuis en santé" (who thought he was going to die here, as had occurred to some members of his household, and of those who did not die, some lost their sight, others their feet, most of the others were never in good health again).[32]

Sociological changes also mark the travelers' entry into a hostile environment well before their arrival at Lanslebourg. Shortly after leaving French territory and entering Savoy on the road from Lyon to Chambery, travelers encountered the goitered inhabitants while passing through the Alpine villages of the Maurienne, Saint-Michel, Saint-Julien, and Saint-Jean, all belonging to Savoy, or Sabaudia, a region that had been the home of the ancient Allobroges and was famous for its inhabitants, known as "grosses gorges" (big throats), who were

> gorgeuz aultrement Goistrez, car à la plus grand part de ceux de ceux du pays, il viens soubz la gorge une sorte de louppe grosse comme les deux poings et plus, appellée la Goestre, ce qui provient de la froiddeur des mauvaises eaux qu'ilz boivent, n'estant aultres que neiges fondues tombantes des montaignes, que les medecins tiennent estre les plus dangereuses.[33]

> (big-throated or goitered, because most of the people of this region develop a sort of loop as big as two fists or more, called the goiter, that comes from the cold of the bad waters they drink, being nothing more than melted snow falling from the mountains, which doctors hold to be the most dangerous.)

The distance of the Savoyard government, transferred to Turin from Chambéry after the signing of the Treaty of Cateau-Cambrésis, and the confusion in France caused by the religious wars and ongoing territorial disputes with Savoy, made the Maurienne the perfect environment for *bandits*, a class of people whose very name defines their existence with the jurisdictional interstices between organized societies.[34] In 1588, the author of the *Discours viatiques* worried about losing his baggage after encountering a group of sixty armed men pretending to be soldiers of the Duke of Maine.[35] The Alps—and the Apennines, described as a natural extension of the master mountain chain—serve as a liminal space occupied by a savage other living at the limits of society whose incivility serves as a counterimage to the emerging civilizations of the globalized world:

> Les Voyageurs qui passent par l'Appennin se garantissent ordinairement des Bandits, ou par escorte ou autrement, s'ils ne veulent estre mis à mort. Ces voleurs se trouvent en grand nombre dans le Royaume de Naples, dont le Viceroy sçait bien se servir dans les occasions. Il y en a en plusieurs autres pays de cette sorte de gens qui sont guerriers et voleurs. Les Iroquois en Canada, les Caribes en Güiane, les Arauguès en Chili, les Quirandies dans le Paraguay: les Mores et les Arabes en Afrique: les Giagues ou Galles dans le Monomotapa: les Alarbes et les Beduins en Arabie: les Curdes aux confins de Turquies et de Perse...[36]

> (Travelers passing through the Apennines normally protect themselves from bandits using an escort or some other means, if they do not want to be killed. These thieves can be found in great number in the Kingdom of Naples, and the Viceroy knows well how to use them on occasion. There are several other nations of these types of people who are warriors and thieves: the Iroquois in Canada, the Caribs in Guyana, the Araucanians in Chile, the Querandí in Paraguay, the Moors in Africa, the Giagues in Monomotapa, the Arabs and Bedouins in Arabia, the Kurds on the border between Turkey and Persia...)

The danger of crossing these territories added to the emotional tension of crossing between civilizations, providing a cultural, sociological, and spatial background to the narrative of exploration and learning. The most important sign of purpose is, of course, the traveler's ability to move through this space, whose symbols give meaning to his journey. The topographical imagery contributes to this sense of transition, a feeling of monumentality captured in the need to write and represent the "vastum, immanemque Cenisium/Rex inter montes" (vast, immense Mont Cenis, King of Mountains).[37]

The official crossing from France into Savoy was at the Pont de Beauvoisin, which crosses the Guier (or Jart) River and was marked by "les armoyrys de France, et de l'aultre costé, sur la porte de la ville" (the arms of France and on the other side, on the city gate), as well as "ceux de son Altesse qui est aultant à dire du Duc de Savoye" (those of his Highness, that is to say, the Duke of Savoy).[38] This ceremonial marker was important, especially to Frenchmen returning from abroad, as can be seen by the fact that during Audebert's departure, the region had been bled dry by celebrations of Henri III's return from Poland. Audebert was thus forced to take an alternative route from Lyon, exiting through the Saint Sebastian Gate and following the Rhône through the "fort aride et sterile" (very dry and sterile) lands of Bresse.[39] Crossing the "impetuous" waters of the Ens River into Savoy (I, 122), he and a Jesuit companion climbed the valley for an entire day, passing through narrow, dramatic passes:

> Et sont les montaignes des deux costez du chemin tellement proches l'une de l'autre, que en plusieurs endroits il ne s'en fault une ject de pierre que les sommitez d'une part et d'aultre ne s'entretouchent, estant en plusieurs endroits aussy droictes qu'une muraille, à cause de quoy, y a un chemin fort estroit le long du torrent, et est fort frais et ombrageux. Souvent se trouvent des fontaines ou petis torrens se precipitans du plus haut des montaignes au milieu du chemin que l'on en est tout le jour estourdy. (122)

> (And these mountains on the two sides of the road are so close together that in several places you could throw a stone from one peak to the other, and in several spots are as straight as a wall, for which, there is very narrow road that follows the torrent, and it is very cool and shady. There are often fountains and small streams falling from the highest peaks of the mountains into the middle of the road from which one is stunned all day long.)

Passing beneath the peaks of the *Monts de Vaterici*, through "bon et gras terroir," and crossing over and following the Rhône through narrow canyons, they sighted the armed garrison of the Duke of Savoy, climbed Mont du Chat past several small villages, and arrived in Bourguet.

The difficult road began near Mont d'Espiere, the site of a small town of the same name, continued through La Chappelle and La Chambre, and crossed numerous small bridges, whose names Audebert records, to Saint-Jean-de-Maurienne:

Depuis La Chappelle jusques au mont Senys, les montaignes sont tellement proches l'une de l'autre qu'il faut cheminer en lieu haut sur le pied d'icelles, costoyant de main droicte la riviere ou torrent d'Arc, qui est fort enserré dans la vallée, et se va precipitant de grande impetuosité parmy les rochers et gros caillous qu'il entrainne avecques un bruit merveilleusement estourdissant, dont aulcuns sentent encore deux ou troys jours après un continu bondonnement d'oreilles, comme si l'on estoit encore sur le lieu.

(From the Chapel to Mont Cenis, the mountains are so close to one another that you have to walk at their foot, leaving on your right the river or stream Arc, which is very deep in the valley and goes falling with great force among the rocks and large stones that it takes with it with a marvelously deafening sound, of which some remain with a buzzing in their ears for two or three days, as if they were still there.)[40]

TURIN: CITY OF TRANSITION

Having escaped the bandits of Maurienne and braved the frozen heights of Mont Cenis, after paying their Marrons and trading their rented horses for their own mounts, travelers into Piedmont faced another danger in Novalesa, "bourg à craindre pour ceulx qui ont esté à Lyon, ou plustot qui n'ont bonnes bulles, car on leur faict faire une miserable quarantaine" (a town to be feared by travelers coming from Lyon, or, rather, by those who do not have good health records, because they will make them do a miserable quarantine).[41] The health certificate—"bollettino" ("bolletta" "bulles," "bulettes," or "bulettin")—was an important document for travelers to Italy in the time of plague, as it recorded every place visited, including overnight stays and towns visited for lunch (*disner*), and was meticulously inspected ("exactement visité") by commissioners (*commissaires*) "establis sur chascun passage" (established at each passage) as far south as Romagna and Florence.[42] The purpose of the document was to ensure travelers had not been to infected towns or regions, but its administration had also become a source of revenue for officials and innkeepers.

The author of the *Discours viatiques* records with humor and verve his experience with capricious officials. Having prepared his documents carefully, he records his satisfaction at having passed Novalesa without a hitch, mocking a predecessor who had inscribed the following words on the wall:

> Heureuz le passager qui fuit le sejour
> des arrestz et prisons de ceste quarantaine
> où plaisir ne se void, mais facherie et paine,
> qui cause d'en fuir à jamais le retour.[43]
> (Happy the passenger who escapes the stay
> of arrests and imprisonment of this quarantine
> where no pleasure is seen, but annoyance and pain,
> that causes him to avoid coming back here at all costs.)

To this, he writes his own wise response:

> Que te plains tu, passant, de ta course arrestee
> et pourquoy maudis tu le sejour merité?
> La faulte t'a conduict a ceste extremitté,
> et non de ce pais la justice ordonnee.
> Sy comme moy garny d'une autenticque bulle
> tu feusses arrivé, ta demeure estoit nulle.[44]
> (Why do you complain about your trip having been stopped
> and why speak badly of your well-deserved stay?
> Your own negligence brought you to this suit
> And not the order and justice of this country.
> If, like me, you had come carrying an authentic bull
> You would have arrived and your stay would have been short.)

These words are spoken too soon, for when the travelers arrive in Susa, where they expect to be waved by, an official begins to scrutinize their passports and bollettes, apparently upset that he can find nothing wrong with them. They offer him a bribe, saying "pigliar un teston" (take a testone),[45] but he condemns the four travelers to three days in the local hotel. On the third day, the travelers manage to win their freedom by losing at cards to the jailkeeper.

From Novalesa, the travelers follow a stony path toward Susa and Turin past memory markers important to French cultural identity:

A la fin de ce bourg (Novalesa) l'on commence à cheminer par quelques petites plaines pierreuses, enserrées de montaignes d'un costé et d'aultre. À costé droicte se descouvre incontinent sur le sommet d'une haute montaigne une Abbaye, en laquelle est ensepulturé *Hedegarde* femme de Charlemagne, de ce mesme costé est Suza.[46]

(At the end of this town, you move over some small, rocky plains, inserted into the mountains that appear on one side and the other. On the right, appears, suddenly, on the summit of a high mountain, an Abbey, in which Hedegarde, wife of Charlemagne, is buried, and on this same side of the road is Susa.)

Audebert passes below the walls of the Castle of Carignano, remembered for the French siege during the war with Charles V,[47] and the small towns and castles of San Giorgio, Susa, Bussoleno, Sant'Ambrogio, Avigliana, and Rivoli. Near San Giorgio, they pass through a very large stone, which, according to popular legend, had been broken in half by Roland. A bit further on, they pass peaks capped by monasteries, such as that of San Michele della Chiusa, a site where Charlemagne had defeated the Lombards in 773, located in

un lieu si hault, qu'il semble que le feste de l'eglise touche les nues, et avec ce est pour sa situation tellement fort que y ayant peu de gens avec munitions, tout un camp n'y pourroit que faire, et ne parviendroit la portée de l'harquebuse jusques là.[48]

(a place so high, that it seems the roof of the church touches the clouds, and for this reason its position is so strong that, even having just a few armed soldiers, an entire army could do nothing to take it, and the shot of an arquebus could not reach it.)

The contrast between France's foundational heroic deeds and the landscape could not be clearer. Audebert mentions the siege only in passing, but his citation of the inadequacy of modern technological warfare reinforces the importance of the deeds of the past. A bit farther, the travelers pass through "l'antique cité de Suze, qui n'a autre embellissement que son antiquité, et de hautes montagnes qui l'environnent, au bas desquelles court la riviere qui descent du mont Senis"[49] (the ancient city of Susa, which has no other decoration than its antiquity and the high mountains that surround it, at the base of which flows the river descending from Mont Cenis). Administered by a governor, it possessed a castle, a citadel, the church of Saint Just (which many travelers took the time to visit),[50] and an old triumphal arch built by "Caesar" (Augustus), which led to the road to Turin.

These heroic memory markers recalling Roland, Charlemagne, the passage of Charles VIII, the descent of the ancient Gauls into Italy, and the wars between France and the empire illustrate the importance of French culture in Piedmont and Italy. The sudden shift of language Montaigne saw when crossing Tyrol into the Veneto is attenuated in the Piedmont by a more or less general bilingualism. Audebert remarks that in Novalesa, "se commence à parler Italien Piedmontese, qui est un langage fort corrompu, et qui a plusieurs pronontiations Bergamasques" (they begin to speak Piedmontese Italian, which is a very corrupted language, and which has several Bergamasc pronunciations).[51] He goes on to add that French and Italian are both spoken all the way to Turin, where French was understood due to the recent transfer of the Savoyard capital. When Montaigne passes through in 1581, he comments on the French intonations of the Piedmontese dialect and what he perceives as the general affection the locals have for the French,[52] but he continues to write in Italian all the way through Sant'Ambrogio, Susa, Novalesa, and Mont Cenis to the bottom of his transport by *ramasse*.

Other markers of the travelers' entrance into a new culture include the shift to the twenty-four-hour ringing of the hours in Italy and the Piedmontese custom of women not rising during the reading of Scripture during Mass.[53] The use of tile roofs, the changing of currency and women's clothing, and the appearance of vineyards grown in the Italian style are other details that attract the travelers' attention as they approach the walls of the fortified city of Turin.[54] Turin was a small city, dominated by a massive, five-pointed *cittadella* almost as large as the city square, "belle, forte et bien campee, bastiee de bricques" (beautiful, strong and well positioned, built in brick),[55] a structure built by the French during the Italian Wars. Approaching the Castello gate, travelers passed the first of many structures built by the victorious Emanuele Filiberto.

The city's massive aqueduct, completed in 1573, provides water for the city's fountains and the daily cleaning of the streets. The fortress is armed, according to Audebert, by three hundred natives of Piedmont and equipped with an interior well in the form of a double helix, a miracle of modern engineering that travelers of the period remembered for its size, which allowed riders on horseback to enter and exit without meeting those coming down from the other direction.

These and other technological innovations showed French travelers the Savoyard dynasty's wealth, culture, and power through symbols they could see and write home about. The luxurious Ducal Palace and Senate, "la Corte," with its elegant galleries and gardens; the duke's cabinet of curiosities; and the city's cleanliness and modernity provided a spatial experience of power, while the city's status as archbishopric, its university, and its ancient Roman origins underlined its connections with Italian structures of culture and power.

REGRETTED MILAN

From Turin, travelers headed to Rome could take a barge down the Po to Ferrara and Venice and then sail to Ancona towards Loreto. Alternatively, they could cross over to Genoa and take a ship to Lucca.[56] The shortest and most popular route, however, was the coach service to Milan that crossed rapidly through Piedmont, the Marquisate of Monferrato, and Lombardy over roads so beautiful, flat, and dry even in a torrential downpour.[57] Passing through Chivasso, Vercelli, Novara, and "Buffalore" (Boffalora sopra Ticino), the route crossed the Orco, Dora Baltea, and Ticino rivers, all tributaries of the Po, as well as a number of political boundaries that mark the conflicted history of this wealthy region.

In the morning, the traveler would reach Chivasso, with its admirable defenses "bastis de bricques et fortiffiez de trois gros boullevers de deux costez" (built of brick and fortified with three large bulwarks on two sides)[58] and a modern aqueduct pouring water into beautiful fountains and moats. In the evening, he crossed the "Bagia" (Dora Baltea) into the Marquisate of Monferrato, a feudatory of the Duke of Mantua, arriving in the "gentille ville" (gentle city)[59] of "Livorne" (Livorno Ferrari). Vercelli, a Lombard town controlled by the Savoy since 1427 and a strategic barrier between the two duchies, was another half-day's ride. A "ville forte" (fortified city),[60] "belle et grande, embellie de plusieurs eglises" (beautiful, large, and decorated with several churches),⁶¹ it was equipped with a small castle, citadel, and fortifications and was noted for its paintings by Gaudenzio Ferrari.⁶²

The "beau pays plein [. . .] fertiles en bled et en prairies" (beautiful, bountiful countryside ... fertile in grain and prairies)⁶³ and straight rows of vineyards into the Duchy of Milan marked the French traveler's first contact with Spanish Italy. Novara was "tres forte et bien bastie, où y a Citadelle et garnison d'Espagnols" (very strong and well built, where there is a citadel and Spanish garrison).⁶⁴ Crossing the Ticino and dining in Boffalora, travelers saw the first arm of the Navigli, canals connecting Lake Garda to Milan, the Ticino, and thus the Po. From there, travelers could continue on one of the abundant boats loaded with passengers and merchandise that led to the great merchant hub of Milan,⁶⁵ admired by all for its abundance of people, artisans, and "marchandise" of all types and regretted by the French as the greatest prize lost in the Italian Wars.

The first impact of the city was its battlements and the system of moats and transport of the swiftly flowing Navigli. The traveler gave his baggage and health certificate for inspection to a customs officer and made his way through the Porta Vercellina, where he found a bustling commercial city that most travelers describe as Italy's largest. A part of this impression comes from moving from the flat, open plains into a populous center decorated with elegant churches and homes, which presented a surprising spectacle:

> Dez cette premiere porte incontinent, combien qu'il y ait eglises et monasteres, mesmement celuy de St. Victor, fort beau, les maisons bien continuées et peuplées d'ouvriers de soyes et autres manufactures, si n'est-ce que le fauxbourg de la ville, laquelle de ce costé commence à la Porte Vercelline.⁶⁶

> (As soon as you enter this first gate, suddenly, there are so many churches and monasteries, including that of San Vittore, very beautiful, the houses well-arranged and populated with workers in silk and other manufacturers, and still, you are only in the suburb of the city, which, from this side, begins at the Vercelli gate.)

"Milan 'la Grande'"⁶⁷ measured ten miles around its outer walls and was home to some three hundred thousand souls, comprising ninety-six parishes, forty monasteries and fifty convents, one hundred confraternities, churches, and elegant homes that impressed visitors by their size and beauty. In 1562, Ferrante di Gonzaga had built a second wall around the city, creating what the French called a *fauxbourg* and allowing the city to accommodate its growing population based on commerce and industry. Travelers were thus surprised by the size of the city as they went through suburbs that formed "comme un corps avec la ville, estans ceints de bastions et de fossez" (as one body together with the city walled in by bastions and moats)[68] This had more than doubled the size of the city, adding an area that included monasteries (usually located outside cities' walls), a variety of shops, and farmland that had been converted into beautiful urban gardens, as can be seen on the map of Milan printed in Georg Braun's 1572 *Civitates orbis Terrarum*.[69]

The city's size, Nordic construction, and gothic cathedral also reminded French travelers of home. It was "très grande et bien peuplée, bastie à la Françoise, et fort ressemblante à Paris." (very large and well-populated, built in the French fashion, and very much resembling Paris).[70] Condé describes it thus: "Une des plus grandes villes qui se puisse jamais voir de tour de murailles, elle est aussi ou plus grande que Paris, mais il y a bien un quart de la ville en jardinage" (One of the largest cities you can ever see measured around its walls, she is as large or larger than Paris, but at least a quarter of the city consists of gardens.)[71] Though it was only half the size of the French capital and ranked second in population to Naples, it gave an appearance of power and wealth that allowed Montaigne to call it the most populated city in Italy, which "non dissimiglia troppo a Parigi e ha molto la vista di Città Francese" (223) (is not too much unlike Paris and has much the appearance of a French city [1035]). Another reason for this reaction, however, has to do with the French history in Milan. Capital of the "Gallia Togata, Cispadana et Transpadana" (Toga-wearing Gaul), a region that was first inhabited by

> Thyrreniens, et Toscans, jusques à ce que, environ l'an 160 de Rome et du monde 3542, les Gaulois Biturges, Hedui, Carinites, Arvernii, Boii, Coenomani, ceux de Berry, Authun, Auvergne, Chartres, Nevers, et aultres, en divers voyages ayans passé premierement les Alpes jusques à Ancone fut appellée Gaule Togate et Cisalpine à cause d'eux. Lors ils fonderent les villes de Milan, Pavie, Come, Bresse, Verone, Bergame, Trente, Vicenze, Modene,

Parme, Boulongne, Lode, Caravage, Senigaglia et Siene, avecq force autres en la Ligurie et Toscane.[72]

(Tyrrhenians and Tuscans until around the year 160 or Rome and 3542 of the world, the Biturgian Gauls, the Hedui, Carinites, Arvernii, Boii, Coenomani, from Berry, Authun, Auvergne, Chartres, Nevers and other, in various journeys having first passed the Alps all the way to Ancona it was called Toga-wearing and Cisalpine Gaul because of them. Then they founded the cities of Milan, Pavia, Como, Brescia, Verona, Bergamo, Trento, Vicenza, Modena, Parma, Bologna, Lodi, Caravaggio, Senigaglia, and Siena, along with many others of Liguria and Tuscany.)

Audebert and Claveson cite Andrea Alciati's *Emblematum libellus* (1531) in affirming that the city itself was "fondée par les Françoys" (founded by the French),[73] repeating the jurist's explanation of the etymology of the Latin *Mediolanum*, deriving from "mi laine" (half wool), in honor of the city's founders from Bourges and Autun.

Milan was coveted for its wealth and size, which were products of the natural abundance of its territory and the industry of its residents. The region, of which Milan, by its shape and position, formed the heart, was described as "fertille (en) toutes sortes de fruicts excellens, bleds et vins" (fertile in all sort of excellent fruits and wines),[74] the "meilleur et plus beau pays de toute l'Italie" (best and most beautiful land of all Italy), producing two crops per year.[75] The productive countryside communicated harmoniously with the hardworking city: "Le *pais* est *paisible* et la ville foeconde et abondante en toutes sortes de marchandise" (emphasis mine) (The country is peaceable and the city fecund and abundant in all sorts of commerce.)[76] Mountains, plains, rivers, and prairies link together as natural extensions of the urban center:

> Ce pays, par la vicissitude et diversité de nature qui fait ores bel, ores laid, ores monts, ores plaines, estant par la fin et proximité des montagnes en la planeure, a par ce mesme voisinage force eaux et rivieres, en ayant ce jour passé 3; la principale fut le Tesin, dont un canal tiré comme une riviere particuliere passe par Buffalore, bourg, continue avec plus de droicteur qu'il est

possible jusque à Milan où l'on va, qui veut, par son eau sur barques chargées de passagers et de marchandises.[77]

(This land, by the vicissitude and diversity of nature that makes, now beautiful, now horrid, mountainous here and plains there, being, by the end and proximity of the mountains in the plains, has because of this same proximity many waterways and rivers, and having this day crossed three, the most important of which was the Ticino, of which a canal, pulled like a type of river, passes through the town of Boffalora, continues as straight as possible all the way to Milan, where one can go, if one wants, by water on boats loaded with passengers and merchandise.)

Villamont remarks on the fertility of the surrounding lands, which transition to "ruës [. . .] belles et spacieuses, et les maisons tres-bien basties" (spacious, beautiful streets and well-built houses) as he enters the city walls, but it is the magnificent construction of "beaux palais et sumptueux edifices" (beautiful palaces and sumptuous buildings) that most impressed the traveler.[78]

Once in the city, the traveler passed the church of Santa Maria delle Grazie, arriving near the corner bastion of Ludovico Sforza's massive citadel on the left, and continued through the old Vercelli Gate. Only the gate remained, the old wall having been dismantled to give access to the old Naviglio that was now used for trade and shipping. After entering the old city, another wide avenue led toward the center and to inns located on the opposite side of the Duomo and Royal (Ducal) Palace.[79] From there, travelers toured the "raretez de la ville" (rarities of the city),[80] visiting Milan's churches, palaces, military defenses, grand hospital, and gardens. While some of Milan's churches dated from the years after the Edict of Milan (the basilicas of San Lorenzo and Sant'Ambrogio) or the Romanesque period (San Francesco Grande and San Celso), the more recent construction of many churches again illustrated Milan's increasing importance and wealth. The reformist archbishop Cardinal Carlo Borromeo (1564–84) had begun restoration of the Church of the Passion in 1573. Construction of the Basilica of San Vittore al Corpo, whose magnificence Florisel de Claveson compares to San Michele in Bosco in Bologna, had begun in 1559.[81] San Fedele was also under construction since 1560, while

Santa Maria presso San Celso (which travelers often confused with San Celso) had been commissioned in 1494, with work ongoing throughout much of the sixteenth century. The author of the *Discours viatiques* describes the result as "la plus jolie, la mieulx doree et la plus plaisant" (the prettiest, best gold-plated and most pleasant), praising the beauty of its sculptures of the twelve apostles, Saint John, and the Virgin Mary and advising his friend to leave half an hour "à la contemplation de sa beauté" (for the contemplation of its beauty).[82]

The focal point of all travelers' tours then, as today, was the Duomo, whose size, design, and construction in marble astounded visitors.[83] Nicolas Bénard remarks on the cathedral's mesmerizing power:

> La voûte et hauteur duquel font esblouyr les yeux des regardans et est directement eslevé presque au mitan de l'Eglise estant de forme ronde, tellement que plus on le regarde et plus on l'admire, tant cest ouvrage est de haute entreprise et d'une ingenieuse structure, et est à croire que l'Eglise de sainct Pierre de Rome ne la surpasse de guere, non plus que saincte Sophie de Constantinople.[84]

> (The vault and height of which bedazzle the eyes of those who look upon it and are directly lifted to the middle of the Church, which is round in shape so that the more one looks at it the more one admires it, such it is a work of high design and ingenious structure and it is to be believed that the Church of Saint Peter in Rome hardly surpasses it, no more than Saint Sophia in Constantinople.)

Most travelers also scaled the three hundred steps to the roof to admire the view of the city:

> C'est une chose toute naturelle de monter haut pour voir de plus loing, et une coustume qui est bone pour considerer d'une seule veue toutes les diverses choses dedans et dehors d'une ville, son paysage, son plan, sa situation, sa closture, ses cartiers, ses rues, de monter en quelque eminent lieu avec homme qui sache deviser de ce qui se voit: ainsi fait-on à Paris du haut des tours Nostre Dame, et à Milan de la sommité du Dome, où l'on void comme

le coeur de cette grosse ville est de forme ronde, ou plustost fait en coeur; et non seulement la ville est-elle circuite entierement comme d'une ceinture par l'eau du canal du Tesin, mais le fauxbourg aussy qui l'entoure et commence au delà dudit canal en est partout distant esgalement et l'estreint derechef en mesme forme ronde qu'un autre grand cercle dans lequel elle est contenue et luy dans la closture du dehors qui est par consequent pareille, de sorte que toute cette ville est comme un grand coeur.[85]

(It is a completely natural thing to climb to a high spot in order to see farther, and a custom that is good for considering in a single view all the many things inside and outside a city, its landscape, its layout, its location, its enclosure, its neighborhoods, its streets, to climb to some high place with a man who knows how to speak about what one sees: people do this in Paris from the top of Notre Dame, and in Milan at the top of the Duomo, where one sees how the heart of this great city is round, or rather in the form of a heart; and not only is the city surrounded completely by a belt of water of the Ticino canal, but the suburb that surrounds it and begins on the other side of the canal is everywhere the same distance around and in the same round form of another great circle forming the shape of a great heart.)

Milan was a modern, functional city defined by the engineering marvel of the Navigli that allowed merchants to ship goods directly from their shops along the interconnected canals to world markets via the Po River. The city's four-thousand-bed hospital was comparable in "magnificence et belle conduitte pour les pauvres, a celuy du Saint Esprit de Rome" (magnificence and usefulness for the poor to that of Santo Spirito in Rome),[86] while its "grande quantité de beaux et superbes palais" (great quantity of superb palaces)[87] were comparable to those of Naples, Venice, or Rome. The most notable were the palazzos Sforza and Trivulzio, as well as the former home of the wealthy merchant Tommaso Marino, a "structure ingenieuse" (ingenious structure) that had already been taken over as the official residence of the Duke of Terranova when Nicolas Bénard passed through in August of 1617.[88]

Another focal point was the magnificent Cittadella, "presque inexpugnable" (almost indestructible)[89] and "une des plus fortes au monde" (one of the strongest in the world),[90] which served as a painful reminder of France's defeat in Italy. Its hexagonal structure of six regular bastions surrounded "de triples fossez fort profonds à fonds de cuve remplis d'eau provenant d'un grand canal tiré du fleuve Thezin" (with triple very deep moats filled with water coming from a great canal taken from the Ticino)[91] and an old castle, or *donjon*, "ouvrage des François" (built by the French).[92] Since Frenchmen could enter only by ruse or using special political connections,[93] Montaigne toured the castle "per di fuora" (from the outside), describing it as "un grandissimo edificio, e di mirabile fortezza" (222) (a very big building and wonderfully strong [1035]). It was guarded by seven hundred Spanish soldiers and more than two hundred cannons, and symbolized France's loss of Milan:

> Amy, sy tu fais oncques le voiage, je t'adverty de monter aussy hault que nous y feusmes, affin que tu voies la citadelle et dessuz et dessoubz, des plus fortes que tu as jamais veue, et en la voyant ne retiens tes larmes pour une telle perte que nous avons faicte, et sy c'est peché que de desirer, peche en desirant le recouvrement d'une sy belle et grande ville.[94]

> (Friend, if you ever make the trip, I advise you climb as high as we did, so that you can see this citadel from the top and the bottom, one the strongest you have ever seen, and, while looking at it, do not hold back your tears for such a loss that we have suffered, and if it is a sin to desire, sin in desiring the recovery of such a beautiful and large city.)

The Duke of Rohan expressed a similar regret:

> je partis de Milan, non sans regret de ne la voir possedée de ses legitimes seigneurs, mais en esperance qu'un jour nous la reconquerrons justement, avec plus de gloire que nous ne l'avons perduë par malheur.[95]

> (I left Milan, not without regret at not seeing it possessed by its legitimate lords, but in hope that one day we will justly reconquer it, with more glory than we lost by bad fortune.)

DIFFERENT PERSPECTIVES OF BOLOGNA "LA GRASSA"

The coachride from Milan to Bologna that cost François Vinchant twenty-one *ducatons*[96] crossed a landscape of fertile plains, shifting wetlands, and rivers populated by beautiful, towered cities. His principal stops on the three-day trip were Lodi, Piacenza, Borgo San Donino, Parma, Reggio (Reggio-Emilia), and Modena. Lodi was "une ville moyennement forte" (a somewhat well-defended city), with a small castle perched above the Adda River and surrounded by "l'étendue des beaux champs et prairies tousjours verdoyants, lesquelles contuellement arousées par des canalx de bois artificiellement bien disposez" (an expanse of beautiful fields and prairies, which are always green and are continuously watered by the wooden pipes that are artfully laid out).[97] The towers and spires of Piacenza could be seen long before arriving at the ferry that crossed the waters of the mighty Po. Parma was also located on a river, while Reggio was "gentile et belle et bastie en un lieu marescageux, à cause de la riviere Crustulo qui costoye ses murailles" (gentle and beautiful, and built in a marshy place, because of the Crostolo stream that passes along its walls).[98] Modena was surrounded by marshlands whose frogs, according to Pliny, were the city's staple food product.

Many of the places along the route had special significance for the French traveler. Between Milan and Lodi Marignano (Melegnano), a small town, "cotoiée de la rivière Abda" (which the Adda river runs along),[99] was the site of François I's famous victory over Italian and Swiss troops.[100] Vinchant cites Guicciardini and provides a short synopsis of the great battle that made the newly crowned king's reputation. In Piacenza, he comments on the fortifications built by Charles V, a city he also criticizes for its abuse of noble titles and the resultant large number of poor noblemen who are "fort courtoise, mais fort adonnée à la vanité" (very galant, but very subject to vanity).[101] Near Borgo San Donino, where the coach often stopped for the night, was the site of the Battle of Fornovo, located at the crossing of the Taro, where a small, ruined bridge marked the famous battle of the first Italian War:

> C'est en cest endroit et du costé droit vers Colorno, que jadis Charles VIII, Roy de France (selon la relation de Belforest), en retournant de la conqueste du Royaulme de Naples, se campa et emporta victoire contre les Lombards, Milanois, Vénétiens et Estradiots qui les

vinrent agresser avec soixante milles hommes; mais, comme je dis, la bonne heure fut que le Roy n'aiant que dix milles hommes, fut victorieux et retorna sans aultre péril en France.

(In this place and on the right toward Colorno, which in times past, Charles VIII, King of France [according to Belforest], returned from the conquest of the Kingdom of Naples, camped and won victory against the Lombards, Milanese, Venetians and Stratioti who came to attack with sixty thousand men, but, as I said, luck had it that the King, with only ten thousand men, was victorious and returned to France without further peril.)[102]

Reggio had the tomb of the historian Prosper of Aquitaine and statues of the Gaulish King Brennus and Charlemagne,[103] and just beyond Modena, Vinchant passed the "chasteau des Franchois ou Castel Franco, où selon les anciens historiens, là emprès estoit Forum Gallorum ou station des Gaulois" (castle of the Franks or Castel Franco, where, according to historians, nearby was the Forum Gallorum or station of the Gauls),[104] just a few miles from the city where Charles V had been crowned.

Bologna was a famous, wealthy, commercial city with an "abondance de vivres, bon air, belles promenades, tout ce qui est necessaire à la vie humaine" (abundance of food, good air, beautiful walks, everything necessary for life).[105] Its large porches and red-brick construction impressed all travelers:

> Boulogne surnommee la grasse, est une grande cité et bien peuplee en laquelle y a douze portes, par le milieu d'icelle passe le torrent Davesa, et est quasi de forme ronde, et situee en une belle campaigne, proche et voisine des hauts monts Appennins, qui n'empeschent la cité d'estre tres riche et marchande, les maisons de laquelle sont presque toutes basties sur porches, de sorte qu'on y peut se pourmener, et faire ses negoces, sans estre incommodé de la pluye, ne aussi de la fange qui y est assez commune, à raison du commerce qui s'y fait, et du peuple qui y resident: principalement pour estudier. (16)

(Bologna, called "the fat," is a large, well-populated city with twelve gates and through which the Torrente Aposa passes, and is almost round in form, and situated in a beautiful countryside, near and next to the high peaks of the Apennines, which does not stop the city from being very wealthy and full of commerce, the houses of which are almost all built on porches, allowing one to walk and conduct business without being inconvenienced by the rain, nor the mud, which are common enough here because of the city's commerce and the people that live here, mainly to study.)

There were many things to see. Its university was, of course, "la plus belle d'Italie" (the most beautiful in Italy)[106] and was believed to have been founded by Saint Petronius under the reign of Theodosius.[107] Visitors all commented on the beauty of the city, its covered sidewalks where merchants sold their wares, the pavement, and many beautiful residential palazzi, all built in the same red brick, and "grande quantité d'eglises que c'est quasi chose innumerable" (an almost numberless quantity of churches).[108]

Bologna's structure and geographical position at the base of the Apennines allowed visitors to view the city from a number of different vantage points. The beginning and focal point of these visits was invariably the Piazza Maggiore, with the Palace of the Podestà, Palazzo d'Accursio, and the Basilica of Saint Petronius. San Petronio and the nearby Duomo dedicated to Saint Peter were filled with the tombs of famous cardinals, bishops, and jurisconsults. Also located here were the fountain of Neptune by Giambologna[109] (erected in 1565), the statue of Pope Gregory XIII (erected the month before Montaigne passed through in 1580), and the twin towers, the Torre degli Asinelli and the Garisenda.

The climb up the Torre degli Asinelli provided a second vantage point:

Ayant asses jouy de si belles veues, fismes dessain, pour mieux particulariser les endroits de la ville, monter a la haulte tour d'Asinelli, posée au milieu de la ville, a la cyme de laquelle arrivasmes par cinq cents degrés de bois, estant, comme j'estime, pour sa grosseur une des haultes Tours du monde, nayant guieres plus de quatorze pieds en carrure, entierement de bricque. De là jugions la ville avoir la forme dung Navire, paroissant ladicte Tour au milieu comme ung mast.

(Having enjoyed these beautiful sights, we made a plan, in order to better inspect the places of the city, to climb up the high tower of the Asinelli, set in the middle of the city, at the top of which we arrived climbing five hundred wooden steps, being, in my opinion, for its width, one of the high towers of the world, measuring no more than fourteen feet square, completely in brick. From there we judged the city to have the form of a ship, the said tower in the middle seeming like a mast.)[110]

Others went to view the city from the church of Monte Oliveto, where "se descrouvre toutte la ville de Bologne et cette grande pleine fertile de la Gaule Cisalpine" (you discover all the city of Bologna and this great fertile plain of Cisalpine Gaul),[111] or at the church of San Michele in Bosco, "située sur ung Cotaud mediocrement relevé, voyant toute la ville et pleyne de Lombardie" (situated on the side of a hill, somewhat elevated, looking over all the city and plain of Lombardy).[112]

The Torre degli Asinelli, in effect, was considered by some as the boundary between "la Gaule Cisalpine" and the region controlled by Rome, or Romagna. Bologna's defining characteristic was its contentious politics, which derived from historic disputes that had only recently been quashed by the election of the Bolognese Pope Gregory. Montaigne compares Bologna to Padua but notes that it is less secure "pour les parts anciennes qui sont entre des partis d'aucunes races de la ville, desquelles l'une a pour soy les François de tous temps, l'autre les Espaignols qui sont là en grand nombre" (77) (because of the old feuds that exist between factions of certain families in the city, one of which has always had the French on their side, [the] other the Spaniards, who are here in great numbers [926]). This proverbial rivalry of Guelfs and Ghibellines, the French, Spanish, and popes and the various families (the Pepoli and Bentivoglio), whose important palaces are also part of the walking tour of the city, was also the reason foreigners were allowed to wear their swords without the permission of the captain of the guard, since members of the various factions wore their caps in a certain direction as a sign of membership and often attacked their rivals in the dark corridors of the city. The symbols of freedom inscribed all over the city in the words *Libertas et S.P.R.B.* continued to roil the local population, whose power had been usurped by papal control, as Claude-Énoch Virey remarks in his *Vers itineraires*:

Bologne apres je veis où des Bentivoli
Avoyent esté seigneurs aussi des Pepoli
Mais lors j'y passay J'y trouvay d'un Gregoire
La statue de bronze effaceant leur memoire.

(Next I saw Bologna where the Bentivoglio
Had been lords as had the Pepoli
But when I passed through, I found a bronze statue
Of Gregory there, erasing their memory.)[113]

Gregory's hand, raised in benediction in the famous statue, was viewed for the symbolic act of control that it was meant to be. But Bologna was not the only city whose political freedom had been compromised, however, as Montaigne would soon find out in his reading of the Grand Duchy of Tuscany.

THE CITY AS SPECTACLE: FLORENCE AND THE RENAISSANCE TRAVELER

Nicolas Audebert concluded his visit to Florence with a tour of the grand duke's *studiolo* of precious stones.[114] Having visited the city for three full days, he had seen many "belles Eglises, Palais, Places" (beautiful churches, palaces, squares)[115] and admired the city's large, straight streets paved in white stone. He had also climbed to the top of the cupola of Santa Maria del Fiore, observed Lorenzo Ghiberti's baptistery doors, and visited the Medici tombs by Michelangelo, so the visit to the Casino di San Marco was almost a codicil to his tour of "Florence la Belle." While there, he was shown two objects worthy of note. The first was a marble table, only partially completed but so richly "couverte de pierres pretieuses rapportées ensemble" (covered in precious stones brought together) that he was told it would cost another forty thousand "escus" to complete.[116] The second object was a piece of agate, small enough to fit into the palm of his hand, carved with an image of the city of Florence "si delicattement et de sorte que jusques à la moindre rue et place s'y cognoist aussy facilement comme l'on feroit en un grand tableau" (259) (so delicately and in such a way that even the tiniest street and square could be easily recognized as one would experience in a large painting.)

The fact that Audebert was shown this piece illustrates the complexity of the art of urban representation in Florence and shows that the

Casino di San Marco, which would later become the *Opificio e Museo delle pietre dure*, was conceived from its inception not only as a laboratory where the grand duke could pass time and satisfy his curiosity but as a means of communicating power and culture. The small object's power as a metaphor is clear enough. It showed how the duke—holding the city, literally, in the palm of his hand—produced, controlled, and manipulated the represented spaces of his city. As a last reminder of Florence's beauty, it presented the city back to the tourist, repeating and recapturing the locations of the itinerary he had just finished visiting in a Mannerist doubling of vision, adding the technical delicacy and showmanship of diminutive size to the manipulative representation of maps and calling the viewer's attention to the precision of its artistry.

Florence is a jewel controlled and transformed by the power and artistry of the Medici dynasty.

THE SPECTACLE OF ARRIVAL

The perception of Florence began long before the traveler arrived at the city gates. Travelers coming from Bologna, as most did, made a crossing that was, after the Alps, the most difficult of the Italian tour. Following a "chemin aspre et montueux" (77) (rugged road and mountainous country [927]), it crossed the so-called spine of Italy, running from "le milieu d'Italie depuis le dessus de Genua jusque en Calabre, tellement ce quy est l'esreste à un poisson" (the middle of Italy from above Genoa all the way to Calabria, in the manner of the skeleton of a fish).[117] This skeleton also served as the geographical and political barrier between the Papal States and Tuscany, marking the "separation de la Lombardie d'avec la Toscane" (separation between Lombardy and Tuscany),[118] a border marked at the mountaintop fortress of Firenzuola. The difficulty of crossing this rugged countryside, followed by the spectacular vision of Santa Maria del Fiore from the hills of Fiesole, created a first impression of Florence's beauty and power.

After leaving the *fauxbourgs* of Bologna the traveler passed through the "beau pays qui est encore de la Lombardie" (beautiful country that is still Lombardy),[119] following the remains of the Roman militia road bordered by beautiful trees, fields, and vineyards:

> . . . belle et unies campagnes de bled et des prairies à longues filieres d'ormes et de peupliers sur lesquels se soustiennent les

vignes, les fleuves ça et là divisés en petits canaux conduits par les prés et heritages et coulants le long des grands chemins qui sont les restes de la milice romaine, droict allignés, souvent recouverts d'arbres, mais tousjours bordé de hayes vives, vertes et espaisses, tondues à niveau comme es parterres des curieux, qui est une beauté autant riante l'esté comme je croy l'hyver.[120]

(. . . beautiful and regular fields of wheat and prairies with long lines of elms and poplars holding up vines, the rivers here and there divided in small canals led through the fields and houses and flowing along the large roads that are what remains of the Roman military road, lined up in straight rows, often covered by trees, but always lined by healthy, green and thick hedges, trimmed and leveled as in the parterres of decorative gardens, that is of such a smiling beauty in summer as, I believe, in winter.)

During the first half-day, the road climbed at a leisurely pace,[121] bringing the traveler to the village of Pianora (modern-day Pianoro), nestled in a valley and named after an Etruscan king who had lived there. From there it climbed rapidly, pushing onto the valley's edge and "sur le dos du grand Mont Appennin/Par devers les Toscans [. . .] approchant le rampant de l'hauteur montaniere" (onto the back of the great Apennine mountain toward the land of the Tuscans, approaching the steep climbs of the mountain peaks).[122] The road to Sabronetta Loiano (Sabbioni, Loiano) climbed very rapidly,[123] following the upper mountains over a road Montaigne's secretary calls "le premier de nostre voyage qui se peut nommer incommode et farouche, et parmy les montaignes plus difficiles qu'en nulle autre part de ce voyage" (78) (the first of our journey that can be called difficult and ferocious, and among the most difficult mountains of any part of our journey [927]). The road topped nine hundred meters near Monte di Fo' before beginning a steep drop-off toward Scarperia and Florence.

This "ferocious" countryside was populated by a number of small, unsavory towns: "Scargalasino" (Monghidoro), whose name derived from the fact that mules had to be unloaded in order to make the steep climb, and Pietramala, or "bad stone," famous for the flames its methane deposits shot from the ground near the road. Bandits and rapacious innkeepers were a problem. Montaigne had chosen to go to Florence because of banditry on the road to Loreto, but arriving in Loiano, he writes of a different sort of theft, where the hostels are famed "entre toutes celles d'Italie de la trahison qui s'y fait aux passans, de les paistre de belles promesses de toute sorte de commodités avant qu'ils mettent pied à terre, et s'en mocquer quand ils les tiennent à leur mercy" (77) (among all those of Italy for the treachery that is practiced on travelers in feeding them with fine promises of every sort of comfort before they set foot to the ground, and laughing at them when they have them at their mercy [927]).

François Vinchant reports nearly being robbed at a "logis seul à l'escart entre ces bois de Monts Appennins" (lone lodging set back among these woods of the Apennine mountains).[124] After he was warned by his innkeeper to watch out for suspicious characters, he and his companion became wary of the owner's familiarity with "5 à 6 païsans" (five or six peasants) and locked themselves in their room, stood guard all night, and escaped in the early morning through the wooded valleys to Scarperia. In the next inn, a guest was killed in his sleep.

These difficulties heighten the spatial drama of travelers' first glimpses of Florence. The author of the *Discours viatiques* recounts wandering "parmy les nues sy obscures qu'à grand peine nous pouvions nous entrevoir" (among the clouds so obscure that we could hardly see one another), until, as if in a vision, he exclaims, "Dieu mercy, [. . .] nous descouvrismes Florence la Belle" (73) (Thank God, we could see Florence the Beautiful).[125] The road between Pratolino and the Val d'Arno descended rapidly,[126] bringing the view of Florence from Fiesole rapidly into sight. Jacques-Auguste de Thou recalls in his *Mémoires*, written years later, that he "se rendit à Florence par l'Apennin, qui étoit tout couvert de neiges" (went to Florence over the Apennines, which were all covered with snow[s]), moving rapidly into "un pays si doux et agréable, qu'il sembloit que l'on fût dans un autre climat, quoiqu'il soit au pied de ces affreuses montagnes" (a country so sweet and agreeable that it seemed as if he entered another climate, even though it was at the foot of these horrifying mountains).[127] For François Vinchant (who had nearly been killed the night before), the movement through this savage land to the sudden view of Santa Maria del Fiore and the walls of Florence was like arriving in a second Eden:

> Or quittant peu à peu lesdits monts, l'on descouvre un beau pays de grande estendue au milieu duquel, comme à son centre, se fait

apparoistre la belle ville de Florence, tellement qu'il me sembloit de veoir un petit paradis terrestre.

(Now, leaving little by little the said mountains, you begin to discover a beautiful, extensive countryside, in the middle of which, in its very center, the beautiful city of Florence appears in such a way that it seemed to me to see a little paradise on earth.)[128]

Most of the French travelers confirmed Vinchant's description, however, taking note of the extensive beautification and management of the Tuscan countryside that had taken place under the Medici rule. Nicolas Audebert describes the rolling hills and well-groomed, tree-lined road leading from Lucca in detail. Sleeping in Boggiano (Borgo a Buggiano) and passing beneath a series of "petites villettes qu'en italien ilz appellent Castelli" (I, 246) (small towns that in Italian they call castles),[129] he passed below Montecarlo, Montecatini, and the "Monte Smano"; crossed the Nevola River; and climbed to Serravalle, perched on "une assez haulte montaigne" (a rather high mountain), where "se descouvre fort à plain Pistoye" (you can see the plain of Pistoia very well).[130] In this "belle plaine" (beautiful plain) (246), he passed Ponte Lungo and Pistoia, following a road he describes as "fort large, des deux costez de laquelle y a hayes et grands arbres plantez à la ligne" (very large, on the two sides of which there were hedges and large trees planted in a row). This tree-lined road continued to within a mile of the city, where the suburbs of Florence began, giving the impression less of a journey than of a pleasant stroll along "une allée de quelque excellent jardin que en un chemin commun" (a pathway of some excellent garden rather than on a common road).[131]

The natural defenses of the sea and mountains allowed Florence a certain openness other cities, such as Bologna or Milan, could not afford. Florence's defense was supplemented by the numerous castelli that dotted the countryside, while the city itself spread out onto the hills outside the walls, communicating to the arriving visitor a sense of the region's prosperity and power. Florence's suburbs had famously been destroyed in 1529 by the forces of Charles V, so Leandro Alberti (1550) and even Belleforest (1575) pined the loss of "les faulxbourgs de Florence abbattuz" (Belleforest 723) (the suburbs of Florence destroyed).[132] By the time of Audebert's (1576) and Montaigne's (1580) visits, Florence had rebuilt these areas to a point that the suburbs once again blurred the borders between countryside and city. This openness, experienced by the French traveler, moreover, had a historical and aesthetic significance that related to the city's past as a thriving republic and center of artistic and industrial innovation.

Florisel de Claveson describes this transition mixing what he experienced with the historical memory of the area. Traveling in 1608, he passed along the "allées couvertes, embellies au long de petits ruisseaux et canaux" (covered roads, beautified all along by small streams and canals). After the grand duke's "mesnagerie du laictage" (milk farm), he arrived at a spot where the plain was filled with "maisons de plaisance, de monasteres et convents, de grands villages et bourgades, qu'on en *sortiroit une armée* de gens" (emphasis mine) (pleasure villas, monasteries and convents, large villages and towns so plentiful that an army of people could be called out of them). The sight of so many bell towers and towns on the hills reminded him of a famous exchange between the Florentine patriot Piero Capponi and the French King Charles VIII, who, in 1494, threatened to lay siege to Florence if it refused to give in to his demands for money and castles. Claveson cites Capponi's "hardie response" (daring response) of grabbing the document being read by the king's secretary, tearing it to shreds, and throwing it at the king's feet, affirming that "puisque lon nous demande choses si deshonestes, vous sonneres vos trompettes, et nous ferons sonner nos cloches" (80) (since you ask us to do such dishonest things, you can sound your trumpets and we will ring our bells).[133] Even for a fervent Catholic like Claveson, the example of Florence's republican patriotism served as a model of political behavior. Florence's peaceful beauty, moreover, was a sign of its latent power, the tranquil, populated countryside contributing to the impression, expressed by many travelers, that Florence was relatively unarmed, defended, as it is, by the natural topography of its surrounding mountains: "Elle est proche des montagnes, assise en une plaine basse, fertile et habitée de plusieurs villages et maisons à l'environ, parfois par petits terres qui en rendent le paysage fort agreable, forte quand à elle" (*1606*, 59) (Florence is close to the mountains, sitting in a low plain, fertile and inhabited by several villages all around, sometimes by small pieces of land that make the landscape quite agreeable, well-defended in itself).[134] The term *paysage* (landscape), still rarely used in this period, appears here in an aesthetic and military context, which, for the noble traveler, are fused. In much the same way that travelers appreciate the aesthetic quality of a city's military defenses, they also view the land as a beautiful space for military endeavors, an aestheticized expression, to cite Deleuze and Guattari, of the smooth space of nomadic freedom.[135] The fact that Florence's walls were "irregulierement fortifiées" (irregularly fortified)[136] and that the strongest of its three fortresses (the Belvedere) was "pas du tout reguliere" (not at all regular) and the other two (San Miniato and San Giovanni) were "guieres fortes" (not strong at all) (Fontenay-Mareuil)[137] were signs of the natural strength of a people and city "scituée en plaine assez longue, mais estroitte et enserrée des haults des monts de l'Apenin" (situated in a rather long plain, but narrow and hemmed in by the Apennine mountains).[138]

THE CITY ON TOUR

Travelers in Florence followed a somewhat standardized tour that began at the Duomo and circled around the city to the churches of San Lorenzo, San Marco, and Santa Maria Annunziata back toward the Duomo to the Palazzo Vecchio and then across the galleria and Ponte Vecchio to the Palazzo Pitti and, very often, returning over the bridge of the Trinità, past the Duomo again to finish up with the Casino di San Marco. Jean Tarde and his companions went to Mass in the church of the Annunziata and then to the Duomo, the Medici collection of wild animals and nearby stables, the Palazzo Pitti, the duke's gallery, back to the "grande place" (Vasari corridor and Uffizi gallery), the grand duke's and duchess's curiosity cabinets, and the grand duke's collection of arms "et les autres" (and other things) all in one afternoon. Florisel de Claveson began at Santa Maria del Fiore, visiting the baptistery and bell tower and then the churches of the Annunziata, San Marco, and San Lorenzo, following a circular itinerary around the San Giovanni district. After San Lorenzo, he crossed the Arno to Pitti Palace, following the galleries back across the Ponte Vecchio to the "vieux Palaix."

These itineraries imply that a rhetoric of presentation was in place, in which the older monuments, Santa Maria del Fiore and the baptistery, and the other churches—Florence's foundations—transitioned to the civic structures now controlled by the Medici dynasty. Francesco Bocchi's *Le Bellezze della città di Fiorenza dove à pieno di pittura, di scultura, di sacri tempii* provided a variety of in-depth tours centered on the various city gates.[139] His first itinerary, or section, began from the Porta San Gallo, the gate used by visitors from the north. This entrance took the traveler to the Casino and church of San Marco and the Medici family home, culminating with a visit to the Duomo and baptistery. The second day passed over to the left bank, where the Palazzo Pitti and its famous statuary are located, and then crossed the Ponte della Trinità to arrive in front of the Palazzo Strozzi, with its column of Justice. Tours three and four covered the Porta del Prato and the Porta di San Minato. All these tours tended to emphasize the importance and logic of the Medici dynasty.

The spaces and statues cited by the French also underline the political importance of these works. After visiting the churches, most visitors then went to the Palazzo Vecchio, renamed the "palazzo d'inverno" (winter palace) by the grand duke, who generally resided on the other side of the river in the Pitti Palace or "palazzo d'estate" (summer palace). The galleria, or walkway, was built by Vasari so that "leurs Altesses peuvent aller a couvert par galleries jusques au vieux Palaix" (their highnesses can go covered by galleries all the way to Palazzo Vecchio) (Claveson 84).[140] The gallery joins practical purposes to a rhetorical, symbolic function. In allowing the duke to walk from his private residence to his ceremonial palace, it connects his private life with the public sphere, confusing the two through the personification of power and conflation of public and private functions. In addition to getting the duke to work, the galleria also prevented him from being assassinated at the hands of the resentful Florentines as he walked through the streets of his city. The masterpieces held in the gallery thus mask the military origins of the "Corridore" (originally a walkway for soldiers defending a castle), substituting the conspicuous consumption of art for the pomp of a ceremonial parade. Leisure has completely conquered civic action.

This increased use of art, moreover, appears to drown out the traditional, more powerfully symbolic use of statues as representations of political allegory. An example of this can be seen in the ambiguous and sometimes flawed readings French travelers made of the statues that mark the entrance to the Palazzo Vecchio. The two statues that greeted the visitor then, as today, were Michelangelo's *David* (today replaced by a copy) and Baccio Bandinelli's *Hercules and Caccus*, statues that represented two different perspectives of government and two different moments in Florentine history. The *David* had been commissioned by the Florentine Republic in 1501 to celebrate its victory over its enemies, the most important of which were the Medici.[141] Bandinelli's sculpture, commissioned by Pope Clement VII (Giulio de' Medici), was a response to Michelangelo's work, so that the two statues, read together, recounted the history of Florence and celebrated the Medici victory over its republican enemies. Aesthetic criticism of Bandinelli's work appears to be related to this emblematic reading of the two statues, which came to represent the Medici victories over their external and internal enemies, as many sources still show today. French travelers of this period, most of whom were probably led around by tour guides, ignored Michelangelo's statue entirely, directing their attention to Bandinelli's work but interpreting it as "Hercule massacrant à ses pieds le Roy" (Hercules killing the King at his feet).[142] The source of this misreading is difficult to say, but it seems clear that the intended message of the Medici statue was misinterpreted or perhaps misdirected through the explanation provided by a tour guide. The future lawyer and Orleanese revolutionary Nicolas Audebert is the only Frenchman who emphasizes that the Palazzo Vecchio "estoit anciennement de la Republique et Seigneurie" (had in the past belonged to the Republic and Signoria) and interprets the two statues as repressed symbols of republican struggle.[143]

PARALLAX

The tour of Florence, beginning with the Duomo and ending at the Casino di San Marco, multiplied the points of perspective from which the tourist could appreciate the city so that the perception of Florence's beauty, confirmed by Audebert in the Casino di San Marco, depended on a guided rhetorical viewing of space.

The Duomo, with its facade, doors, and cupola, served as an important communicative device, dazzling travelers as they arrived on horseback from the hills of Scarperia and Fiesole. Condé describes Santa Maria del Fiore as "la plus belle chose du monde toute de marbre blanc et noir toute achevée hors la façade" (the most beautiful thing in the world, all built of white and black marble completed everywhere except on the façade).[144] Travelers place it above all the churches of Bologna and even the Duomo of Milan[145] and wonder at the delicacy of its marble work, and Montaigne notes that he can already see signs of erosion.[146]

Nicolas Audebert, on the other hand, uses an anecdote to underline how the monument plays on the sense of perspective of the viewer through the voice of King François I during his visit to Florence in 1515:

Voyant ce temple et en approchant, l'estima merveilleusement; et attendu ce qui de loing luy apparoissoit et se rendoit plus beau quand plus il approchoit, il se promettoit de veoir encore davantage et choses plus riches et pretieuses dedans. Où estant arrivé et ne trouvant ce qu'il attendoit, il commença à louer fort le dehors comme le plus beau vaisseau qu'il eust jamais veu, n'y trouvant qu'une chose à redire, qui est que pour un si bel oeuvre il eust desiré un estuy pour deffence de l'injure du temps, ou que l'autheur d'iceluy, l'eust basty en sorte que l'on eust peu en faire comme des manches d'un pourpoinct, lesquelles on retourne affin que la doubleure, qui est de moindre estoffe, serve de toylette pour conserver le dessus.

(King François I, seeing this temple and approaching it, considered it marvelously; and, since that which from far away seemed and made itself even more beautiful the closer he approached it, he expected to see even richer and more precious things inside. Where, upon arriving and not finding what he expected, he began to praise the exterior as the most beautiful vessel he had ever seen, finding only one thing wrong with it, that for such a beautiful work, he would have wanted a case to protect it from the damage of time, or for the architect to build it in a way that one could turn it inside out like the sleeves of a doublet whose lining, which is made of less valuable fabric, serves as a protection for the outside.)[147]

François I's confusion comes first from the excessive delicacy and fineness of the cathedral's marble decoration, which, in its use of inlay, becomes more beautiful as one comes closer to it. Its comparison to a fine doublet turned inside out reinforces the gentlemanly comparison, while the king imagines constructing a case to protect the delicate object.

The Duomo also turns on itself and is both an instrument for viewing and an object to be viewed. As the bedazzled tourist arrived, gazing at the church's minute finery, his tour guide would direct his attention to the golden ball at the top of the dome. Travelers wrote in their journals that it looked the size of a soccer ball—not big enough for a man to enter nor large enough for "moitié d'un petit enfant" (half a small child).[148] After observing the church's interior and the underside of the dome, they climbed five hundred steps to the "lanterna," enjoying the view of the Val d'Arno as far as the Medici villa of Pratolino. Then they were shown a secret passageway, which the jeweler Brunelleschi had ingeniously hidden, which allowed them to climb up another flight of stairs and into the bronze ball itself. Montaigne claims that forty people fit into the 2.4-meter diameter space (82, 930). Claveson claims that "nous fussions logés facillement 20 hommes" (twenty of us fit easily in),[149] and Bergeron, who often uses secondhand testimony, claims the ball can hold sixteen or seventeen men, and Villamont, twenty. Audebert, who rarely, if ever, records anything he did not see with his own eyes, writes that the ball could hold thirty-five or forty people "estans rangez tant en hault que bas sur ladicte charpenterie" (arranged on two levels on the said framework).[150] He also claims to have peered out the trap door at the top of the ball, observing the large cross at the ball's top. Claveson looks down at unrecognizably small priests and visitors walking around the church floor and the view of Pratolino and is "unable" to leave the enchanting location.[151]

The themes of the visit to Florence juxtapose beauty and artistic refinement over the trappings of power. This aspect includes an emerging mythology of the importance of the artist, which, while somewhat present in the description of other cities, is raised to another level in the artisan city of Florence. The second theme, present in almost all the artworks, is the political and social value of art itself. The physical structure of the city—its landscape and churches, its public structures and functional beauty, its statues and tombs of famous people—is used to present aspects of Florence's contrasted political history, known to French travelers through works such as Guicciardini.

THE POLITICAL CITYSCAPE

Arriving "par le haut de certaines collines" (80) (over the top of certain hills [929]), Montaigne entered Florence on a Saturday evening, November 22, 1580, through the San Gallo gate and made his way to the Agnolo Inn in the Borgo di San Lorenzo. He passed two kidney stones and some sand and then went out to inspect the city. He does not seem to have followed an itinerary, wandering down the street to see the grand duke's menagerie of wild beasts; then to the church of San Lorenzo, right outside his inn, and the Duomo just a few blocks away; and then the

Casino di San Marco, also nearby. He does not seem overly impressed, complaining about his food and lodging and remarking that few nations had "si peu de belles femmes que l'Italienne" (81) (so few beautiful women as the Italian [929]).

On his second day, Montaigne climbed the Duomo, visited the "palais du Duc" (Palazzo Vecchio), and dined with the grand duke in Palazzo Pitti. In both the church of San Lorenzo, where Michelangelo's shrine celebrated the Medici's glory and Montaigne sighted the banners of the Maréchal Strozzi lost in the defense of Siena, and the Palazzo Vecchio, where he saw Vasari's famous paintings, Montaigne was reminded of France's losses to the Medici, noting with nostalgia that "les fleurs de lis tiennent le premier rang d'honneur" (82) (the fleur de lys hold the first rank of honor [930]). The secretary insists that he went out of his way, however, to see the houses of the Gondi and Strozzi, two important Florentines with strong ties to France. It is at this point that the *Journal* records the following observation, assumed to be that of Montaigne and not his secretary:

> Je ne sçay pas pourquoi cette ville soit surnommée belle par privilege; elle l'est, mais sans aucune excellence sur Boulongne, et peu sur Ferrare, et sans comparaison au dessous de Venise. Il fait à la vérité beau descouvrir de ce clochier l'infinie multitude de maisons qui remplissent les collines tout autour à bien deux ou trois lieues à la ronde, et cette plaine où elle est assise qui semble en longueur avoir l'estendue de deux lieues: car il semble qu'elles se touchent, tant elles sont dru semées. (83)

> (I do not know why this city should be privileged to be surnamed "the beautiful"; it is so, but without any advantage over Bologna, and little over Ferrara, and it is incomparably inferior to Venice. True it is fine to discover from the bell tower the infinite multitude of houses that cover the hills all around for a good two or three leagues, and this plain where the city is situated, which seems to extend to a length of two leagues; for the houses seem to touch each other, so thickly are they sown.) (930–31)

Montaigne's skepticism is strongest when he faces compulsion. His patriotism and nostalgia for the age of heroic French action instigate his objection to Florence claiming a "right" to a title. Rather than deny Florence's beauty, however, Montaigne opens a question around it, balancing his underlying skepticism of the regime that had contributed to France's defeat while examining with objectivity the structures of the new Florence, transforming the view from the Duomo and the populated suburbs covering the surrounding mountains into a space of perceptual aesthetic debate.

Chapter 6

MAPPING MONTAIGNE'S ROME

Traveling through Italy with the same spirit of reverie and adventure announced during his arrival in the Veneto, Montaigne continued to resist Rome's call as he headed south, wandering along "chemins divers et contrées" (61) (various roads and regions [915]) and enjoying the various pleasures of the road. In Rovereto, the gentlemen of the troop rented horses to visit Torbole and took a three-hour boat ride to admire the view of the length of Lake Garda. They also stopped in Battaglia, where Montaigne inspected the baths, and in Montalcino. They spent extra time in the major cities along their route,[1] where vectors of Montaigne's dreams of beyond continued to feed the geographical discourse of the *voyage*.[2] Montaigne "n'eust sceu arrester ny à Rome, ny ailleurs en Italie" (71) (would not have stayed peacefully in Rome or anywhere else in Italy [922]) without visiting Venice. In Bologna, too, he planned to head for Loreto, until reports of banditry pushed him back to the quicker route over the Apennines toward Florence. After leaving Siena, Montalcino, and the val d'Orcia behind, however, the troop finally entered the Papal States near Viterbo, where Montaigne was jolted from his pleasant story by a hardworking mule:

> Viterbo, qui avoit une partie de son assiette couchée sur une croupe de montaigne. C'est une belle ville, de la grandeur de Senlis. Nous y remerquasmes beaucoup de belles maisons, grande foison d'ouvriers, belles rues et plaisantes; en trois endroits d'icelle, trois très-belles fontaines. Il s'y fust arresté pour la beauté du lieu, mais son mulet qui alloit devant estoit déjà passé outre. (89)

(Viterbo, which is in part situated on the crest of a hill. It is a beautiful town, of the size of Senlis. We noticed here many beautiful houses, a great abundance of workmen, beautiful and pleasant streets; in three parts of town, three very beautiful fountains. Monsieur de Montaigne would have stopped here because of the beauty of the place, but his mule, which went ahead of him, had already passed on.) (934–35)

The following day, "tant il avoit envie de voir le pavé de Rome" (ibid.) (so eager was he to see the pavement of Rome [935]), Montaigne sped up his pace, rousing the troop three hours before dawn to travel the fifty-nine kilometers to the gates of the eternal city.[3]

This humorous incident shows Montaigne's symbiotic absorption into the spaces of his journey. Like his determined pack animal, he is pulled by space, pushing obliviously onward even as his traveling companions bicker or tag along, losing himself in the details as the others dream of arriving at their destination. Montaigne's "affective itinerary" is magnified as he approaches the Eternal City, as multiple and conflicting political, temporal, and cultural dimensions of Rome pull him in multiple directions and elicit a revisitation of self that is neither here nor there.[4] After considerable resistance to the commonplace of Roman dominance, Rome becomes the focal point of his journey in the reading of Eric MacPhail, allowing the essayist "to formulate the unlocalized, itinerant persona that emerges from the end of the *Essais*."[5] The mental wanderer, in other words, is able to achieve with his feet what he had done in words by visiting a city he had come to know through reading.[6] At the same time, it is through the local and specific contexts of each moment that Montaigne is able to achieve a spotty form of cosmographic spatio-political discourse akin to the writing of his *Essais*.[7] The written details of his journey and, as we shall explore in this chapter, the often unwritten or underwritten spatial contexts of his experience help Montaigne's imagination move out into space, asserting a displaced sense of personal, social, and political identity, caught between the varying facets of an ever-changing *moy*.[8]

The purpose of this closing chapter is to highlight, through a detailed tracking of Montaigne's movements, how a sense of spatial dispersion contributes to and modifies an evolving sense of identity. Using maps printed between 1551 and 1625, Roman guidebooks and other historical sources, this chapter attempts to give shape, *pas à pas*, to Montaigne's wanderings in the Eternal City in order to better understand how the material aspects of his experience relate to his imaginary vision of Rome. Montaigne's journey from Florence to Rome anticipates his political readings of Roman space and prepares his continued contemplation of his home country's role in the world. His sense of identity as a soldier, administrator, diplomat, and Frenchman are also tested in his exploration of the cities of Siena and Montalcino and his continuation on the road to Rome. Montaigne's approach to space, moreover, is starkly different from those of other French travelers, who generally apply erudite, textual readings to Roman spaces. Montaigne refuses this restrictive approach in favor of a vision of a cosmopolitan, dislocated sense of citizenship that develops during his wanderings between the organized streets of the New Rome and the empty desolation of its uninhabited "sepulture" (tomb). The second section of this chapter examines the neighborhood where Montaigne lived during his lengthy stay in order to understand the material and spatial contexts of the visitor's political meetings and studies of the Eternal City. Montaigne's stay can be divided into two parts: the first, passed in the company of his secretary, involving political activities and wandering through Rome's empty quarter, or *disabitato*, in search of an understanding of the ancient city, and the second, in which Montaigne is occupied with the activities of Lent, which forms the subject of the final section of this book. In this section, I cite two rarely used sources—the Catholic Missal of 1570 that established the Roman religious calendar and Pompeo Ugonio's guide of the Roman "Stational Masses," both of which help us trace Montaigne's path through Rome.[9]

ROME'S PULL

The territory Montaigne was crossing when his mule got away from him included the southern portion of the Grand Duchy of Tuscany and the northern stretches of the Campagna Romana. Montaigne followed the standard route along the Via Francigena through the Orcia and Paglia valleys that led into the volcanic lake region leading to the last stretches of the Via Cassia toward Rome. Here he passed from the fertile, cultivated landscape of the Campagna Senese, across mountains and river gorges, into lands that descended widely into the increasingly barren spaces once occupied by the periphery of Rome. The lay of the land and an ever-denser presence of Roman ruins punctuated by official markers of the papal political space exerted a sort of pull on the traveler, preparing him for a dramatic arrival into the Eternal City.[10]

Nicolas Audebert, who traveled just a few years before Montaigne, describes the transition from the fertile plenitude of Tuscany to the barren ruin of the Campagna Romana in characteristic detail.[11] Leaving Siena through the Porta Romana, he descended rapidly into the Val d'Arbia, heading southeastward through "haultes et fascheuses collines fertiles" (I, 267) (high and bothersome fertile hills), entering a "beau et plat chemin" (ibid.) (beautiful and flat road), and crossing the Arbia River before arriving in the small village of Ponte d'Arbia. Passing a small mountain, he forded the Ombrone River at the town of Buonconvento and entered "une assez belle grande plaine" (ibid.) (a rather large plain) leading to Torrenieri and down a "colline qui est assez droict" (ibid.) (rather straight hill), where he forded the Asso, another affluent of the Orcia that also flows into the Ombrone. In the Val d'Orcia, from San Quirico, he followed a newly paved road through "une terre grasse" (I, 268) (a fat land). All through this land, Audebert comments on the presence of distant hilltop cities and towns, "que les Italiens appellent castelli, pour les distinguer de celles qui ont Evesché, qu'ilz nomment Cità" (ibid.) (which the Italians call castelli, to distinguish them from towns with a bishopric, which they call città): Montalcino, Pienza, and San Pietro (Rocca d'Orcia), as well as the eight-hundred-meter peak of Radicofani that towered on his left near Ricorso.

The landscape changed at the entry point to the Papal States near Acquapendente. The last piece of territory controlled by the Grand Duke of Tuscany entered a gorge following and crisscrossing a "tres gros et furieux torrent" (I, 269) (very large and furious torrent), making for a wet and difficult road that ended in Ponte Centino (Centeno).[12] The road led rapidly down to the crater of Lake Bolsena, a body Audebert describes as "de si grande largeur et estendue qu'il semble plustost une mer qu'un lac" (I, 270) (of such size and extent that it seems more a sea than a lake) with waves lapping against the walls of the town of Bolsena, where he followed the ancient Via Cassia connecting Arezzo to Rome. After Montefiascone, Viterbo, and a hefty climb above Lake Vico, the road fell off rapidly from more than 800 meters along the rim of the extinct volcano to 450 at Ronciglione, 150 at La Storta, set amid a "grande plaine descouverte, où n'y a aulcuns arbres" (I, 271) (large uncovered plain, where there are no trees), and leading to Rome at an elevation of 8 meters.[13] This descending road is the stretch where Montaigne lost control of his mule.

In addition to the drastic drop-off that pushed the traveler downward, Roman ruins progressively invaded the landscape along the Via Cassia. Audebert describes the pavement of this famed road, whose polygonal stones remind him of Rome's glory:

> En quoy ay remerqué qu'ils n'usoyent aulcunement de quarrez, mais bien quelques foys septemgulaires, ce que—en mon opinion—ilz faisoyent pour plus grande durée, ne trouvant rien plus ferme que une quantité d'angles rapportés ensemble qui se gardent et tiennent l'un l'aultre, ce qui ne peult venir au quarré. Et est à presupposer qu'ilz pouvoyent avoir ceste consideration, tant pour raison naturelle qui le demonstre, comme aussy que tout ce que faisoyent les anciens Romains estoit pour laisser memoire de leur nom. (I, 275)

> (In which I noted that they did not use square paving stones at all, but rather sometime heptangular ones, which, in my opinion, they did because they last longer, having found nothing stronger than a quantity of angles fit together, which fix and hold one another, which does not happen with square stones. And this can be shown to be true as much by natural logic as well as because everything the Romans did was to leave a memory of their name.)

These reminders of Rome's past increase near Bracciano, where "se descouvre un peu Rome" (I, 276) (Rome shows itself a bit) amid fields and hillsides, where "se voyent encore des ruines de plus en plus" (ibid.) (more and more ruins appear), culminating in the large monument known as the Nero's tomb, "assez entier, tout massif et couvert d'une grosse tombe et chapisteau de marbre" (ibid.) (rather intact, quite massive and covered by a large tomb and marble capital). Montaigne blows right by this large monument, while his humanist predecessor Audebert dutifully copied its inscriptions and described its sculptures. The rest of the road leading to the Ponte Milvio followed "assez fascheux passages" (rather difficult passages) where "ne sont que toute ruines qui sont parmy les collines infertiles" (278) (there is nothing but ruins lying between the barren hills).

The emptiness of the last stretch of the road to Rome contrasts with the textual plenitude of a landscape marked by the physical and written signs of history. From Montefiascone, famed for its white wine "jadis tant celebrez des anciens Romain" (22r–v) (once so celebrated by the Ancient Romans),[14] travelers began to read into the landscape, tracing the beginnings of Rome's influence and its progressive expansion. Montefiascone was known for its surrender to Rome under the consul Camillus in 396 BCE, as Florisel de Claveson recalls in a gloss of Livy's *Books from the foundation of the City*.[15] A few miles on, the small stream of the Cremera marked the sacrifice of the gens Fabia for the Roman *patria*.[16]

Bookish as these references may seem, they have legal value in the readings of sixteenth-century Frenchmen marking political borders that continue to divide the various regions of Italy. Pliny, Strabo, and even Livy mark the limits between the various Italian states, informing the actions of the future diplomat or politician. The crossing from Etruria ("anciennement appelez Falisci" [Audebert, I, 269]) into Roman territory occurring at the Ponte della Paglia also marked the border between the Papal States and Tuscany. Pierre Bergeron marks Radicofani "à 32 mil de Siene, fort chasteau sur les confins du Sienois, *Radicofanum castellum*" (at 32 miles from Siena, a strong castle on the confines of the Senese region, *Radicofanum castellum*), and describes it as a castle built by the Lombards and rebuilt by Cosimo de' Medici, which formed the "limites du patrimoine de S. Pierre, vendu par la comtesse Mathilde à l'Esglise" (limits of the patrimony of Saint Peter, sold to the Church by the countess Mathilde).[17] As late as 1641, the Marquis of Fontenay-Mareuil, on his way to the ambassadorship in Rome, commented on this long-standing border dispute.[18]

A number of authors use this historic subtext to celebrate French history, emphasizing the actions of the Gauls and Franks in Italy. The Paglia River (Latin, Allia) was the location of the Celtic King Brennus's victory over the Romans in the fourth century BCE.[19] Bergeron describes the river's flow from the *Monts Crustumoniens* (monte Amiata) to the Tiber near Orvieto, writing that the Gaulish king, "avecq les Gaulois senonois, desfirent entierement l'armée romaine, et en suitte de cette victoire allerent prendre et brusler la ville de Rome, *anno 364 ab urbe condita*" (with the Galli Senones, completely defeated the Roman army, and after their victory went to take and burn the city of Rome).[20] The Romans labeled the river "*horrificus, infaustus*" and named unlucky days after the river and terrible battle. Bergeron stretches phonetic similarities between the Senones, who had come from the Seine-et-Marne, Loiret, and Yonne regions and had founded Senigallia on the Adriatic coast, and the city of Siena, affirming it to be of French foundation even though "autres disent que ce furent les anciens Toscans qui la bastirent" (others say it was the ancient Etruscans that built it).[21] Henri de Rohan also notes the disagreement regarding the city's origins, but opts for an Etruscan foundation followed by the establishment of a Roman colony in 290 BCE, noting that "bien qu'il y en aye qui disent que ceste premiere *Sena* de quoy parle Tite Live soit *Sena Gallica* et non Siene en Toscane, il est toute certain qu'elles ont esté toutes deux Colonies Romaines" (although there are those who say that this first Siena that Livy mentions is *Sena Gallica* [Senigallia] and not Siena in Tuscany, it is certain that both were Roman colonies).[22] Rohan also mentions the city's liberation from Lombard control by the Holy Roman Emperor Charlemagne.

These Gallican readings conducted in the wake of the Italian Wars explain why some travelers confuse the ruins of these wars with ruins of antiquity. The visual experience of passing through Siena's destroyed defenses melded with older ruins created the effect of desolation that extended from the Roman *disabitato* to the cities that surrounded it at various distances. Shortly outside Siena's Porta Romana, Audebert comes upon the ruined bastions of Isola (Isola d'Arbia), which he describes as having been "une foys comme une petite ville" (once like a small city) but "maintenant est desmantelée" (now is dismantled). A few miles later, he finds Monterone, a "bourg fort ruiné et desmantelé" (town very much ruined and dismantled), and Lucignano, a "gros bourg comme petite ville, mais ruinée, comme aussy tous les environs, ce qui provient et est encor du temps de la guerre des Florentins et Siennois" (I, 267) (large town or small city, but ruined, like the rest of the surroundings, which are still from the time of the war between the Florentines and the Sienese). Fontenay-Mareuil, writing fifty years later, still sees this area as "environnee de quantité de ruines des maisons du temps des Romains" (surrounded by a lot of ruins of houses from Roman times).[23]

Montaigne's reading is patriotic, though he transforms Siena's beauty into symbols of a freedom lost during the Italian Wars. He spent all of November 25 studying Siena, "pour le respect de nos guerres" (86) (in respect to our wars [932]), participating in a form of personal, military tourism focused on an idealized memory of the "temps de nos pere" (the time of our fathers).²⁴ His secretary describes Siena as very old, located on top of a hill, and "du nombre des belles d'Italie, mais non du premier ordre" (ibid.) (among the beautiful towns of Italy, but not of the first rank [ibid.]). It is decorated with fountains, cellars, streets going up and down, and a cathedral "qui ne cede guieres à celuy de Florence" (86) (that scarcely yields to that of Florence [933]). The convergence of this irregular form onto the great public square weaves the names of Siena's great families into the city's fabric:

> La plus belle piece de la ville, c'est la place ronde, d'une tres-belle grandeur, et allant de toutes parts se courbant vers le palais qui fait l'un des visages de cette rondeur, et moins courbe que le demeurant. Vis à vis du palais, au plus haut de la place, il y a une très-belle fontaine qui, par plusieurs canals, remplit un grand vaisseau où chacun puise d'une très-belle eau. Plusieurs rues viennent fondre en cette place par des pavés tissus en degrés. Il y a tout plein de rues très-anciennes: la principale est celle de Piccolomini; de celle là, de Tolomei, Colombini, et encore de Cerretani, nous vismes des tesmoingnages de trois ou quatre cens ans. Les armes de la ville se voyent sur plusieurs piliers, c'est la Louve qui a, pendus à ses tetins, Romulus et Remus. (86–87)

> (The handsomest part of the town is the round plaza, very beautiful and grand, curving in from all directions toward the palace that forms one of the fronts of this circle and is less curved than the rest. Opposite the palace, at the upper end of the place, there is a very beautiful fountain, which, through several conduits, fills a great basin where everyone can draw very fine water. Several streets converge in this circle by graded stone steps. There are plenty of very ancient streets and dwellings: the principal ones are those of the Piccolomini, the [one over there], the Tolomei, Colombini, and that of the Cerretani. We saw evidences of three or four hundred years of age. The arms of the city, which you see on many pillars, are the she-wolf with Romulus and Remus hanging at her teats.) (933)²⁵

The public square is the most beautiful "piece" of the city, receiving a harmonious and natural flow of people, traffic, water, and symbols of the city's nobility into its "curved" and "curving" form. It is illustrated and fed by the streets and houses of its most ancient families, many of which recall Siena's Guelph, pro-French history.[26] Montaigne had met Silvio Piccolomini, a member of the most illustrious of these families, son of the Sienese general Enea Piccolomini, who had chased the Spanish from Siena in 1555.[27] Montaigne describes the son as "le plus suffisant gentilhomme de nostre temps à toute sorte de science et exercice d'armes" (the most able nobleman of our time in every kind of knowledge and exercise of arms [933]) but is surprised that the Medici now entrust the descendant of their enemy with the grand duchy's defenses. Montaigne snidely describes the grand duke's popularity as that of "celuy qui a principalement à se garder de ses propres sujects" (87) (one who has to guard himself principally against his own subjects [933]).[28] This formal recognition of freedom is seen also in the Sienese coats of arms that are allowed to remain in the city that "sonnent partout *Liberté*" (ibid.) (everywhere ring[s] of liberty [ibid.]). At the same time, more subtle changes of the urban iconography have been made in the displacement of the French tombs of fallen soldiers, moved "sous couleur de quelque reformation du bastimant & forme de leur eglise" (87) (under color of some improvement in the building and shape of their church [933]).

This reading continues as Montaigne and the other gentlemen leave the baggage train to visit Montalcino, "pour l'accointance que les François y ont eue" (87) (because of the associations the French have had with it [934]). In his description of the fortified hilltop town, Montaigne seems eager to explain the French defeat, noting that while Montalcino is located at the top of the highest mountain in the region, it is poorly built, "accessible," and "guiere fort, etant ledict lieu commandé d'une part par une autre montaigne voisine de cent pas" (88) (not very strong, for the place is commanded on one side by another higher mountain within a hundred paces of it [ibid.]) He again inquires about French tombs and is told that they had been in the church of Saint Augustine but that the duke had had them moved. His interviews with locals confirm French valor, leading him to conclude (as he would as he left Piedmont the following year) that the French were everywhere loved for their heroic actions:

> On maintient la memoire des François en si grande affection, qu'on ne leur en faict guiere souvenir que les larmes leur en viennent aux yeux, la guerre mesme leur semblant plus douce

avec quelque forme de liberté, que la paix qu'ils jouissent sous la tyrannie (88).

(The memory of the French is maintained with such great affection that you can scarcely remind the people of the French without tears coming to their eyes; for even the war seems sweeter to them, if accompanied by some form of liberty, than the peace they enjoy under tyranny.) (934)

Montaigne's attention to his nation's engagement in the peninsula and his interest in questions of valor, honor, and service underline the Essayist's particular take on the question of freedom. In a passage of the *Essais* relating to the defense of Siena, Montaigne had depicted honor, service, and power as commodities, while freedom remained something unquantifiable. Through the voice of King Hyeron, Montaigne notes how nobility creates a prison for the monarch who is unable to "voyager en liberté" (I, 26, 265) (go about and travel freely), while wealth, military honors, and administrative powers compare unfavorably to convenience and ease:

Et ne m'est jamais tombé en fantaisie que ce fut quelque notable commodité à la vie d'un homme d'entendement, d'avoir une vingtaine de contrerolleurs à sa chaise percée, ny que les services d'un homme qui a dix mille livres de rente, ou qui a pris Casal, ou defendu Siene, luy soyent plus commodes et acceptables que d'un bon valet et bien experimenté.

(And it has never struck me that it was any special advantage in the life of a man of understanding to have some twenty people watching him go to the toilet, nor that the services of a man with an income of ten thousand pounds, or who has taken Casale or defended Siena, are more convenient and acceptable to him than those of a good and experienced valet.)[29]

This complex comparison marks how Montaigne values his own freedom above anything else. On the one hand, he cites the taking of Casale Monferrato and the defense of Siena,[30] both events of the final years of France's engagement in Italy, as social advantages as important as possessing immense wealth or holding major public office. That said, all these advantages are debunked as less important than the freedom to travel or the help of a good valet. These latter freedoms are in fact threatened as Montaigne approaches Rome, as his pleasant, free movement along the irregular and uncontrolled meanders of his ambulant mind move toward a walled space where he would return to work as a servant of the state.

Montaigne's scorn for erudition and technical and bureaucratic forms of writing also relates to this desire for freedom. His readings of space have neither the erudition nor the painstaking diligence of observation of the accounts of the jurist Nicolas Audebert, the geographer-historian Pierre Bergeron, or even the noble erudite Florisel de Claveson. Montaigne takes a philosophical stance against pedantic learning, much as Du Bellay had done, writing and observing the things that captured his imagination as he travels

> non pour en rapporter seulement, à la mode de nostre noblesse Françoise, combien de pas a Santa Rotonda, ou la richesse des calessons de la Signora Livia, ou, comme d'autres, combien le visage de Neron, de quelque vieille ruyne de là, est plus long ou plus large que celuy de quelque pareille medaille, mais pour en raporter principalement les humeurs de ces nations et leurs façons, et pour frotter et limer nostre cervelle contre celle d'autruy.

> (not merely to bring back, in the manner of our French noblemen, knowledge of the measurements of the Santa Rotonda, or of the richness of Signora Livia's drawers, or, like some others, how much longer or wider Nero's face is in some old ruin there than on some similar medallion; but to bring back knowledge of the character and ways of those nations, and to rub and polish our brains by contact with those of others.)[31]

French soldiers' tombs fit into this discourse of freedom, while the tombs of popes and theologians buried in Bologna or Rome, or even of Erasmus's grave in the cathedral of Basel and in Rome, do not. The fight for Siena, viewed from the perspective of its unsuccessful conclusion, becomes an idealistic, exasperated resistance to the impending *realpolitik* that eventually crushed the city's independence.

Montaigne's observations on the road to Rome exert a continued discourse in favor of personal and civic freedom, and he engages only casually with the signs of Roman grandeur and antiquity as he passes through Acquapendente, San Lorenzo, Bolsena, Montefiascone, and Viterbo. Crossing the mountains of Viterbo and Vico and traveling through a "plaisant vallon entourné de petites collines" (89) (very pleasant valley surrounded by low hills [935]), the woods near Ronciglione and the area. Making his way through an area Audebert had described as a jumble of ruins, with his mind *ailleurs*, Montaigne notes only that Rome appears and then disappears and "ne nous faisoit pas grand'montre à la recognoistre de ce chemin" (90) (did not make a great show to see it from this road [935]), while he considers Italy a good place "pour les paresseux" (ibid.) (for lazy people [ibid.]), a trait he finds to be "selon son humeur" (ibid.) (in accordance with his humor [ibid.]).

"VIS À VIS DE SANTA LUCIA DELLA TINTA"

Arriving in Rome in the midafternoon of November 30, 1580,[32] Montaigne checked into one of the city's best and most popular inns, where he stayed for two days before moving into rented apartments his secretary describes in detail:

> Nous prismes des chambres de louage chez un Espaignol, vis à vis de Santa Lucia della Tinta. Nous y estions bien accommodés de trois belles chambres, salle, garde manger, escurie, cuisine, à vingt escus par mois: sur quoy l'hoste fournit de cuisinier et de feu à la cuisine. (91)

> (We took rented rooms in the house of a Spaniard, opposite Santa Lucia della Tinta. Here we were well accommodated with three handsome bedrooms, dining room, larder, stable, and kitchen, at twenty crowns a month, out of which the host provided a cook and fire for the kitchen.) (936)

These seemingly minor details about lodging tell us much about the nature of Montaigne's interests. The secretary describes the size and layout of a space that Montaigne would use for the following months, describing an *arrièr-boutique* that would assume the functions of his castle-tower library and fulfill his social, political, and personal needs during his lengthy stay in Rome. These rooms were located, as we shall see, at a crucial juncture in the city's complex and varied topography, sitting at the fulcrum between the old, medieval city and the radial streets of modern papal Rome. They placed Montaigne minutes from the Vatican, allowing him a continued political commerce. They also show that he intended to make himself at home and stay a while, with a room for himself, one for his secretary, and a third room where he could lay out books and maps for his study of the city. An extra room allowed him to receive visitors, while the secretary's details regarding bedding, a kitchen, stable space, wood, and a cook show that Montaigne largely preferred comfort to luxury. He was, moreover, in need of privacy and convenience, preferring a private entrance that would allow him to receive visitors and enter and exit as he pleased.

The physical location of Montaigne's apartments informs his readings of the Eternal City and allows us to understand not only the essayist's daily routine but the background and reasoning of his psychological, sociological, and political interactions with Roman space. Montaigne appears to need to feel at home and to live in Rome not as a Frenchman but as a Roman and is annoyed to find "en la rue quasi personne qui ne le saluast en sa langue" (91) (no one in the street who did not greet him in his own language [936]). His need for books and a study is at once personal and an attribute of his social and political class. His need for a space in which to receive guests allows us to imagine him receiving the historian Marc Antoine Muret, the ambassador Louis Chasteigner, or Paul de Foix before any number of erudite or political outings. Understanding where Montaigne lived thus goes to the heart of understanding the nature of his Roman experience as well as the material aspects of his philosophical assertions made regarding Roman society and the ruins of Rome.

But where was this residence?

The area around the church of Santa Lucia della Tinta, located on the via di Monte Brianzo (called Via Trinitatis in Montaigne's time), on the edge of two of Rome's *rioni*, the Campo Marzio and the Rione Ponte, has changed significantly since Montaigne's time. The main difference between Montaigne's neighborhood and today's Via di Monte Brianzo is its relationship to the Tiber, altered after the dismantling of the Aurelian wall for the construction of the Lungotevere Marzio in the late nineteenth century. Period maps, such as Antonio Tempesta's 1593 representation of Rome,[33] nonetheless allow us to confirm many of the secretary's impressions of the city as "toute plantée le long de la rivière du Tibre, deça et delà" (91) (built all along the river Tiber, on both sides [936]). Antoine Du Pérac's 1577 *Novae urbis descriptio*, a map Montaigne might have used during his stay, gives an even stronger idea of the contact this area had with the Tiber, showing openings in the Aurelian wall that gave the area its nickname of *Le Quattro Porte*.[34] These small ports allowed the area to thrive as a center for the for the commerce of firewood, mentioned in Montaigne's rental agreement, and gave river access to the cloth-dyers who gave their name to the mentioned church.

The noted maps also force us to contextualize our understanding of the area within a period of rapid transformation and growth that transformed the medieval city, "ruinosa e cadente," into the "Roma restaurata" of Pope Sixtus V (1585–90). These changes were particularly notable for the *Quattro Porte* area, where frequent flooding and the central location made urban renewal a priority.[35] Leonardo Bufalini's map of 1551, the first two-dimensional ground survey of Rome, shows the contrast between the order and symmetry of Rome's new urban planning, the disorder of the medieval *abitato*, and the empty desolation of the *disabitato* under which Montaigne's Roman "sepulcher" was buried.[36] The streets and major buildings of the area in the schematic plan are suggestive of an urban plan whose details are still in need of refinement that later maps will be called to define. The plans of Mario Cartaro (1576), Étienne Du Pérac (1577), Antonio Tempesta (1593), and Giovanni Maggi (1625) chart continued growth, mapping the changes around the Santa Lucia della Tinta with an accuracy that permits speculation as to which building Montaigne might have lived in during his five months in Rome.

Rereading the secretary's description of Montaigne's residence, we know it (1) was equipped with stables, (2) was large enough to have three rooms, (3) had independent access, and (4) was rented from a Spaniard. The secretary later adds the detail that a papal procession passed under the apartments' window, allowing an assumption that they were located on an important street, probably the Via Trinitatis. While looking at the three-dimensional maps of Rome, moreover, we can probably assume that Montaigne, regardless of his official capacity in Rome, would have avoided staying in small, one-story buildings that were more suitable for shops.

The various maps show that the area around Santa Lucia della Tinta was transformed in the years before and after Montaigne's visit, but they also allow us to identify two possible locations for Montaigne's residence.

The church of Santa Lucia della Tinta, located on the corner of today's Via di Monte Brianzo and Via del Cancello (today's Via Trinitatis and an unnamed street/piazza in Montaigne's time), was restored and perhaps even rebuilt several times over the centuries, but most significantly in the very year of Montaigne's visit.[37] In Leonardo Bufalini's map, we see the church as a small rectangle running parallel to Via Trinitatis, perpendicular to its current orientation, suggesting it faced Via del Cancello and had a side entrance on the main thoroughfare and a rounded choir on the church's east end. In the maps produced just prior to Montaigne's visit (Mario Cartaro and Étienne Du Pérac), the church appears in its present-day orientation. Several years later, Antonio Tempesta shows the church facing the Via Trinitatis and covered by a roofed structure or vestibule, but with a large facade facing the Via del Cancella. Finally, Giovanni Maggi's map of 1625 shows a much smaller, almost square church facing the Via Trinitatis and backed by a walled garden absent in the other maps. Complicating matters further, each of these three-dimensional maps places the church's steeple on a different corner of the church, allowing us to question the accuracy of the maps themselves.

Considering these various positions, the buildings "facing" the church, where Montaigne lived for some six months, could have included now demolished buildings located across from the church of Via Trinitatis; structures located on the Via del Cancello, which today look at the side of the church; or even some more significant structures that, when considered within the changing topography of the area, may have reasonably been described as "looking onto" the church of Santa Lucia della Tinta.[38]

Period maps show that the buildings surrounding the church changed more than the church itself. In Bufalini's line drawings, we see the footprint of the churches of Santa Lucia della Tinta and Sant'Antonio dei Portoghesi, as well as the major residences still present in Montaigne's time of Antonio Massimo ("D[omus] Antoni de Maxim[i]" [Palazzo Massimo]), Romulus Amaseus, and the Soderini family. Bufalini provides no information on the areas surrounding these buildings, however, leaving the spaces lined off from the streets and piazzas open for interpretation. The general impression is that of recently drawn lots hosting major structures surrounded by land that was under the master house's purview.[39] Du Pérac's map of 1577 shows a church of Santa Lucia still appears to dominate the structures occupying its block, leaving the possibility that these ancillary structures (refectory, residences, etc.)

might have been considered part of the church. These shorter buildings are blocked by newer, larger buildings built around the church but would have permitted a view of all of the church structures in the years preceding the rebuilding of the area (1585–90). Most notably, the Palazzo Aragonia, or Aragona-Gonzaga (a.k.a. Balami Galitzin, a.k.a. Negroni, a.k.a. Mancini), facing onto the piazza Nicosia to the east of the church of Santa Lucia, and Palazzo Massimo, on Via dell'Orso, both appear to look onto the church and its attached properties.[40]

If we take the *Journal*'s words literally, then Montaigne stayed in the buildings facing Santa Lucia della Tinta, making their most likely location on the other side of the Via Trinitatis. These now-destroyed buildings, were, however, built during the late sixteenth century and appear as late as Du Pérac's (1577) map to be low, humble buildings, perhaps even one-story shops.[41] Tempesta's map of 1593 shows the effects of the building spree of Sixtus V (1585–90), with rows of more significant structures all along the Via Trinitatis near Santa Lucia. These buildings, which appear to be respectable enough as rental properties, begin to cut off the view of the church of Santa Lucia. If these buildings existed in Montaigne's time, then his rooms would have looked, as the secretary's words indicate, directly onto the church. His horse would have been stabled in the courtyard behind the building and, with the Tiber just a few steps away, Montaigne could probably have seen the "vigne" lining the other side of the Tiber and perhaps even the Castel Sant'Angelo from the windows at the back of his building.

Yet these now-demolished buildings were probably built after Montaigne's stay, making it more probable that Montaigne might have stayed in more important structures, most particularly in the nearby Palazzo Aragonia, which appears to look onto the church in the 1577 map. This is in fact the only residence that meets all the requirements described in the *Journal*. Not only is it large enough to meet Montaigne's needs, possessing an inner courtyard providing stable space and rooms that fit the secretary's description, but it also has an independent entrance looking onto Piazza Nicosia and the Via Trinitatis. A corner apartment in Palazzo Aragonia could have both looked onto the church of Santa Lucia and Via Trinitatis/Piazza Nicosia and been located on street likely to host a papal procession. The most intriguing point, moreover, is the building's Spanish connection, having belonged, at the time of Montaigne's stay, to Giambattista (Titta) d'Aragona, who later sold the prestigious home to Scipione Gonzaga, patron of the epic poet Torquato Tasso.[42] This same building would later be used by the French ambassador *pro tempore* François de Luxembourg, Duke of Piney, who came to Rome in 1596 to negotiate the delicate questions of King Henry IV's formal recognition by the papacy.[43] Is it possible the secretary would refer to rooms at the rear of the Palazzo Aragonia as a "logis" and that the Spaniard in question was a servant of or Giambattista (Titta) Aragona himself? Were Montaigne's lodgings, like those of the Duke of Piney, the base for political negotiations during a period of tense negotiation, as Philippe Desan has recently affirmed?[44]

The description of the residence in the *Journal*, in any case, does not provide enough details to say for sure, insisting, rather, on the aesthetic dimensions of Montaigne's stay, of his apartment's location on the edge of the Tiber, surrounded by too many Frenchmen and priests, and ideally situated for the pursuit of "mille promenades" through the "quartier montueux" of the tomb of ancient Rome.[45]

"À BOUT DE CETTE SCIENCE": MEASURING ROME'S GRANDEUR IN THE *VOYAGE D'ITALIE*

Many holes in Montaigne's *Journal* blur the exact details of his stay in Rome. After arriving, the secretary and Montaigne took a break, transforming the journal into a notebook of sporadic observations. We know that Montaigne arrived in Rome and settled into his house near Santa Lucia della Tinta on December 2, after which there were no entries until December 25, when Montaigne attended Mass in Saint Peter's Basilica. After this, the record is somewhat more regular, with entries occurring every six days or so. The secretary continues to write on his favorite themes: changes in his master's health, social or moral observations attributed to Montaigne, household expenses, and the mention of a few highly formal meetings. On December 29, Montaigne met the pope and had dinner with the cardinal of Sens.[46] He later went on horseback to the banking district, witnessing of the execution of the bandit Catena on the Ponte Sant'Angelo on his way back. A few days later, he (or his secretary) saw another execution. In the final weeks before he left Montaigne's employ, the *Journal* turns to the preparations for Lent, describing Carnival races in the Via Lata (Via del Corso) and festivities in the Castel Sant'Angelo, where he comments on the "fort grand apprest, et notamment un amphitheatre très artificiellement et richement disposé pour le combat de la barriere" (105) (good deal of preparation . . . notably an amphitheater very artfully and richly disposed for combat in the lists [947]). On January 28, an attack of colick does not keep him from "ses actions ordinaires" (101) (his ordinary actions [944]), a physiological detail that could just as easily be applied to Montaigne's other unmentioned (and perhaps unmentionable) activities.

The political record of the *Journal* is, in fact, minimal, implying either that Montaigne was involved in matters so delicate he could not write about them or that he was simply biding time in the capitol and enjoying a vacation among Rome's ruins and festivities. The few meetings he does mention are of the most formal type: a papal audience, a dinner with the cardinal of Sens, Nicolas de Pellevé. Perhaps tellingly, however, we learn of Montaigne's circle of friends who became his companions during his leisured strolls through the city and countryside. The tension of the nobleman's performance, in essence, is seen in the fact that Montaigne gives every appearance of being on vacation while keeping company of the highest political order.

His pastimes are at once intellectual extensions of his personal culture and emanations of social class. Much of the first half of his stay was taken up by the study of Rome, which the secretary sums up a month into their stay:

> Tous ces jours là, il ne s'amusa qu'à estudier Rome. Au commencement, il avoit prins un guide François, mais celuy là, par quelque humeur fantastique, s'estant rebuté, il se piqua, par son propre estude de venir à bout de cette science, aidé de diverses cartes et livres qu'il se faisoit lire le soir, et le jour il alloit sur les lieux mettre en pratique son apprentissage: si que, en peu de jours, il eust aysément reguidé son guide. (99–100)

> (All these days he spent time only in studying Rome. At the beginning he had taken a French guide; but this man quit because of some fancy or other, he made it a point of pride to learn all about Rome by his own study, aided by various maps and books that he had read to him in the evening; and in the daytime he would go on the spot to put his apprenticeship into practice; so that in a few days he could easily have guided his guide.) (943)

Like Rabelais, Montaigne tries hard to arrange the pieces of the Roman puzzle, dedicating himself to the study of numerous maps and guides in order to get to the bottom of "this science."

This study, therefore, is presented again as an attempt to rectify the reading of books with spatial representations and Montaigne's practical experience of the city. Each of the maps he could have used—Pirro Ligorio, Bufalini, Cartaro, Pérac—presented particular rhetorical and spatial advantages while posing different problems of interpretation. A look at Bufalini's map, for example, proposes an abstract, two-dimensional vision of the city that was revolutionary in its time. Bufalini's technique of indicating the shapes of Rome's hills with hatched lines and Rome's ancient monuments as floor plans or reconstructions of what they once had been can also be used as a justification of Montaigne's famous description of Rome as the "sepulcher" of its ancient self. Pirro Ligorio's *Antiquae urbis imago accuratissimae ex vetusteis monumenteis* of 1561 was even more likely to cause a shock to Montaigne's attempts to find traces of the ancient city, providing a fabricated image of what Rome was supposed to look like at its height.[47] Du Pérac, on the other hand, shows the archeological area more realistically, as a series of vineyards and pleasure palaces built on remains of antiquity. None of these maps is easy to relate to the descriptive representations contained in the guides of Lucio Mauro,[48] Lucio Fauno,[49] the Roman chapter of Leandro Alberti,[50] or even Marliani.[51] Their abstract nature combined with the rhetorical presentation of the antiquarian guides thus work together to give Montaigne an impressionistic image, not of the city, but of a number of possible constructions of pieces of the once-magnificent city.[52]

Montaigne's "commerce" with ancient Rome begins shortly after his arrival, when his secretary writes that he "faisoit tous les jours milles promenades et visites" (91) (went every day and took a thousand walks [936]) among the churches, houses, and gardens of the "quartier montueux" (hilly quarter). The only record of these daily excursions is a general observation regarding the morphological changes affecting the city:

> Il jugeoit par bien claires apparences, que la forme de ces montaignes et des pentes estoit tout changée de l'ancienne, par la hauteur des ruines; et tenoit pour certain qu'en plusieurs endroits nous marchions sur le faiste des maisons tout entieres. Il est aisé à juger, par l'Arc de Severe, que nous sommes à plus de deux

piques au dessus de l'ancien planchier; et de crai, quasi partout, on marche sur la teste des vieux murs que la pluie et les coches descouvrent (92)

(He judged by very clear appearances and by the height of the ruins that the shape of these mountains and of the slopes was completely changed from the old shape; and he held it as certain that in many places we were walking on the tops of entire houses. It is easy to judge, by the Arch of Severus, that we are more than two pikes' length above the ancient street level; and in truth, almost everywhere, you walk on the top of old walls which the rains and the coach ruts uncover.) (936)

Montaigne lacks the discipline of earlier authors who measure the steps from one spot to another, instead preferring a more generalized, moralizing analysis of the passage of time. His mention of the Arch of Septimius, while not erudite, is nonetheless significant. Written after only a few weeks in Rome, it shows Montaigne's familiarity with city, which makes "l'Arc de Severe" a part of his everyday understanding of the city. Montaigne mentions the arch, not because he admires its structure, but as a measure (covered by two "pikes" of dirt) of the changes that have transformed the city.[53] More importantly, Montaigne strips the monument of its iconicity, inserting its broken form into a relativized spatial context. Montaigne digests the fragments of ancient Rome and sews them into his own personal narrative.

Montaigne later returns to give a more detailed reading of this same spot on the forum, this time inserting it within a larger discursive contemplation and adding details about the other monuments nearby. Focalizing on the point where the Via Sacra climbs up from the forum, he chooses a spot of high symbolic and spatial value where the verticality of the Capitol viewed from below combines with the implied motion of the Via Sacra connecting the Coliseum and the Temple of Saturn. Montaigne is confounded by the distances that separate the complex topography of the ruins he sees, the reconstructions artists had given to this spot, and his own imagined vision of Roman grandeur:

Il disoit ne pouvoir aysemant faire convenir, veu le peu d'espace & de lieu que tiennent aucuns de ces sept mons, & notammant les plus fameux, comme le Capitolin & le Palatin, qu'il y rangeast un si grand nombre d'edifices. A voir seulemant ce qui reste du Temple de la Paix, le long du Forum Romanum, duquel on voit encore, la chute toute vifve, comme d'une grande montaigne, dissipée en plusieures horribles rochiers: il ne semble que deux tels batimens peussent tenir en toute l'espace du mont du Capitole, où il y avoit bien 25 ou 30 temples, outre plusieurs maisons privées. Mais, à la vérité, plusieurs conjectures qu'on prend de la peinture de cette ville antienne n'ont guiere de verisimilitude, son plan mesme estant infinimant changé de forme; aucuns de ces vallons estans comblés, voire dans les lieux les plus bas qui y fussent; comme pour exemple, au lieu du Velabrum, qui pour sa bassesse recevoit l'esgout de la ville et avoit un lac, s'est tant eslevé des monts de la hauteur des autres monts naturels qui sont autour delà, ce qui se faisoit par le tas et monceau des ruines de ces grans bastimens; & le Monte Savello n'est autre chose que la ruine d'une partie du theatre de Marcellus. (101)

(He said he could not easily make people agree, seeing the small space occupied by some of these seven hills, and notably the most famous ones, like the Capitoline and Palatine, that so great a number of buildings had been arrayed there. Merely to see what remains of the Temple of Peace, beside the Forum Romanum, of whose quite recent fall you still see evidence, as of a great mountain broken up into many horrible rocks, it does not seem that two such buildings could fit into the whole space of the Capitoline Hill, where there were fully twenty or thirty temples, besides many private houses.

But in truth many conjectures that we make from the description of this ancient city have hardly any verisimilitude, since even its site has infinitely changed form, some of the valleys having been filled up, even in the lowest places that were there; as for example, in the place of the Velabrum, which because of its lowness received the sewage of the city and had a lake, hills have arisen of the height of the other, natural hills that are round about, as a result of the piling and heaping up of the ruins of these great buildings; and the Mount Savello is nothing but the ruin of a part of the Theater of Marcellus.) (944)

The spatial complexity of his description before, through, and after the quoted passage shows how Montaigne dismantles antiquarian representations of Roman *grandeur*, transforming a moral observation into a sociopolitical commentary on papal reconstructions of ancient Rome. Repeating commonplaces regarding Rome's destruction by barbarians, Montaigne goes further in representing the city's monstrous, "horrific" entombment. To the conventional citation of the "world's" envy of Roman "domination," he adds the image of a broken cadaver whose disfigurement horrifies its murderer, forcing the madman to bury the evidence of his crime—an amazing image that shows Montaigne's scorn for a modernity that can never measure up to his conception of the accomplishments of Rome's dead heroes. His choice of Monte Savello (Palazzo Savelli sul Teatro di Marcello) points to an underlying disquietude that is as moral as it is introspective in its appropriation of specific spatiocultural points of reference. Whereas Du Bellay had cited the Testaccio, a mountain made only of debris from broken pots, Montaigne adds the image of modernity's frivolous encroachment on the ancient glory. The members of the Savelli family, whose ancestors included popes, cardinals, senators, and generals, become birds nesting atop destroyed monuments, "monstres" that reiterate the shapelessness of our conceptions of the "quartier montueux" (hilly quarter) in our reading of "ces petites montres de sa ruine" (these small showings of its ruin).

The other monuments Montaigne mentions—the Temple of Peace, the Velabrum, and Monte Savello / Theater of Marcellus—are also products of Montaigne's critical reading of Roman spaces. From both a topographical and a textual standpoint, these symbols serve as a rhetorical introduction to Rome, marking the vista from which Rome's maximum splendor should be imagined, as Lucio Mauro explains in the opening of his *Le antichità di Roma*:

> Su questo colle si saliva da molte parti, ma la piu celebre sallita, e per laquale si conducevano sul colle i Trionfi; era la parte che risponde a Santo Giorgio in Velabro. Vi si saliva anco dalla parte, che risponde al Foro Romano, et a l'arco di Settimio, e dalla parte verso la città piana, che hoggi piu ch'altrove s'habita.[54]

> (One ascended this hill from diverse directions, but the most famed climb, and the one through which the Triumphs were

carried onto the Capitoline, was the part that communicates with San Giorgio in Velabro. One could also climb from the other side, which communicates with the Roman Forum and with the Arch of Septimius Severus, and from the other side toward the flat part of the city, where today more people live.)

Montaigne chooses Rome's most famous heroic site to underscore the city's collapse and nothingness, reversing the image of Rome as a heroic space. Where Mauro describes a climb up the Via Sacra, Montaigne cites "la chute toute vifve, comme d'une grande montaigne, dissipée en plusieures horribles rochiers" (the living collapse, as if from a great mountain, dissipated into horrifying rocks [translation mine]). Embedded in this reading are Montaigne's personal issues with death and stones, his tendency toward melancholy and unfulfilled filial reverence for Rome's heroes, and the state of affairs in France and the Périgord.[55] As ever, these archaeological ruminations are reworked into the expression of Montaigne's personal referential space, calling to mind the Motte de Gurson, a ruined castle just sixteen kilometers from his Saint-Michel de Montaigne on the lands of Frédéric and Diane de Foix.

All told, then, Montaigne takes an approach to Rome that is rooted in his leisurely approach to space and reading. Using Rome as a form of learned entertainment to "amuse himself," he reads his books and maps in his study in the Quattro Porte district, following them up with long rides and walks among the "quartier montueux" (mountainous neighborhood). He leaves no signs, in fact, of having ever taken his guides with him on these ramblings, producing an overall vision of the Eternal City that is less erudite than "abstraite et contemplative" (ibid.) (abstract and contemplative).[56] Montaigne reads Roman space in the same way he reads books, enjoying them with leisure and citing them only when he is able to recall their content.[57]

"JE VIS . . . À STATION"

If Montaigne's approach to the spatial experience of reading and topography is undisciplined, coupled with long periods of ambulant contemplation followed by sudden revelations, it is not necessarily fragmentary in a mimetic way. Rather, Montaigne seems to develop an affinity with Rome's fragmentary nature, producing a narrative that is itself a series of broken observations, often removed from their narrative or spatial context.

When Montaigne takes up the task of writing his own diary, he follows a similarly sporadic method of writing things down as they occur to him, making it challenging to reconstruct all of his activities.[58] The work does shift, however, from an account of diplomatic meetings, comments on Roman ruins, questions of accounting, and surprisingly, even the record of his own health to a sporadic record of Montaigne's cultural and moral observations. Like his servant, Montaigne provides few specific spatial references, so on the few occasions he does tell us where he is, space becomes an ancillary support for his anthropological interests. It is almost as an aside that he records where he was when he makes these singular observations: "Le 16 Février, revenant de la station, je rencontray en une petite chapelle, un prestre revestu, embesoigné à guerir un spiritato" (109) (On February 16th, returning from the station, I came across a priest in vestments in a little chapel curing a possessed man [947]). Here Montaigne makes no mention of going to Mass, which was part of his daily routine. His casual mention of the "station," moreover, suggests that he probably regularly attended the Stational Masses, whose location and date we can reconstruct using the *Roman Missal* of 1570 and guides such as Pompeo Ugonio's *Historia delle Stationi* of 1588.[59]

These references allow us to place Montaigne on February 16, the first Thursday of Lent, in the church of San Lorenzo in Panisperna, on the Viminal Hill, a location that informs his description of the exorcism, since it is there that Saint Lawrence had been grilled alive for not refusing to worship demons.[60] We can even visualize Montaigne's route, which would have been conducted among throngs of participants, from his apartments in Via Trinitatis to the church's location among the hills using Du Pérac's 1577 map. Passing from Rome's historic center, he would have followed a touristic itinerary that passed by the Pantheon (Santa Maria Rotonda), the Column of Marcus Aurelius on Via del Corso, to the Trevi Fountain, before climbing Monte Cavallo, passing the vineyard of the d'Este family, the Palazzo Vercelli (belonging to the Cardinal Ferrero), and the Baths of Constantine at the base of the Viminal Hill. Once inside the temple, he would have seen the martyr's relics exposed to the worshippers—"un braccio [. . .] delle sue ossa e del suo grasso" (an arm, some of his bones and fat)—as well as the grate the saint had been roasted on.[61] After witnessing this spectacle, Montaigne would have turned around to leave the recently remodeled church, finding his priest in one of "alcune cappellette à nuovo modello" (a few small chapels in the new style).

Continuing this reading, we can place Montaigne in many other locations at specific dates and times. On March 1, Wednesday of the third week of Lent, Montaigne mentions meeting the amazingly ignorant ambassador from Moscow at the "station de Saint Sixte" (station of Saint Sixtus), a location confirmed by the *Roman Missal* and Ugonio.[62] To get to this church on the Coelium, Montaigne would have passed through the Velabrum and beside the Coliseum before entering the rural hills around the Baths of Caracalla. Another example occurs on the Saturday of the Passion (March 18), when Montaigne records, without saying he went, that that station had been held at San Giovanni in Porta Latina,[63] while on Palm Sunday, he makes the interesting observation that he had seen some transparent marble in the Basilica of San Giovanni in Laterano, the location of that day's Stational Mass.[64] On Holy Saturday, Montaigne records seeing the heads of Saints Peter and Paul at San Giovanni's Basilica, where the Stational Mass had been performed.[65]

As the week of the Passion approached, Montaigne's activities would have been filled with the Lenten processions. On March 6, in fact, we read that he visited the Vatican Library, located minutes from his house and only 3.7 kilometers from that day's station at the church of Quattro Santi Coronati on the Coelium. In an entry that appears to be written on the Tuesday of Passion Week, he mentions seeing the Huguenots' lost banners in Saint Peter's Basilica, the site of that day's Mass. In all these cases, Montaigne either makes no mention of Mass at all or does so only as a way of locating his anecdotal or moralist observations in space and time, allowing us to assume that on most days, when Montaigne makes no journal entries, he was probably attending the Stational Mass and participating in the Lenten processions and festivities.

THE DISTANCE OF COMMON SPACE

This combination of politics, religion, and leisured consumption are what lead to Montaigne's conclusions that despite Rome's being "la plus commune ville du monde" (the most common city in the world), a certain distance separated him from feeling he truly belonged. The distance Montaigne keeps from Roman ceremony, or that this ceremony keeps from him, can be felt in his concluding statements that Rome is a "pleasant place," and he regrets that he had only seen "son visage publicque, & qu'elle offre au plus chetif estrangier" (126) (its public visage, which it offers to the meanest stranger [961]). Montaigne appears to have organized his journey around this public face and to have understood its advantages and limitations, summing up the things he had said during his conversations about Rome:

> Je disois des commodités de Rome, entre autres, que c'est la plus commune ville du monde, et où l'estrangeté & difference de nation se considere le moins; car de sa nature c'est une ville rapiecée d'estrangiers; chacun y est come chez soy. Son Prince embrasse toute la Chrestienté de son authorité; sa principale jurisdiction oblige les estrangiers en leurs maisons, comme icy; à son election propre; & de tous les Princes & Grands de sa Court, la consideration de l'origine n'a nul poids. (126–27)

> (I used to say about the advantages of Rome, among other things, that it is the most universal city in the world, a place where strangeness and differences of nationality are considered least; for by its nature it is a city pieced together out of foreigners; everyone is as if at home. Its ruler embraces all Christendom with his authority; his princely jurisdiction is binding on foreigners in their own homes just as here; at his own election and that of all the princes and grandees of his court the consideration of their origin has no weight.) (961)

Montaigne's dream of common citizenship is achieved as much as it can be in his experience of Roman political and ceremonial life. This fleeting identity, "pieced together" from those of various nations, is perhaps the best solution possible when compared to France's struggles with national identity. Rome remains, however, a distant abstraction when compared with the living image of the ancient city or the painful memories of his homeland, whose struggles he would witness soon enough.

CONCLUSIONS

In his now famous talk titled "Des espaces autres: Hétéropies" (Other spaces: Heterotopias), Michel Foucault declared that "space itself has a history," asserting the importance of understanding the "fatal crossing of time with space."[1] To this end, he cites the Renaissance and, in particular, Galileo's opening of the world to the possibilities of an infinitely open space that helped put an end to the localization characteristic of the Middle Ages. If his declaration of the end of localism seems today a bit premature, there is no doubt that conceptions of space underwent significant changes during the Renaissance. Rather than a shift from localism to its opposite, however, the Renaissance studied here has shown itself to be a space of contention and struggle between politics, religion, the individual and local, translocal, linguistic, regional, national, and supranational definitions of space that contend for one another in a constant mixing and extension of questions of identity. The importance of what Foucault calls "mixed spaces," or heterotopias, are essential in periods of extreme change because of their functioning as mirrors of society and the self. These spaces are different because they provoke a struggle between mythological spaces and the real spaces in which we live. The heterotopia combines the functions of the utopia with a real, lived space, juxtaposing seemingly incompatible places and creating spaces of purification that communicate and signify the rest of the world through a paradoxical combination of inclusion and exclusion. All these qualities pertain to the French experience of Italy, centered on the great heterotopic space of Rome as a contested space of translocality.

In the analysis of Montaigne's Alpine passage, we saw the many of the contradictions that travel through and toward such a space entails—a voyage without a center, a conflicted sense of purpose and national identity, the contemplation of one's own mortality linked to conflicted desires for absolute (spatial) freedom, grandeur, military valor, peace, and solitude. Montaigne's journey through Italy is nothing less than a spatial *psychomachia*, a struggle for and assertion of identity that responds to a question Tom Conley posed some years ago: "We can wonder if Rabelais's universe of the 1530s is not only a chorography of Chinon and its environs in the Touraine but also a totality that mimes the construction of a world map that valorizes the author in the view of the contemporary politics of statecraft."[2] Substituting Montaigne and Villamont for François Rabelais allows us to answer in the affirmative that not only the virtual representations of maps but also the individual's ongoing negotiation of a relationship with space involves and defines concepts of nation and selfhood. If Montaigne's sense of self is in constant movement, it appears to be movement itself that permits this understanding in a visceral, physical, and metaphysical way. Montaigne understands, more than most, that his being is always located in the *au-delà* of becoming.

The signs of Montaigne's semiconscious self-staging that occurs during these dramatic changes of scenery have also illustrated how the weight of historical memory—in Montaigne's case, of the most personal and heartfelt sort—comes to bear on French readings of Italian space. Italy is a desired space, defined by its relationship to a lost world of classical unity represented by ancient Rome, but it is also a space of transition, a borderland through which the French define their own national identity. André de la Vigne provided an early example of this contest that involves the rewriting and rhetorical appropriation of space as a function of national objectives. The fact that his *Voyage de Naples* unites a new concept of authorship as a condition for producing this openly propagandistic narrative in favor of a questionable war anticipates the increasing interdependence of evolving modes of self-representation and questions of national and international territorial desire. Self-representation develops not only out of knowledge of the other but also as a function of the assertion of the nonself, whose strongest forms of expression are politics, diplomacy, and war.

Du Bellay's conflicted sense of purpose confirms the contentiousness of this ongoing negotiation and its relationship to the discourse of travel and movement. If Du Bellay's *Regrets* anticipates Montaigne's satirically painted self-portrait, it is perhaps due to the fact that the two authors both share a contentious relationship with politics and selfhood, both work within a realm of practical exigency that involves lending oneself while seeking to carve out an *arriere-boutique* that is both distinct from and dependent on the outside world. Both authors travel to Italy in a conflicted state of mind, demanding a form of introspection that is also a conditioned public display within the political world.

The increased attention given to space in the early modern period owes much to the Age of Discovery, in which text anticipated the discovery of previously unknown worlds. At the same time, these forces of expansion and macroscopic spatialization (to avoid the term *globalization*) create tensions that seem to require a spatially contingent assertion of self. The link between narrative and space nonetheless represents a major shift from a rhetorical, what Foucault would call hierarchical, view of space to an articulated, multidimensional, and individually created space. Both Joseph Catin and Jacques de Villamont create space in the furtherance of political self-representation. Villamont, in particular, proposes the traveler as an image of the divine Creator due to his ability to recognize, describe, and embody traversed spaces, while Joseph Catin views space as a rhetorical device to be manipulated and deployed in the depiction of personal narrative.

The sociopolitical implications of the French journey to Italy thus mandate a rewriting of space by which experienced Italy becomes a function of national and personal interests. The vast majority of French travelers view Italy through the lens of collective experience and yet begin to weave the elements of this commonality into what Montaigne had called a "narration particuliere" (personal narrative). As a lost piece of French national identity, Italy becomes a space to be conquered, experienced, and digested, an accessory of class, as Pierre Du Val seems to imply, but also a space of self-exploration and understanding.[3] It is for this reason that Montaigne, who seeks to carve out his own piece of Rome in his choice of apartments, his wanderings among Rome's ruins, and his participation in the festivities of Lent, never quite gets there, finding Rome's universalism at odds with the inner image created through reading and the imagination. More importantly, the constantly changing spaces of the Italian journey force French travelers to negotiate a new sense of identity that is no longer dependent on fixed national borders forcing them to create imaginary spaces of contingent desire.

NOTES

INTRODUCTION

1. MS 222 R 424 of the Bibliothèques Méjanes d'Aix-en-Provence, ed. Luigi Monga. *Discours viatiques de Paris à Rome et de Rome à Naples et Sicile (1588–1589)* (Genève: Slatkine, 1983), 138.
2. A native of Haute-Garonne, Hugues Loubenx de Verdalle was a member of the Order of the Hospitaliers de Saint-Jean de Jérusalem and served as the order's ambassador to Rome (1579–82) before being appointed Grand Master of Malta. He had been ordained into the College of Cardinals in 1587, along with, among others, Juan Hurtado de Mendoza, Pierre de Gondi, and Scipione Gonzaga.
3. Frank Lestringant, *L'Atelier du cosmographe: Ou l'image du monde à la Renaissance* (Paris: Albin Michel, 1991); Frank Lestringant, *Le huguenot et le sauvage: L'Amérique et la controverse coloniale en France, au temps des guerres de religion (1555–1589)* (Paris: Klincksieck, 1990); Stephen Greenblatt, *Marvelous Possessions: The Wonder of the New World* (Chicago: University of Chicago Press, 1991).
4. Jean Balsamo, "Le Voyage d'Italie et la formation des élites françaises," *Renaissance and Reformation/Renaissance et Réforme* 27, no. 2 (2003): 9–21.
5. Élizabeth Schneikert, *Montaigne dans le labyrynthe: De l'imaginare du Journal de voyage à l'écriture des Essais* (Paris: Champion, 2006); Olivier Pot, "Lieux, espaces et géographie dans le *Journal de voyage*," *Montaigne Studies* 15 (2003): 63–104; Normand Doiron, "L'Art de voyager: Pour une définition du récit de voyage à l'époque classique," *Poétique* 73 (1988): 91.
6. Philippe Desan, *Montaigne: Une biographie politique* (Paris: Odile Jacob, 2014).
7. Ibid., 317–94.
8. George Hoffmann, *Montaigne's Career* (Oxford: Clarendon, 1998).
9. Virginia Krause, *Idle Pursuits: Literature and Oisiveté in the French Renaissance* (Newark: University of Delaware Press, 2003).
10. William Beik, *A Social and Cultural History of Early Modern France* (Cambridge: Cambridge University Press, 2009), 134–63.
11. "Tutta Italia vi andava in preda, et si sottoponeva a gente gallica, la qual, scundo l'antiche hystorie, mai potuto longamente dominar in quella." Marino Sanudo, *La Spedizione di Carlo VIII in Italia* (Venice, 1883), 15–16.
12. See Michael Mallett and Christine Shaw, "Introduction," in *The Italian Wars, 1494–1559* (Harlow: Pearson, 2012), 1–5. After Charles VIII's conquest and subsequent loss of Naples, Louis XII also found a reason to invade, asserting his claim to the throne of Milan in 1499. While in Italy, he helped Florence take Pisa and invited Spain to join in the conquest and cutting up of the Kingdom of

Naples. The French lost the Neapolitan kingdom to the Spanish with the battles of Cerignola and Garigliano in 1503. During the War of the League of Cambrai, King Louis invaded Venice, lost and then recaptured Milan from the Swiss, and was followed by his successor Francis I, who furthered these successes at the Battle of Marignano. After Charles V of Spain was chosen Holy Roman Emperor over the French king, the rivalry between these two monarchs dominated much of the next two decades, with little net gain for France. In the War of the League of Cognac, France joined the Papal States, England, Venice, Florence, and Milan in fighting the Spanish menace only to lose Milan (1529). In 1535 and 1544, the French attempted to retake the Lombard capital, and Francis's successor Henri II executed an ambitious plan to regain control of Italy during the last Italian war, resulting in the French defeat in Marciano and Saint Quentin.

13. Siena had been the site of the strongest French-led resistance to the Empire. See my chapter 5. Alfonso II d'Este, Duke of Ferrara (r. 1559–98), was the son of Ercole II d'Este and Renée of France and had fought in the service of his uncle Henri II against the Habsburgs.

14. Duke Emmanuel-Philibert (r. 1553–80) obtained his Duchy's independence by defeating the French at Saint-Quentin. He repaired his relationship with France by marrying Marguerite de Valois, daughter of Francis I and sister to Henri II, but simultaneously moved the Savoy capital from Chambéry to the other side of the Alps in Turin.

15. Anthropologists define embodied space as places where local/global power relations are embedded in transnational or translocal space. According to this reading, language and discourse transform space into place. Setha M. Low, "Towards an Anthropological Theory of Space and Place," *Semiotica* 175 (2009).

16. See Henri Lefebvre, *The Production of Space* (Cambridge, MA: Blackwell, 1991). Leibniz is in a sense the father of the relative view of space as an "accidental whole" or contingent phenomenon. See Jeffrey K. McDonough, "Leibniz's Philosophy of Physics," in *The Stanford Encyclopedia of Philosophy*, ed. Edward N. Zalta (Spring 2014), http://plato.stanford.edu/entries/leibniz-physics/#Aca. For a more complete discussion of spatial theory and how it relates to the travel narrative, see my first chapter.

17. See Terence Cave, *The Cornucopian Text: Problems of Writing in the French Renaissance* (Oxford: Clarendon, 1979); and Numa Broc, *La geografia del Rinascimento* (Ferrara: Panini, 1986), chapters 1 (9–15) and 5 (41–49).

18. See Frédéric Tinguely, *L'Écriture du Levant à la Renaissance: Enquête sur les voyageurs français dans l'empire de Soliman le Magnifique* (Geneva: Droz, 2000), 27; Tzvetan Todorov, *The Conquest of America: The Question of the Other* (New York: Harper & Row, 1987).

19. Marie-Madeleine Martinet, *Le voyage d'Italie dans les littératures européennes* (Paris: Presses Universitaires de France, 1996), 3.

20. Edward Saïd describes Orientalism as a "correspondence, or lack thereof, with a 'real' Orient." Edward W. Said, *Orientalism* (New York: Vintage Books, 1979), 3.

21. The Age of Discovery was prompted by the rediscovery of classical geographical texts that included not only Ptolemy's *Geography* but also Strabo's *Geography* and the works

of Pomponius Mela and Dionysius Periegetes. Numerous editors also prepared erudite, commented editions, in which commentary and cross-referencing displace linear reading. As an example, one can cite Vadianus's edition of Mela's *De situ orbis*, first published in 1518 but reprinted as late as 1556, where commentary and intertextual reference surround the text to the point of suffocation. Pomponius Mela, Joachim Vadianus, and Joannes Camers, *Pomponii Melae De orbis situ libri tres* (Paris: C. Wechelum, 1540), 18.

22. Marc Bizer, *Les lettres romaines de Du Bellay* (Montreal: Les Presses de l'Université de Montréal, 2001).

23. On the importance of the Roman journey, see Eric MacPhail, *The Voyage to Rome in French Renaissance Literature* (Stanford: Stanford French and Italian Studies, 1990); Margaret M. McGowan, *The Vision of Rome in Late Renaissance France* (New Haven: Yale University Press, 2000).

24. Michel de Montaigne, "Des cannibales," in *Les Essais* (Paris: Quadrige/PUF, 1992), I, 31, 205.

CHAPTER 1

1. All quotations of the *Journal*, except where otherwise indicated, are from *Journal de Voyage* (Paris: Presses universitaires de France, 1992). Translations, except where otherwise indicated, are by Donald Frame, *The Complete Works of Montaigne: Essays, Travel Journal, Letters* (Stanford: Stanford University Press, 1958).

2. Theorists of landscape all underline its subjective quality as distinguished from the objective reality of the land. See Michael Jakob, *Il paesaggio* (Bologna: Il Mulino, 2009), 15–26. Cosgrove defines landscape as "a way of seeing the world." Denis Cosgrove, *Social Formation and Symbolic Landscape* (Totowa, NJ: Barnes and Noble Books, 1984), 15. Clearly borrowing from Montaigne, Alain Roger uses the term *artialisation*. Alain Roger, *Court traité du paysage* (Paris: Gallimard, 1997), 11, cited in Jakob, *Il paesaggio*, 15.

3. The land is "beautiful," "pleasant," and "inaccessible." The attested usage of *rencontrer* in Renaissance French is as a military encounter or battle asserting the nobleman's power over space. Robert Estienne translates the noun *rencontre* as "offensio, occursus" (a striking against [attack], tripping, stumbling), adding the idea of a fortuitous encounter. *Dictionnaire Francoislatin, contenant les motz et manieres de parler François, tournez en Latin* (Paris: Robert Estienne, 1539), s.v. "rencontrer."

4. Henri Lefebvre, "La production de l'espace," *L'Homme et la société* 31–32 (1974). Translated in his *The Production of Space* (Cambridge, MA: Blackwell, 1991).

5. The original reads, "Le beau temps et serein *nous nous* y aidant fort" (the beautiful weather and calm [we] helping us). Michel de Montaigne, *Journal du voyage en Italie, Par la Suisse et l'Allemagne en 1580 et 1581* (Rome: Le Jay, 1774), 153–54. Printed recently by Philippe Desan, ed., in Montaigne, *Journal du voyage en Italie (1774)* (Paris: Société des textes français modernes, 2014).

6. Martin Savransky, "Will There Be a Place for My Life? Cities, Subjectivities and Geographies of Resistance / ¿Habrá un Lugar mi Vida? Ciudades, Subjetividades y Geografias de Resistencia," *Athenea Digital* 12, no 1 (2012): 191.

7. The effect of the building of this route in 1492 on Bavarian trade

was immediate, with Venice shifting its trade to the Mittenwald Market. Several separate roads funneled into the Mittenwald route as a result, connecting Augsburg, Weiheim, and Munich (through Lindau) to the Kesselberg route heading to Innsbruck. "Historisches Lexikon Bayerns," https://www.historisches-lexikon-bayerns.de/Lexikon/Kesselbergstraße.

8. Commemorative plaques were an integral part of Albrecht IV's self-promotion of his public persona. The only plaque erected outside an ecclesiastical context, it underlines the duke's strategic alliance with the patrician classes of Bavaria. Andreas Dahlem, "The Wittelsbach Court in Munich: History and Authority in the Visual Arts (1460–1508)" (University of Glasgow, Faculty of Arts, 2009), 23–24.

9. The year is written in Latin ("año dm mccclxxxxII Jar"), while Duke Albrecht's name is abbreviated "alb'echt" and the engineer Heinrich Bart's as "hairch part." "Historisches Lexikon Bayerns."

10. Readers as early as Meusnier de Querlon have noted the symbiosis between Montaigne and his servant. See Craig B. Brush, "La composition de la première partie du *Journal de voyage* de Michel de Montaigne," *Revue d'Histoire Littéraire de la France* 71 (1971); Brush, "The Secretary, Again," *Montaigne Studies: An Interdisciplinary Forum* 5, nos. 1, 2 (1993); Richard Keatley, "Le statut du valet dans le *Journal du voyage de M. de Montaigne en Italie, par la Suisse et l'Allemagne en 1580 et 1581*" (Univeristé de Paris IV–Sorbonne, 1997). Sainte-Beuve notes, in the passage through Kesselberg cited above, that "c'est le secretaire de Montaigne qui écrit, mais qui visiblement s'inspire de ses impressions et se teint de son langage." Louis Lautrey and Michel de Montaigne, *Journal de Voyage* (Paris: Hachette, 1906), 133, note.

11. Foucault alludes to the connections between space and power. He points to "three great spatial variables—territory, communication, and speed"—as having spaces of the "practice" of liberty or oppression. Foucault also sees the state as an extension of the city. Michel Foucault and Paul Rabinow, "Space, Knowledge and Power," in *The Essential Works of Michel Foucault, 1954–1984*, vol. 3 (London: Penguin, 2002); Erica Carter et al. identify the centrality of the city as the "site of contestation between groups of distinct, located identities." Erica Carter, James Donald, and Judith Squires, *Space and Place: Theories of Identity and Location* (London: Lawrence & Wishart, 1993).

12. Certeau defines space as a practiced, or narrated, place, going so far as to assert that "every story is a travel story" and citing Merleau-Ponty, who distinguishes geometrical space from an anthropological space "situated by a desire" and forming a "direction of existence." Michel de Certeau, *The Practices of Everyday Life* (Berkeley: University of California Press, 1984), 115–17. See also Fernando Cabo Aseguinolaza, "The Spatial Turn in Literary Historiography," *CLCWeb: Comparative Literature & Culture: A WWWeb Journal* 13, no. 5 (2011).

13. "This Italian expedition was not leisurely, for Montaigne was not taking a vacation—as has been suggested—; rather, he was going on a mission to Rome, the destination of his travel having been approved by the monarch." Henri III sent Montaigne to Rome to serve as the interim ambassador until Pope Gregory could be convinced to accept the nomination of Montaigne's fellow Perigordin Paul

de Foix. Philippe Desan, "The Public Life of Montaigne," in *The Oxford Handbook of Montaigne* (Oxford: Oxford University Press, 2016), 124–27. See also *Montaigne: Une biographie politique* (Paris: Odile Jacob, 2014), 317–94.

14. For descriptions of Montaigne's château and the surrounding area, see Anne-Marie Cocula and Alain Legros, *Montaigne aux champs* (Bordeaux: Éditions Sud Ouest, 2011); "MONLOE: Montaigne à l'oeuvre," https://montaigne.univ-tours.fr/centaine-de-livres/.

15. The inscription placed at the entrance of his library proposes "une sorte de programme à trois points: *libertas, tranquillitas, otium*." Alain Legros, "Inscriptions du 'cabinet' et dédicace perdue de la librairie," MONLOE: MONtaigne à L'Œuvre (2015), https://montaigne.univ-tours.fr/autres-inscriptions-de-la-tour/.

16. Hoffmann, "Working at Home," in *Montaigne's Career* (Oxford: Clarendon, 1998), 8–38.

17. Desan, "Vivre noblement," in *Montaigne: Une biographie politique* (Paris: Odile Jacob), 51–58; Virginia Krause, *Idle Pursuits: Literature and Oisiveté in the French Renaissance*; Robert Sayre, *Solitude in Society: A Sociological Study in French Literature* (Cambridge, MA: Harvard University Press, 1978).

18. If Michel Bideaux underlines the newness of Montaigne's interactive way of traveling, Montaigne's description of his motivations for traveling also makes him a first proponent of escapism and travel as an antidote to boredom: "Cette humeur avide des choses nouvelles et inconnues ayde bien à nourrir en moy le desir de voyager, mais assez d'autres circonstances y conferent. Je me destourne volontiers du gouvernement de ma maison" (III, 9, 948) (This greedy appetite for new and unknown things indeed helps to foster in me the desire to travel, but enough other circumstances contribute to it. I gladly turn aside from governing my house [733]). Michel Bideaux, "La description dans le *Journal de voyage* de Montaigne," in *Études seiziémistes offerts à M. le Professeur V.-L. Saulnier par plusieurs de ses anciens doctorants* (Geneva: Droz, 1980).

19. Built on the outer reaches of the jurisdiction of Bordeaux, Montaigne's château had served as part of a defensive chain built along the English-French border during the conflict over Guyenne. The Hundred Years' War (1337–1453) had begun near its walls and ended with the signing of the treaty of Castillon just a few miles down the banks of the Dordogne. Guyenne had passed into French hands at the end of the war, at first as a Royal apanage and finally as fief of the Crown in 1472, just five years before Montaigne's great-grandfather Ramon Eyquem purchased the lands of Montaigne and Balbeys with all their adjoining property, vineyards, and mills. Donald Murdoch Frame, *Montaigne: A Biography* (New York: Harcourt, Brace & World, 1965), 3–8.

20. "Geographically Huguenotism found its stronghold in the square roughly formed by the Rhone and Saône, the Loire and the Bay of Biscay, and the Pyrenees, the northern border running from Chalons to the mouth of the Loire. . . . In Poitou and Guyenne in some towns Huguenots formed a majority. At Rochelle Catholicism almost ceased to exist." E. Armstrong, *The French Wars of Religion, Their Political Aspects* (New York: Russell and Russell, 1971 [1892]), 23.

21. The Baron d'Uzeste, Sarran de Lalan writes, "(L)'orage et les troubles

subsistent toujours et nous menacenet d'ung naufrage. Si vous, Madame, qui tenez le gouvernail de ce roiaume, par votre prudence et singuliere dexterité n'appaisez ceste tourmente, et surtout en ceste province et duché de Guyenne, si longuement agitée." *Archives historiques du département de la Gironde*, t. 3, 1861–62, no. 86, February 13, 1580, p. 210, cited in Desan, *Montaigne*, 318.
22. Jean de Saint-Sulplice, *Guerres de religion dans le Sud-Ouest et principalement dans le Quercy* (Geneva: Slatkine Reprints, 1975), 484–94.
23. Charles Estienne, *La guide des chemins de France* (Paris: Estienne, 1552), 197–99.
24. On the conflicts in Limoges, see Annette S. Finley-Crosswhite, *Henry IV and the Towns: The Pursuit of Legitimacy in French Society, 1589–1610* (Cambridge: Cambridge University Press, 1999), 153. A map of League towns as they were a few years after Montaigne's journey also gives an idea of the geographical boundaries of the conflict. Ibid., 64.
25. Estienne, *La guide des chemins de France*, 179.
26. During negotiation for the treaty of Fleix, the king is said to have refused to even speak of peace until Mende (in Languedoc-Roussillon), Cahors, and La Fère had surrendered. Léonce Anquez, *Histoire des assemblées politiques des Réformés de France (1573–1622)* (Paris: Auguste Durand, 1859), 144.
27. On the development of French identity in the early modern period, see Colette Beaune, *Naissance de la nation française* (Paris: Gallimard, 1985). More recently, see Marcus Keller, *Figurations of France: Literary Nation-Building in Times of Crisis (1550–1650)* (Newark: University of Delaware Press, 2011); Phillip John Usher, *Errance et cohérence: Essai sur la littérature transfrontalière à la Renaissance* (Paris: Classiques Garnier, 2010).
28. Philippe Desan has recently pointed out the improbability of Niort, lying on the route between Saintes and Poitiers, appearing in these first two pages, proposing a reading of "Mours." Philippe Desan, oral presentation, April 24, 2014.
29. In 1477, Ramon Eyquem, a wealthy merchant in Bordeaux, purchased the lands of Montaigne and Belbeys that became Montaigne's estate; Charles le Téméraire, who aspired to reconstitute the ancient province of Lotharingia, died at the siege of Nancy that same year, at which point his lands were divided between French Burgundy and the Low Countries, which fell to the empire.
30. Since the 1419 marriage of René of Anjou with Isabelle of Lorraine, the Duchy of Bar, swearing fielty to France, and Lorraine, land subject to the empire, were united under one sovereign while maintaining their independence.
31. Concetta Cavallini, *L'italianisme de Montaigne* (Paris: Schena/Presses de l'Université de Paris-Sorbonne, 2003), 67–87.
32. Montaigne makes no mention of Piero's son Filippo di Piero Strozzi, lord of Épernay, who was probably not present at the time.
33. Cavallini, *L'italianisme de Montaigne*, 51–115.
34. Ibid., 61.
35. Jean Balsamo, *Les rencontres des muses: Italianisme et anti-italianisme dans les lettres françaises de la fin du XVIe siècle* (Geneva: Editions Slatkine, 1992).
36. See chapter 6.
37. Homi Bhabha, *The Location of Culture* (London: Routledge, 1994), 1.

38. See my forthcoming chapter on this topic: "Alpine Cannibals: French Renaissance Representations of the Alps and their Residents," in *Monstrous Borders in the Renaissance* (Abingdon: Routledge, in press).
39. On the role of the imagination and the *mythos* of Montaigne's journey, see Schneikert, *Montaigne dans le labyrynthe: De l'imaginare du Journal de voyage à l'écriture des Essais* (Paris: Champion, 2006).
40. Montaigne describes his progression through life without any major health problems, in terms of a traveler: "J'avoy pensé mainte-fois à part moy que j'alloy trop avant, et qu'à faire si long chemin, je ne faudroy pas de m'engager en fin en quelque malplaisant rencontre." All passages from the *Essais* are from Montaigne, *Les Essais* (Paris: Quadrige/PUF, 1992), 759 (A). Translations are from Donald Frame, cited edition.
41. Fredric Jameson's description of the decentered, postmodern hyperspace is equally valid in the contestatory geopolitical environment of the sixteenth century. Jameson underlines how space is "embodied" in the individual's environment, thereby creating a sense of identity linked to processes of political change and globalization. Fredric Jameson, *Postmodernism, or, The Cultural Logic of Late Capitalism*, Post-contemporary Interventions (Durham: Duke University Press, 1991), 44.
42. Francois Rigolot, "La situation énonciative dans le *Journal de voyage de Montaigne*," in *Poétique et Narration. Mélanges offerts à Guy Demerson* (Paris: Champion, 1993), 465.
43. Ibid., 469–72.
44. By "discourse," I mean the signs of subjectivity used in language but also in a Foucaultian sense as a way of constituting knowledge and relations of power through language. See Emile Benveniste, "De la subjectivité dans le langage," in *Problèmes de linguistique générale*, Bibliothèque des sciences humaines (Paris: Gallimard, 1966–74, 1966), vol. 1, 258–66; Pablo Iannone, *Dictionary of World Philosophy* (New York: Routledge, 2001), 156–57.
45. Montaigne's enthusiasm was evidently difficult for Meusnier de Querlon to grasp, his edition transcribing "M. de Montaigne disoit que c'estoit la lune de ses tretes" and adding in the note that "Parce que cette poussiere obscurcissant le jour, ne lui laissoit, ainsi que la lune, que ce qu'ill falloit de clarté pour se conduire." Montaigne, *Journal*, ed. Meusnier de Querlon (Paris: Chez le Jay, rue Saint-Jacques, au Grand-Corneille, 1774), 158.
46. *Traite* derives from the verb *traire*, in turn from the Latin *trahere*, meaning "to pull."
47. Sarga Moussa sees these readings as a confirmation of Montaigne's paradoxical reading of alterity (described by Claude Blum) in which the *essayist* seeks strangeness in his own culture and universality in distant places. I see Montaigne more as a contrarian averse to accepting conventional dogma. Moussa, "Une rhétorique de l'altérité: La représentation de la Suisse dans le *Journal de voyage* de Montaigne," in *Montaigne, Journal de voyage en Alsace et en Suisse (1580–1581); Actes du colloque de Mulhouse/Bâle* (Paris: Champion, 2000), 3–29; Claude Blum, "Montaigne, écrivain du voyage: Notes sur l'imaginaire du voyage à la Renaissance," in *Autour du Journal de voyage de Montaigne, 1580–1980*, ed. François Moureau and René Bernoulli (Geneva: Slatkine, 1982), 7.
48. The concept of self-fashioning in Renaissance society and its links to performance have been studied by

Stephen Greenblatt, *Renaissance Self-Fashioning from More to Shakespeare* (Chicago: University of Chicago Press, 1980). For Montaigne, see David Posner, "Montaigne and the Staging of the Self," in *The Performance of Nobility in Early Modern European Literature* (Cambridge: Cambridge University Press, 1999), 22–79; Krause, introduction to *Idle Pursuits*, 15–26.

49. Fausta Garavini, ed., "Introduction," in Michel de Montaigne, *Journal de Voyage* (Paris: Gallimard, 1983), 10.
50. François Rigolot, ed., "Introduction," in Michel de Montaigne, *Journal de Voyage* (Paris: Presses universitaires de France, 1992), xxi.
51. Meusnier de Querlon, ed., "Discours preliminaire," in Michel de Montaigne, *Journal du voyage en Italie, par la Suisse et l'Allemagne en 1580 et 1581* (Rome: Le Jay, 1774), lviii.
52. Frédéric Tinguely, *Les ruses de l'écriture à la Renaissance* (Paris: Champion, 2014), 183–94.
53. See Alain Legros, "Comme un désir de Grèce," in *Montaigne à l'étranger: Voyages avérés, possible et imaginés*, ed. Philippe Desan (Paris: Classiques Garnier, 2016); Élizabeth Schneikert, "Montaigne et l'appel de la Pologne," ibid.

CHAPTER 2

1. Robert D. Cottrell, *Sexuality/Textuality: A Study of the Fabric of Montaigne's Essais* (Columbus: Ohio State University Press, 1981).
2. Ibid., xii.
3. Ibid., xiii.
4. All quotations of the *Ressource*, except where indicated, are from André de la Vigne, *La Ressource de la Chrestienté* (Montréal: CERES, 1989).

Critical edition by Cynthia Brown, 107–8. Translations mine.

5. For the history of the expedition, see Silvio Biancardi, *La Chimera di Carlo VIII (1492–1495)* (Novara: Interlinea, 2009); David Abulafia, *The Western Mediterranean Kingdoms, 1200–1500: The Struggle for Dominion* (London: Longman, 1997), 246–62; Michael Mallett and Christine Shaw, *The Italian Wars, 1494–1559* (Harlow: Pearson, 2012), 6–37; Didier Le Fur, *Charles VIII* (Paris: Perrin, 2006), 296–375; Yvonne Labande-Mailfert, *Charles VIII et son milieu (1470–1498): La jeunesse au pouvoir* (Paris: Klincksiek, 1975), 169–438.
6. Charles's claim to the throne came through his father's inheritance through King René d'Anjou, to whom Queen Giovanna had offered the throne. He occupied the throne for only three years (1438–1441) and spent the rest of his life in exile in France, having been expelled by Giovanna's adopted son Alfonso of Aragon.
7. See Le Fur, *Charles VIII*, 266–68. Mallet and Shaw note regional differences, with Paris and the north generally opposed to the expedition and Angevins (who had the most to gain) and Provencals in favor. Mallet and Shaw, *Italian Wars*, 13–14.
8. Guicciardini describes the instability created by Lorenzo de' Medici. Francesco Guicciardini, *Storia d'Italia*, 3 vols., vol. 1 (Turin: Einaudi, 1971), cap. 2, 10–14. Charles's strongest allies were Savoy under the regency of Bianca di Monferrato, Ludovico Sforza's Milan, and Ercole d'Este's Ferrara. Venice remained neutral, while Piero de' Medici had close ties with the Neapolitan king. The Borgia pope, Alexander VI, who had used the threat of French invasion to counterbalance his concerns over the Neapolitan kingdom's expansion of interests around Rome and to

the north, was subsequently firmly opposed to Charles's plans. See Mallet and Shaw, *Italian Wars*, 9–10.
9. With the death of the "bon roi René" of Anjou in 1480, the Angevin claim to the Neapolitan kingdom had passed to Charles's father Louis XI, who died on August 30, 1483. See Mallet and Shaw, *Italian Wars*, 6–8; Labande-Mailfert, "Les Origines des Guerres d'Italie et le vouloir du roi," in *Charles VIII et son milieu*, 169–218; Marino Sanudo, *La Spedizione di Carlo VIII in Italia* (Venice, 1883); Guicciardini, *Storia d'Italia*, I, cap. 4, 24–37.
10. On the literary influences on the *Ressource*, see Cynthia Brown, "Introduction," in *La Ressource de la Chrestienté* (Montreal: CERES, 1989), 28–43.
11. Roland's popularity, moreover, not only was a relic of the past but had become, through the pen of Matteo Maria Boiardo, court poet of Charles's strongest ally, Ercole d'Este, a vehicle for the discussion of chivalric values in the face of changing societal and military realities. Having published the first two volumes of *Orlando innamorato* in 1483, Boiardo died during the French invasion, his last words referring to the destruction of Italy's garden paradise:

Mentre che io canto, o Iddio redentore,
Vedo la Italia tutta a fiama e foco
Per questi Galli, che con grave valore
Vengon per disertar non so che loco;
Però vi lascio in questo vano amore
De Fiordespina ardente a poco a poco;
Un'altra fiata, se mi fia concesso,
Racontarovi il tutto per espresso.

Orlando innamorato (Turin: Einaudi, 1974), III, 9, 36, p. 1495. Jo Ann Cavallo points out the importance of Boiardo in renewing interest in the chivalric ethic not only through his melding of Arthurian and Carolingian traditions but through a "creative rewriting" and transformation of sources including epic, romance, history, tragedy, comedy, and the novella and lyric forms, creating a dialogue between contemporary knights and the heroic past. Jo Ann Cavallo, "L'*Orlando innamorato*: Un romanzo per la corte ferrarese," in *Boiardo*, ed. Silvano Vinceti (Rome: Armando, 2003), 17.
12. Mallet and Shaw, *Italian Wars*, 12.
13. Ibid.
14. Labande-Mailfert, *Charles VIII et son milieu*, 160–64.
15. Philippe de Commynes describes Charles as "tres jeune, foible personne, plain de bon vouloir, peu accompaigné de sages gens ne de bons chiefz." *Mémoires* (Geneva: Droz, 2007), 514. Guicciardini describes him as "di complessione debole e di corpo non sano, di statura piccolo, di aspetto, se tu gli levi il vigore e la degnità degli occhi, bruttissimo, e l'altra membra proporzionate in modo che e' pareva quasi più simile a mostro che a uomo: né sono cogniti delle lettere; animo cupido di imperare ma abile a ogn'altra cosa, perché aggirato sempre da' suoi non riteneva con loro né maestà ne autorità." Guicciardini, *Storia d'Italia*, I, 78–79. The Venitian Marino Sanudo describes him as "cupido di augumentare el regno" and "desideroso innanzitutto di reclamare l'apanaggio francese." Sanudo, *La Spedizione di Carlo VIII in Italia*, 19–20.
16. Le Fur, *Charles VIII*, 259–62.
17. Sanudo writes that Charles's ambassadors to Florence were instructed to remind the town of "li benefici che la città di Fiorenza in diversi tempi havea ricevuti da la casa di Franza, et maxime da Carlo Magno che, come si legge ne le hystorie, essendo Fiorenza ruinata da Totila re de Gothi,

la redificoe et amplioe di circuito di mure." Sanudo, *La Spedizione di Carlo VIII in Italia*, 32–33.
18. Mallet and Shaw, *Italian Wars*, 12–13.
19. Commynes writes that "l'emprise sembloit a tous gens saiges et experimentez tres deraisonable" (the project seemed very unreasonable to all wise and experienced people). *Mémoires*, 513.
20. See Abulafia, *Western Mediterranean Kingdoms*, 246–53; Labande-Mailfert, *Charles VIII et son milieu*.
21. The Ottomans had taken Constantinople in 1453. After signing a treaty with Venice in 1479, they concentrated their efforts on the Balkans and the eastern Italian coast, capturing Otranto in the massacre of 1480.
22. Abulafia, *Western Mediterranean Kingdoms*, 259–62.
23. Naples became a singular example of tolerance in this brief period before the arrival of the Spanish, granting Jews full civic rights in 1468 and seeing the opening of Joshua Soncino's printing press in 1490. Naples and the Ottoman Turks both received Jewish refugees expelled from Spain in 1492. Adri K. Offenberg, "The Printing History of the Constantinople Hebrew Incunable of 1493: A Mediterranean Voyage of Discovery," *British Library Journal* 22, no. 2 (Autumn 1996): 225. See also Abulafia, *Western Mediterranean Kingdoms*, 230–31.
24. La Vigne had published a version of the *Ressource de la Chrestienté* before its inclusion in the *Vergier d'honneur* in 1500. This earlier version, composed prior to the military expedition, survives in a partial fragment and two manuscript copies. Brown, "Introduction"; "The Evolution of André de la Vigne's *La Ressource de la Chrestienté*: From the Manuscript Tradition to the Vergier d'Honneur Editions," *Bibliothèque d'Humanisme et Renaissance* 45, no. 1 (1983).
25. Despite its suggestive homophony, the French *vergier* derives from its greenness (viridarium) and not from any relationship to the phallus (verge). The *pourpris*, or enclosed garden space, derives from the Old French verb *porprendre*, meaning to "invest, occupy, take by force or usurp." Algirdas Julien Greimas, *Dictionnaire de l'ancien français: Le Moyen Age* (Paris: Larousse, 1994), s.v. "porprendre."
26. Brown, "Introduction," 18–19.
27. Giovanna Trisolini, *Introduction to Le Voyage de Gênes by Jehan Marot* (Geneva: Droz, 1974), 22.
28. André de la Vigne, *Le Voyage de Naples* (Milan: Pubblicazioni della Università Cattolica del Sacro Cuore, 1981).
29. Charles began collecting the documentation relating to his claim as early as 1490. Le Fur, *Charles VIII*, 259.
30. After the death of his commander Pierre d'Esquerdes, Charles took personal charge of the preparations on April 22, 1494. Guicciardini shows him "fervently" managing the provisioning of the troops and the collection of money. Guicciardini, *Storia d'Italia*, I, 61.
31. "(Il) assembler *fist* des nobles ung grant tas" (131, v. 52) (had a large number of noblemen assemble), "*fist* venir d'Espaigne aucunes gens" (vv. 65–66) (ordered men from Spain), and "souldoya gendarmes et archiers" (132, v. 97) (contracted soldiers and archers). La Vigne's account makes no mention of the king's famous libido, pursued, according to Marino Sanudo, at the expense of the operation: "El re di Franza in questo mezzo essendo a Lion dove era venuto l'April, et quivi stette zerca mexi cinque, provvedendo a molte cose era bisogno a questa impresa, et non tanto lui quanto li suoi principali, zoè Samalla et mons.

Di Beucher, però che el Re stava su piaceri et innamoramenti, secondo il costume di Franza. Et accidit che sé innamoroe in una lì à Lion pur di bassa conditione, a la quale volse dar di molti scudi, tamen li fratelli mai voler sopportar questo." Sanudo, *La Spedizione di Carlo VIII in Italia*, 47.

32. Cynthia Brown, "Books in Performance: The Parisian Entry (1504) and Funeral of Anne of Brittany," *Yale French Studies, No. 110: Meaning and Its Objects Material Culture in Medieval and Renaissance France* 110 (2006).

33. For the political, artistic, and sociological importance of the royal entry, see Robert J. Knecht, *The French Renaissance Court* (New Haven: Yale University Press, 2008), 99–112; Richard Cooper, "Triumphal Entries under Henri II," in *Court Festivals of the European Renaissance: Art, Politics and Performance* (Aldershot: Ashgate, 2004), 51–75; Nicolas Le Roux, "The Politics of Festivals at the Court of the Last Valois," ibid., 101–17.

34. The triple function of the *entrée royale* under Henri II joined a symbolic taking of possession, the projection of the royal image, and extraction of money from the town. Cooper, "Triumphal Entries."

35. Sandra Provini, "Les Entrées de Charles VIII à Chieri et à Florence en 1494 vues par André de La Vigne," in *Vérité et fiction dans les entrées solennelles: À la Renaissance et à l'Age classique*, ed. John Nassichuk, Collections de la République des Lettres: Symposiums (Collections de la République des Lettres: Symposiums) (Quebec: PU Laval, 2009); Julie-André Rostand, "L'*ekphrasis* ou de l'efficacité de la description dans les relations d'entrées françaises," ibid.

36. Sandra Provini, "Les Entrées de Charles VIII à Chieri et à Florence en 1494 vues par André de La Vigne," ibid.

37. See Luigi Monga, "Travel and Travel Writing: An Historical Overview of Hodoeporics," *Annali d'Italianistica* 14 (1996).

38. The so-called Palazzo Gotico, the palazzo comunale of Piacenza.

39. In Turin, the king parades from the suburbs to its castle; in Chieri, from the fields into the city's decorated piazzas; in Moncalieri, the visitors witness "l'une des plus belles places, / des gorgïases et des bien acoustree/de grosses tours, rivieres, boys et chasses/ qu'on saiche point en toute la contree" (178, vv. 1791–94) (one of the most beautiful squares, the most gorgeous and best equipped with large towers, rivers, woods, and hunting grounds that are known in any part of the country) surrounded by "grans pons levis, bouloars et lucernes / meurtris-soueres de haulteur succombes / larges fossez a basses barbacanes, / artillerie, grosses boulles plombees" (178, vv. 1799–1802) (large drawbridges, bulwarks and high archer towers, large moats with low barbicans/artillery, large leaded balls).

40. The Middle French *acteur* is "celui qui administre les biens d'un mineur jusqà sa majorité" (someone who administers the property of a minor until he/she comes of age), "régisseur d'un domaine, d'un patrimoine" (the administrator of property or an estate), or a "receveur de deniers publics" (recipient of public funds). "Dictionnaire du Moyen Français (1330–1500)," Analyse et traitement informatique de la langue française, http://www.atilf.fr.dmf.

41. "Celui qui a une part active dans une affaire." Ibid., s.v. "acteur."

42. La Vigne was one of the first authors to sue and win protection for the copyright of his poetic work.

Cynthia Brown, "Du manuscrit à l'imprimé en France: Le cas des Grands Rhétoriqueurs," in *Les Grands Rhétoriqueurs: Actes du Ve Colloque International sur le Moyen Français. Milan, 6-8 mai 1985. Vol. 1* (Milan: Pubblicazioni della Università Cattolica del Sacro Cuore, 1985); Frank Lestringant, "André de la Vigne et *Le Vergier d'honneur*," in *Le poète et son oeuvre: De la composition à la publication*, ed. Jean Eudes (Geneva: Droz, 2004).

43. Brown, "Introduction," 23. See also "La prose poétique," *Ressource*, 54–57. A few examples: perscruter, antipodes, baccanales exactions, asopy, lingonique, reonance, prepostillant, revolucion, consolative hemee. La Vigne, *Ressource*, appendix 1, 167.

CHAPTER 3

1. Olfa Abrougui, *Du Bellay et la poésie de la Ville: Rome n'est plus Rome* (Paris: L'Harmattan, 2013), 279.
2. Francois Rigolot, "Du Bellay et la poesie du refus," *Bibliotheque d'Humanisme et Renaissance* 36 (1974): 492. See also William Franklin Panici, "Rejection and Indirection: Du Bellay's *Regrets*," *Journal of Evolutionary Psychology* 9, nos. 1–2 (1989).
3. On Du Bellay's ambivalence to French national identity, see Eric MacPhail, "Nationalism and Italianism in the Work of Joachim Du Bellay," *Yearbook of Comparative and General Literature* 39 (1990); Marc Bizer, "'Qui a païs n'a que faire de patrie': Joachim Du Bellay's Resistance to a French Identity," *Romanic Review* 91, no. 4 (2000). Margaret Ferguson describes Du Bellay's ambivalence toward ancient literature as conflicted "filial piety." Ferguson, "The Exile's Defense: DuBellay's La Deffence et illustration de la langue françoyse," *PMLA: Publications of the Modern Language Association of America* 93, no. 2 (1978).
4. Thomas M. Greene, *The Light in Troy: Imitation and Discovery in Renaissance Poetry*, Elizabethan Club series (New Haven: Yale University Press, 1982), 62.
5. Philippe Desan, "De la poésie de circonstance à la satire: Du Bellay et l'engagement poétique," in *Du Bellay*, ed. Georges Cesbron (Angers: P de l'Univ. d'Angers, 1990).
6. See, for example, the lively debate regarding the importance or nonimportance of Du Bellay's social engagement that occurred in response to Ullrich Languer's presentation at the Colloque international d'Angers. In Ullrich Langer, "Le Discours de la souveraineté dans Les Regrets," ibid., 388–90.
7. Bizer describes the tension of this referentiality as a force that "dépoétise les *Regrets*" even as they contribute to the creation of "un monde poétique clos." Marc Bizer, *Les lettres romaines de Du Bellay* (Montreal: Les Presses de l'Université de Montréal, 2001), 75.
8. G. Dickinson, *Du Bellay in Rome* (Leiden: Brill, 1960).
9. See, for example, V. L. Saulnier, *Du Bellay* (Paris: Boivin, 1951). L. Clark Keating sees the *Regrets* as an attempt to "escape from reality," describing a "rising crescendo of contempt for Italy and the Italian way of doing things." L. Clark Keating, *Joachim du Bellay* (New York: Twayne, 1971), 80.
10. During his first year in Rome, the French were on the ascendant, using their alliance with the Ottomans to gain control of Corsica, conquering assets in Piedmont, and protecting the independence of the Republic of Siena. From 1555 onward, this progress

was halted as the succession of Popes Marcellus and Paul IV placed France in a political dilemma. After Henri II broke his word with Pope Paul by signing the treaty with Philip of Spain at Vaucelles, relations with the papacy turned sour. France's final move of sending troops led by the Duke of Guise to take Naples, proved a mistake, leading to the French loss at home at the Battle of Saint Quentin. Dickinson, *Du Bellay*, 107–54; Michael Mallett and Christine Shaw, *The Italian Wars, 1494–1559* (Harlow: Pearson, 2012), 250–88.

11. Keating, *Joachim du Bellay*, 64. See also William Franklin Panici, "Du Bellay's *Regrets* and Magny's *Souspirs*: Satire or Vituperation?," *Romance Notes* 23, no. 1 (1982); Ruth Calder, "Montaigne as Satirist," *Sixteenth Century Journal* 17, no. 2 (1986); Philip Ford, "Du Bellay et le sonnet satirique," in *Le Sonnet à la Renaissance: Des origines au XVIIe siècle*, ed. Yvonne Bellenger (Paris: Aux Amateurs de Livres, 1988); Marie-Madeleine Fontaine, "Rire comme Ulysse," in *La Naissance du monde et l'invention du poème*, ed. Jean-Claude Ternaux and Isamu Takata, Etudes et Essais sur la Renaissance: 21 (Paris: Champion, 1998).

12. Richard Katz, *The Ordered Text: The Sonnet Sequences of Du Bellay* (Berne: P. Lang, 1985); Jerome Schwartz, "The Poet in Bivio: Du Bellay's Spiritual Itinerary in the *Regrets*," in *Lapidary Inscriptions: Renaissance Essays for Donald A. Stone, Jr.*, ed. Barbara C. Bowen and Jerry C. Nash, French Forum Monographs (FrFM): 74 (Lexington, KY: French Forum, 1991).

13. Abrougui, *Du Bellay et la poésie de la Ville: Rome n'est plus Rome*, 34–42.

14. Panici follows Screech in excluding the remaining sonnets after 130 from the "*Regrets* per se." Panici, "Du Bellay's *Regrets*"; Michael Screech, ed., "Introduction," in *Joachim Du Bellay, Les Regrets et autres oeuvres poëtiques* (Geneva: Droz, 1966), 29–30. Bizer, on the other hand, illustrates how these "cartes postales poétiques" and the "sonnets courtisans" relate to the poet's sociopoetical network. Bizer, *Les lettres romaines de Du Bellay*, 86, 115–87.

15. Estienne writes, "Pource que la profession de nostr'art nous enhorte a faire tousjours quelque chose qui soit utile en general a tous ceulx qui entendent au faict des lettres" (Since the profession of our art incites us to always make something that is generally useful to those who understand literature). Estienne, *Dictionnaire Francoislatin, contenant les motz et manieres de parler Francois, tournez en Latin* (Paris: Robert Estienne, 1539), preface, (2).

16. Regarding productive work, Estienne lists "labeur que une personne prend d'elle mesme (*verus labor*), [...] labeur et travail (*industria*), [...] labeur plus fortuné (*industria foelicior*), [...] labeur continuel (*labor continens*), ... etc."; for difficulty and quality of work, "relaschement de labeur (*laxamentum*), [...] un labeur extreme (*summus labor*), [...] chose de grand labeur, et difficile, ou penible (*res operosa*),"; and for distribution of work, "accroistre d'ung an le labeur [...] ton labeur est prolongé d'ung an (*additus est annus tuo labori*) [...] achever son labeur ordonné, [...] alleger et diminuer le labeur, [...] etc." Ibid., s.v. "labeur."

17. The word's origin, *tripalium*, was a medieval instrument of torture. Estienne gives the word complex psychological connotations, resulting in lengthy French locutions that in Latin are contained in a single adverb such as "travail d'esprit qui ne laisse

point l'homme en repos, principalement quand il luy vient de remors de conscience (*intemperiae*)." Ibid., s.v. "travail."
18. Virginia Krause, *Idle Pursuits: Literature and Oisiveté in the French Renaissance* (Newark: University of Delaware Press, 2003).
19. "L'ouvrage compose et escript (*liber*), [...] ouvrage faict apres qu'on a besonge (*Factura*), [...] ouvrage antique (*opus antiquum*), [...] ouvrage a miel, [...] ouvrage de cuyre, ou d'airain, [...] de marqueterie (*emblema*), [...]." Estienne, *Dictionnaire Francoislatin*, s.v. "ouvrage."
20. Ibid.
21. All citations are from Joachim Du Bellay, *Les Regrets et autres œuvres poëtiques suivis des Antiquitez de Rome, plus un Songe ou Vision sur le mesme subject*, ed. Michael Screech (Geneva: Droz, 1979). Translations from Du Bellay, *The Regrets with The Antiquities of Rome, Three Latin Elegies and The Defense and Enrichment of the French Language*, trans. Richard Helgerson (Philadelphia: University of Pennsylvania Press, 2006).
22. Estienne, *Dictionnaire Francoislatin*, s.v. "travail."
23. Ibid.
24. Langer, "Le Discours."
25. George Hugo Tucker, *The Poet's Odyssey: Joachim Du Bellay and the Antiquitez de Rome* (Oxford: Clarendon, 1990), 17–18.
26. Du Bellay's imprisonment meets all the parameters of what Foucault calls "hétéropies de crise." These "other" and "unreal" spaces (prisons, mental hospitals, the military, colleges) offer "une espèce de contestation à la fois mythique et réelle de l'espace ou nous vivons" (a sort of contestation that is both mythic and real of the space where we live). Michel Foucault, "Des espaces autres (1967), Hétérotopies," *Architecture, Mouvement, Continuité* 5 (October 1984): 47.
27. Schwartz, "Poet in Bivio."
28. On the changing role of work in Renaissance France, see Philippe Desan, "Work in the Renaissance," *Journal of Medieval and Renaissance Studies* 25, no. 1 (1995); Laure Chantrel, "Les Notions de richesse et de travail dans la pensée économique française de la seconde moitié du XVIe et au début du XVII siècle," ibid.
29. In particular, *Canzoniere* 7, "La gola e'l sonno, e l'oziose piume."
30. It is interesting that Du Bellay cites Hannibal as the first to cross the Alps from Gaul into Italy, ignoring the model, cited by most other travelers, of Brennus, chief of the Galli Senones who defeated the Romans at the Battle of Allia in 387 BCE.
31. Estienne, *Dictionnaire Francoislatin*, s.v. "travail."
32. Desan describes the situation of Louis Chasteigner, who desperately awaited reimbursement and replacement in 1580. Desan, *Montaigne: Une biographie politique* (Paris: Odile Jacob, 2014), 356–71.
33. Floyd Gray, *La poétique de Du Bellay* (Paris: Nizet, 1978), 59–78.
34. See chapter 4.
35. Jean Balsamo, "Le Voyage d'Italie et la formation des élites françaises," *Renaissance and Reformation/ Renaissance et Réforme* 27, no. 2 (2003). The *peregrinatio academica* had, since the Middle Ages, allowed students to frequent courses at any European university. Horsemanship, fencing, and dance were taught at centers across Italy.
36. Horace, *Satires, Epistles and Ars Poetica*, trans. H. Ruston Fairclough, Loeb Classics (Cambridge, MA: Harvard University Press, 2005), Epistles, I, 11, 27.

37. See also Krause, *Idle Pursuits*, 66–67.
38. In La Vigne's heroic account, the Lombards change their clothing, becoming French. For Du Bellay, the French have lost their identity by taking on the habits of the Italians.
39. Lionello Sozzi, "La polémique anti-italienne en France au XVIe siècle," *Atti della Accademia di scienze di Torino* 189 (1972).
40. Jerome Turler, *The Traveiler of Jerome Turler, devided into two Bookes . . . conteining a notable discourse of the maner, and order of traviling oversea, or into straunge and forrein Countreys. The second comprehending an excellent description of the most delicious Realme of Naples in Italy* (Gainseville: Scholars' Facsimiles and Reprints, 1951). Originally published as *De peregrinatione, et agro neapolitano. Libri II. Scripti ab Hieronymo Turlero. Omnibus peregrinantibus utiles ac necessarii: Ac in eorum gratiam nunc in primum editi* (Strasbourg, 1574).
41. Turler, *The Traveiler*, 4.
42. Ibid., 5.
43. Justus Lipsius, "Epistola de ratione cum fructu peregrinandi et praesertim in Italia," in *Miscellanea litteraria*, ed. Adam Heinrich Lackmann (Hamburg, 1721), 152.
44. Justus Lipsius and John Stradling, *A Direction for Travailers taken (by Sir J. Stradling) out of J. Lipsius and enlarged for the behoofe of . . . the young Earle of Bedford, being now ready to travell* (London, 1592), B.
45. Ibid., B (1).
46. Ibid., A 3.
47. For a list of travelers, see my bibliography. In chronological order, narratives of travel during the Wars of Religion were as follows: Joseph Catin (traveled 1568), Jacques-Auguste de Thou (1573–74), Nicolas Audebert (1574–78), Michel de Montaigne (1580–81), Charles de Neufville (1583–84), *Discours viatiques* (1588–89), *Voyage de Provence et d'Italie* (1588–89), and Jacques de Villamont (1588–89, 1591).
48. Joseph Catin, Claude-Énoch Virey, and Nicolas Audebert were lawyers who studied in Italy, returning to France to serve in the government. Audebert, Virey, Montaigne, Jacques-Auguste de Thou, and Jacques de Villamont were all members of France's various parliaments. Audebert and Villamont served in the Parliament of Brittany, with Audebert stepping down when Mercoeur took over the institution in 1589.
49. The name of Achille de Harlay, the great French magistrate and *président à mortier* of the Parisian Parliament from 1572 until 1611, who gained fame for defending the monarchy during the *Journée des barricades*, figures prominently in his relations with a number of travelers. Harlay's second wife, Anne de Thou, was the sister of the historian and parliamentary maître de requêtes Jacques-Auguste de Thou, who traveled to Italy in 1573 in the company of the French ambassador Paul de Foix. Claude-Énoch Virey went to Padua with Harlay's son Christophe and later became secretary to the Henri II de Bourbon-Condé through this connection. Harlay is also listed as "le puissant seigneur Achille de Harlay, sieur de Sancy, comte de Dourdan, baron de Molle, vicomte de Mailleboys" (the powerful lord Achille de Harlay, lord of Sancy, count of Dourdan, Baron of Molle, Viscount of Maillebois) on the parish record of the baptism of Jacques de Villamont's son. Département de Maine-et-Loire, *Inventaire sommaire des archives départementales antérieures à 1790* (Angers, n.d.), 350–51.

CHAPTER 4

1. "Nam quod maxime mihi fuit optatum iam inde ex quo in literis politioribus aliquem sensum habui, ut Italia, peragrare, Romámque orbis caput invisere possem." François Rabelais, "Franciscus Rabelaesus Medicus Cariss. doctissimóque viro D. Ioanni Bellaio Parisiensi Episcopo, Regísque in sanctiori consessu consiliario S.P.D.," in *Topographiae antiquae Romae* (Lyon: Gryphius, 1534), * 2.
2. "Deinde (quod artis erat meae) plantas, animantia, et pharmaca nonnulla contueri, quibus Gallia carere, illi abundare dicebantur." Prefatory letter to *Topographiae antiquae Romae* (Lyon: Gryphius, 1534), unnumbered.
3. "Postremo sic Urbis faciem calamo perinde ac penicillo depingere, ut ne quid esset, quod non peregre reversus municipibus meis de libris in promptu depromere possem." Ibid.
4. See chapter 3, "Je me feray sçavant en la philosophie." Joachim Du Bellay, *Les Regrets et autres œuvres poëtiques suivis des Antiquitez de Rome, plus un Songe ou Vision sur le mesme subject*, ed. Michael Screech (Geneva: Droz, 1979), 32.
5. "Plantas autem nullas, sed nec animantia ulla habet Italia, quae non antè nobis et visa essent et nota." François Rabelais, "Franciscus Rabelaesus Medicus Cariss. doctissimóque viro D. Ioanni Bellaio Parisiensi Episcopo, Regísque in sanctiori consessu consiliario S.P.D.," in *Topographiae antiquae Romae* (Lyon: Gryphius, 1534).
6. Horace's aphorism "Caelum, non animum mutant qui transmare currunt" (*Epistles*, I, 11) appears in introductions and advice for travelers as early as Breydenbach's *Peregrinatio Terrae Sanctae* of 1486, published in France as *Le saint voyage et pelerinage de la cite saincte de hierusalem* in 1489.
7. "Quod erat postremum, id sic perfeci diligenter, ut nulli notam magis domum esse suam, quàm Romam mihi Romaéque vicolos omneis putem." Rabelais, "Franciscus Rabelaesus Medicus Cariss.," in *Topographiae antiquae Romae* (Lyon: Gryphius, 1534), * 3.
8. Ibid.
9. "A Dictionary of Greek and Roman Antiquities" (Perseus Digital Library, 1890), s.v. "AGRIMETA´TIO," http://www.perseus.tufts.edu/hopper/text?doc=Perseus:text:1999.04.0063:entry=agrimetatio-cn.
10. "Ego ex Thaletis Milesii invento, sublato Sciothero Urbem vicatim ducta ab orientis ab obeuntísque solis, tum Austri atque Aquilonis partibus orbita transversa partiebar, oculísque designabam: Ille à montibus graphicem maluit auspicari. Hancce tamen scribendi rationem, tantum abest ut reprehendam, ut valde ego ipsi gratuler, quòd id ipsum cum agere conarer, anteverterit. Plura enim unus praestit, quàm expectare quis ab omnibus seculi huiusce nostri quamlibet eruditis potuisset." Rabelais, "Franciscus Rabelaesus Medicus Cariss.," 3 v.
11. Alberti's purpose was to create a portable image of Rome so that "anyone, of however mediocre talent, may be able to draw very well and easily Rome in whatever dimensions he may desire" ("excogitavi quo pacto quivis vel mediocri ingenio praeditus bellissime et commodissime pingere, quantacumque voluerit in superficie, possit" / "j'ai aussi imaginé un moyen pour que n'importe qui, fût-il doué d'un médiocre talent, puisse les dessiner tout à fait bellement et commodément, aux dimensions qu'il désire"). Leon Battista Alberti, *Descriptio urbis Romae* (Geneva: Droz, 2000), English translation mine, 27, 47.

12. Richard Cooper, "Rabelais and the Topographia Antiquae Romae of Marliani," *Etudes Rabelaisiennes* 14 (1977).
13. The sciotherum or gnomon was a surveyor's tool described by Vitruvius. "Dictionary of Greek and Roman Antiquities," s.v. "AGRIMETA'TIO."
14. See Numa Broc, *La geografia del Rinascimento* (Ferrara: Panini, 1986).
15. The most important development in the representation of space is the discovery of perspective in painting and architecture, attributed to Alberti and Filippo Brunelleschi, which shifts the Aristotelian idea of space as "containing" objects to the modern conception of extensible space. See Martin Kemp, *Seen and Unseen: The Visual Ideas behind Art and Science* (New York: Basic Books, 2001), 13; Susan Bordo, *The Flight to Objectivity: Essays on Cartesianism and Culture* (Albany: State University of of New York Press, 1987), 68.
16. In Montaigne's time, the Copernican revolution had begun to displace the Ptolemaic vision of the universe. Kuhn argues that this shift in perspective does more than offer an alternative version of space; rather, theory and observation are so intertwined as to modify reality itself. Thomas S. Kuhn, *The Structure of Scientific Revolutions* (Chicago: University of Chicago Press, 1970), 110.
17. Frank Lestringant, "Chorographie et paysage à la Renaissance," in *Le Paysage à la Renaissance*, ed. Yves Giraud (Fribourg: Eds. Universitaires, 1988).
18. Montaigne, *Les Essais* (Paris: Quadrige/PUF, 1992), "Des cannibales," I, 31, 205. Translation mine. Frame translates "topographers who would give an exact account of the places they have been." Frame, *Montaigne: A Biography* (New York: Harcourt, Brace and World, 1965), 152.
19. The French adjective *particulier* defines property, things that are "propre, à un chacun, Proprius, Peculiaris." Jean Nicot, "Le Thresor de la langue francoyse, tant ancienne que moderne" (Paris: David Douceur, 1606), 463. On the importance of Montaigne's use of economic language, see Philippe Desan, *Les commerces de Montaigne: Le discours Èconomique des Essais* (Paris: Libr. A.-G. Nizet, 1992).
20. See Mieke Bal, *Narratology, Introduction to the Theory of Narrative*, 2nd ed. (Toronto: University of Toronto Press, 1997), especially "From Place to Space," 132–42, and "Focalization," 42–62.
21. Though Montaigne's argument in "Des Cannibales" is moral, he uses a spatial argument to make this point. "Internet Encyclopedia of Philosophy, A Peer-Reviewed Academic Resource," https://www.iep.utm.edu, s.v. "Cognitive relativism."
22. Jessica Maier, *Rome Measured and Imagined: Early Modern Maps of the Eternal City* (Chicago: Chicago University Press, 2015).
23. Marliani had almost certainly studied Pausanias under his master Stefano Negri. At Yale University's Beinecke Rare Book and Manuscript Library, I was able to consult one of the very rare copies of Stefano Negri's *Dialogus apud Pausaniam*, a Platonic dialogue that purports to study "everything worth knowing" in Pausanias, whose *Description of Greece* had been published in Greek the previous year. The most inquisitive student, and the one who asks the master Negri for help understanding Pausanias, is named Ioannes (Marliani's first name). Negri, *Dialogus in quem quicquid apud Pausaniam scitu dignum legitur quem diligentissime congessit Stephanus*

Niger tam graece quam latine opidoque, eruditus (Milan: Minutianus, 1517), 44.

24. Biondo and Fulvio both use a modified version of the categories (walls, gates, temples, etc.) of the twelfth-century *Mirabilia urbis Romae*. After describing Rome's situation (book I), Biondo, dedicated his chapters to the various types of structures contained in ancient Rome: baths (*thermae*), religious and public monuments (book II), amphitheaters, circuses, various monuments, the Domus aurea, Aedes Fortunae, Septizonium, the Arch of Septimius Severus, and so on.

25. Based on a search on worldcat.org of "topographia" from 1450 to 1550, Marliani's appears to be the only published *topographia* until Pierre Gilles's *De topographiae Constantinopoleos, et de illius antiquitatibus*, published in Lyon in 1561. Gabriele Simeoni and Jean Chaumeau produced a map of Berry titled *Limaniae topographia Gabriele Symeoneo* in 1566. Antoine Vacher, *Le Berry. Contribution à l'Etude géographique d'une région française* (Paris: Armand Colin, 1908), 77–81.

26. See Margaret M. McGowan, "The Guidebook," in *The Vision of Rome in Late Renaissance France* (New Haven: Yale University Press, 2000), 33–55; Ludwig Schudt and Oskar Pollak, *Le guide di Roma: Materialien zu einer Geschichte der römischen Topographie, unter Benützung des Handschriftlichen Nachlasses von Oskar Pollak, hrsg. von Ludwig Schudt*, Quellenschriften zur Geschichte der Barockkunst in Rom (Wien: B. Filser, 1971).

27. While Biondo was arguably the most important, he too wrote in a well-established tradition. His predecessors include Giovanni Dondi dell'Orologio's *Iter Romanum* (1375); the *Tractatus de rebus antiquis et situ urbis Romae*, also known as *Anonimo Magliabecchiano* (ca. 1411); Niccolò Signorili's *Descriptio urbis Romae eiusque excellentiae* (ca. 1430); as well as Leonbattista Alberti's *Descriptio urbis Romae* (ca. 1445).

28. See Marc Laureys and Anna Schreurs, "Egio, Marliano, Ligorio, and the Forum Romanum in the 16th Century," *Humanistica Lovaniensia* 45 (1996).

29. Giovanni Barlolomeo Marliani, Dedicatory letter to Cardinal Domenico Cupo, in *Antiquae Romae Topographia* (Rome: Bladus, 1534), n.p. (1).

30. Laureys and Schreurs describe the feud between Pirro Ligorio, who mocked Marliani for his (correct) location of the Roman Forum, calling him "Merlianus," or "Merdianus," as an opposition between Marliani's "strictly philological *Quellenforschung*" (citation of sources) and Ligorio's "creative-interpretative handling of non-textual documentation." Laureys and Schreurs, "Egio, Marliano, Ligorio, and the Forum Romanum," 404.

31. See Philip Joshua Jacks, *The Antiquarian and the Myth of Antiquity: The Origins of Rome in Renaissance Thought / Philip Jacks* (Cambridge: Cambridge University Press, 1993), 175–204.

32. Andrea Fulvio, *Antiquaria urbis* (Rome, 1513), A iv.

33. Andrea Fulvio, "Praefatio" to Pope Clement VII, *Antiquitates urbis Romae* (Rome, 1527), B ii.

34. Ibid.

35. Book I deals with Rome's foundation, Book II the Capitoline, Book III the Palatine, Book IV the Forum and Coelium, V the Aventine, VI the city center, and VII the Tiber.

36. See my bibliography. Albertini was author of *Septem mirabilia orbis et urbis Romae et Florentinae civitatis* (1510); Leto, *De antiquitatibus*

urbis Romae libellus (1510); Fulvio, *Antiquaria Urbis* (1513) and *Antiquitates Urbis*; Ponto, *Rhomitypion* (1524); and Calvo, *Antiquae urbis Romae cum regionibus simulachrum* (1532).

37. Giovanni Bartolomeo Marliani and Ercole Barbarasa, *L'Antichità di Roma di M. Bartholomeo Marliano tradotti in lingua volgare per M. Hercole Barbarasa* (Rome, 1548), ii v.
38. Ibid., ii.
39. Joseph Catin and Luigi Monga, *Voyage aux champs phlégréens (1568) (de l'Antiquité de Pezoles)* (Moncalieri: Centre interuniversitaire de recherche sur le Voyage en Italie, 1997) (hereafter cited as *Catin*).
40. See Normand Doiron, "Les rituels de la tempête en mer," in *L'Art de voyager: Le déplacement à l'époque classique* (Sainte-Foy: Les Presses de l'Université Laval, 1995), 163–75; Friedrich Wolfzettel, "La Renaissance: La naissance d'un discours du voyage," in *Le discours du voyageur: Pour une histoire littéraire du récit de voyage en France, du Moyen Age au XVIIIe siècle* (Paris: Presses universitaires de France, 1996), 35–120.
41. *Catin*, 27.
42. Catin mentions his studies in Paris and Bourges, where he received his degree in law; his travels to Rome and Naples; and having succeeded his father as royal secretary (27–30).
43. *Catin*, 28. The priest Hugon was the confessor of Kings Charles IX and Henri III. He participated at the Council of Trent in 1562.
44. The traditional bow to the authority, present in travel accounts as early as that of Bernard von Breydenbach's *Peregrinatio in terram sanctam* (1486), translated in 1489 by Jean de Hersin as *Le saint voyage et pelerinage de la cité saincte de Hierusalem*, both recognizes and undercuts authority by underlining the traveler's independent, semisacred status. Frank Lestringant describes it as setting up an opposition between the totalizing vision of the cosmographer and the practical experience of the traveler. Lestringant, *L'Atelier du cosmographe: Ou l'image du monde à la Renaissance* (Paris: Albin Michel, 1991), 44.
45. Doiron, *L'Art de voyager*, 163.
46. Monga points this out but does not analyze the consequences. *Catin*, 85, note.
47. François Rabelais, *La quart livre* (Geneva: Droz, 1947), 31–34.
48. The spatial metaphors that populate the language suggest a profound link between human perception of space and discourse. Turler, cited above, had condemned travelers who "vagari, lustrare, *discurrere*" (wander, traverse, roam) without direction. See Georges Matoré, *L'Espace humain: L'expression de l'espace dans la vie, la pensée et l'art contemporains* (Paris: La Colombe, 1962).
49. Benedetto Di Falco, *Descrittione dei luoghi antichi di Napoli e del suo amenissimo distretto* (Napoli: Giovanni Francesco Sugganappo, 1549), (I ii + 3-k ii + 5).
50. Benedetto Croce, "Il primo descrittore di Napoli, Benedetto di Falco," in *Nuove curiosità storiche* (Naples: Riccardo Ricciardi, 1922). An earlier text (apparently held only at the UCLA library) by Francesco Priscianese exists, titled *Descrittione della illustre et generosa città di Napoli e suoi contorni* (Rome: Priscianese, 1544).
51. "Della antichità di Pezzuolo" is the title of the section covering the tour.
52. Di Falco, *Descrittione*, n.p. "A Parthenope," (1).
53. Catin divides them into the following categories: "Historiographi Latini: Plinius secundus, Polibius grecus,

Petrarca, D. Hieronimus, Festus, Eusebius, Suetonius tranquillus, Seb. Munsterus, Plutarchus, Dion Cassius et alïtr(os?), Blondus, Strabo; Itali: Mr Bandolpho Colenuccio, Mr. Benedetto di Falco, Mr. Elisis Medico, Mr. Boccaccio, Poetae: Virgilius, Pontanus, Horatius, Silius Italicus, Martialis, Laurea Tullus," followed by "Le Sr. De fontenailles ès Histoires de Naples" (fol. 1 v.).

54. The use of marginal references is a characteristic of humanist writing in general. I mentioned the extreme example of Vadianus's commented edition of Pomponius Mela's *De situ orbis* (Paris, 1540) in my introduction. An example of the listing of "authores" is Sebastiano Marliani's *Antiqua Romae topographia* (Rome, 1534). Catin lists "Historiographi Latini: Plinius secundus, Polibius grecus, Petrarca, D. Hieronimus, Festus, Eusebius, Suetonius tranquillus, Seb. Munsterus, Plutarchus, Dion Cassius et alïtr(os?), Blondus, Strabo; Itali: Mr Bandolpho Colenuccio, Mr. Benedetto di Falco, Mr. Elisis Medico, Mr. Boccaccio, Poetae: Virgilius, Pontanus, Horatius, Silius Italicus, Martialis, Laurea Tullus," followed by "Le Sr. De fontenailles ès Histoires de Naples." Joseph Catin, "De l'Antiquité de Pezoles," ed. Biblioteca Marciana (1573), fol. 1 v.

55. Catin was a lawyer and secretary to the king in 1573. He filed lawsuits in Tonnerre, May 7, 1571, and December 31, 1583. Archives nationales, "Inventaire de la Collection de Chastellux," *Bulletin de la Société des sciences historiques et naturelles de l'Yonne* 58 (1904): 271/329, 285/343. See also Catin and Monga, introduction to *Catin*, 12–15.

56. Deborah N. Losse, *Sampling the Book: Renaissance Prologues and the French Courtiers* (Lewisburg: Bucknell University Press, 1994), 27.

57. Losse describes the sixteenth-century narrative prologue as a "locus of mediation" that ensures a good reading of the narrative, follows and preempts criticism, establishes a "contract" with the reader, declares the literary genre, explains the work's title, and declares authorial intention. Ibid., 13, 57–77.

58. The other significant aspect that recalls the prayer is the resemblance of Catin's *navigatio* to a *peregrinatio*, or pilgrimage, which its linear format moving *in crescendo* toward the site of the Sibyll's cave.

59. Rather than a language "déposé dans le monde" that "en fait partie à la fois parce que les choses elles-mêmes cachent et manifestent leur énigme," antiquarian discourse seems to me skeptical of all links to the supernatural except those written by proper authorities. This belief in the importance of the source, in turn, frees the use of "fictions poétiques" for play and self-referential display.

60. Mieke Bal, in his description of the functioning of narrative focalization, notes that most typologies of narrative perspective fail to distinguish between those who see and those who speak, noting that "it is possible, both in fiction and in reality, for one person to express the vision of another." Bal, *Narratology*, 143.

61. Four to six meters wide and seven hundred long, the *Crypta neapolitana*, or *grotta vecchia*, dates from the first century BCE. After the Grotta di Seiano in Cuma, it was the longest ancient Roman road tunnel. Following Benedetto Di Falco and others, Catin believes the grotta to be even older than it is, attributing its construction to the Chalcidians of Negroponte (founders of Cuma in the eighth century BCE). Di Falco does mention "Coceo" (L. Cocceius Auctus), the Roman architect credited

with the construction of both tunnels (25, unnumbered [B ii verso]). For Di Falco's *Descrittione*, due to the work's very difficult page numbers (lacking for many pages at a time), I refer to the page number of the PDF file of the work as copied by the Bibliothèque Nationale de France, followed by the page number in the work.
62. Michel Foucault, "La prose du monde," in *Les mots et les choses* (Paris: Gallimard, 1966), 32–40.
63. Joseph Catin, "Tombeau du hault et puissant seigneur, Monseigneur de Clermont, decedé pour l'honneur de Dieu au service du Roy devant la Rochelle ceste année 1573, À Madame de Clermont, sa Vefve" (1573), Biblioteca Marciana, Cod. franc., App. 15 (280), fol. 70–79. Henri Antoine de Clermont, Duke of Tonnerre, was from one of France's oldest families. Charles IX named him peer of France in 1571. The Siege of La Rochelle, following the St. Bartholemew's Day massacre, was the most important event of the fourth religious war.
64. Jacques de Villamont, *Les Voyages du Seigneur de Villamont de l'ordre de Hierusalem, Gentilhomme ordinaire de la chambre du Roy. Divisez en trois livres, comme il se voit dans la page suivante. Derniere edition reveuë, corrigee, et cotee par l'autheur* (Paris: Claude de Montroeil and Jean Richer, 1600), "Preface au Lecteur," (a iii v).
65. See chapter 2, p. 40.
66. Roche-Melon (3,538 m) is 1,500 meters taller than Mont Cenis, which Villamont had crossed on his way to Novalesa and was scaled for the first time in 1358 by Bonifacius Rotarius of Asti, who built the small chapel in which Villamont will pray on arriving at the peak's summit. It is considered the "first Alpine peak to be either attempted or successfully climbed." World Mountain Encyclopedia Peakware, "Roche Melon," http://www.peakware.com/peaks.html?pk=1012.
67. See also *Voyage d'Italie* of 1606, which describes it as an "image de la mort et miroir de nostre chestifvité humaine, où on les enterroit par une fenestre my pourris et exhalants une odeur la plus infecte qui se puisse imaginer" (image of death and mirror of our human insignificance, where they inter them through a window half rotten and emitting the foulest odor one can imagine). *Voyage d'Italie (1606)* (Geneva: Slatkine, 1982), 38–39.
68. The influence of climate on the appearance and character of the various nations is a mainstay of travel literature of the period. Discussed by Pliny (*Natural History*, II, LXXX) as a function of the varying combinations of the four elements within the individual, this theme was developed throughout the Renaissance, most importantly in Jean Bodin's *Methodus ad facilem historiarum cognitionem* (1566), whose influence Olivero notes in Audebert's *Voyage d'Italie*. See Adalberto Olivero, "Le fonti di informazione dell'Audebert," in Nicolas Audebert, *Voyage d'Italie (1574–78)* (British Museum, Ms. Lansdowne 720) (Roma: Lucarini, 1981), I, 70–73.
69. Wes Williams traces this interpretation from Burkhardt, followed by Cassirer, Kristeller, and P. Burke. Other critics (H. Blumenberg, T. Greene) underline Petrarch's "hesitation" between eras. Williams interprets Petrarch's climb as a pilgrimage in which "the most evident sign of pilgrimage [. . .] is the gesture of reader aloud *ad locum.*" Williams, *Pilgrimage and Narrative in the French Renaissance: The Undiscovered Country* (Oxford: Clarendon, 1998), 29–34, 30. Luigi Monga sees Petrarch as apologizing for a guilty pleasure. Monga,

"Travel and Travel Writing: An Historical Overview of Hodoeporics," *Annali d'Italianistica* 14 (1996): 39.
70. What Gérard Genette calls a diegetical or narrative metaphor. Genette, *Figures III* (Paris: Éditions du Seuil, 1972), 48.
71. The king's letters from August 1591 are posted from various places outside Paris: Chaillot, Saint-Denis, and Saint-Antoine-des-Champs. See *Recueil des lettres missives de Henri IV* (Paris: Imprimerie Royale, 1843), p. 55.
72. Merdrignac (1591), Craon (1592), Quimper, and Crozon and Morlaix (1594).

CHAPTER 5

1. Sirmond went to Rome to act as secretary to Claudio Acquaviva, *Preposito generale* of the Jesuit order, and later mentions being involved in affairs of great interest for France. See Luigi Monga, "L'Hodoeporicon de Jacques Sirmond, S.J.," *Humanistica Lovaniensia* 42 (1993): 301–13.
2. Jean-Jacques Bouchard, *Les Confessions, suivies de son Voyage de Paris à Rome en 1630, publiées pour la première fois sur le ms. de l'auteur* (Paris: Liseaux, 1881). Because of the similar titles of many of the *voyages d'Italie*, I will cite the full title only once, using the short title provided in parentheses, generally the author's name, if known.
3. Jean Tarde, *À la rencontre de Galilée: Deux voyages en Italie* (Geneva: Slatkine, 1984) (hereafter cited as *Tarde*).
4. Departing from Paris, he traveled over Mont Cenis in 1589, visiting Turin, Asti, and Genoa before returning to France to Nice, Antibes, Cannes, and Aix-en-Provence. *Voyage de Provence et d'Italie: Ms. fr. 5550, BN Paris* (Geneva: Slatkine, 1994) (hereafter cited as *Provence*).
5. Duval Fontenay-Mareuil, *Voyage faict en Italie par Monsieur le Marquis de Fontenay-Marueil [sic] ambassadeur du Roy près de Sa Saincteté en l'année 1641 ... ensemble la façon d'eslire les Papes, le tout recueilli par le S.r de Vologer Fontenay* (Paris: L. Boulanger, 1643) (hereafter cited as *Fontenay-Mareuil*).
6. Tarde mixes up the order, showing he wrote his journal rapidly at the end of the day.
7. On Jean Tarde's motivations and itinerary, see François Moureau's préface to *Tarde*, 12–27.
8. *Voyage d'Italie (1606)* (Geneva: Slatkine, 1982) (hereafter cited as *1606*). On the importance of the voyage to Naples, see Richard Keatley, "Lo spazio campano dei viaggiatori francesi di fine Cinquecento," in *Viaggio e comunicazione nel Rinascimento*, ed. Luisa Rotondi Secchi Tarugi (Florence: Franco Cesati, 2017), 301–10.
9. *Provence*.
10. Nicolas Audebert, *Voyage d'Italie (1574–78)*. (British Museum, Ms. Lansdowne 720) (Roma: Lucarini, 1981) (hereafter cited as *Audebert*).
11. On the style and political implications of Virey's "fiction auto-biographique," see Anna Bettoni's Introduction to her critical edition. Anna Bettoni, "Introduction," in *Claude Enoch Virey: Vers itineraraires: Allant de France en Italie. 1592; allant de Venise à Rome. 1593* (Paris: Société des Textes Français Modernes, 1999) (hereafter cited as *Virey*).
12. Florisel de Claveson, *Voyage d'Italie (1608–1609)* (Moncalieri, Italy: Centro Interuniversitario di ricerche sul viaggio in Italia, 2001) (hereafter cited as *Claveson*).
13. See Luigi Monga's introduction to Pierre Bergeron, *Voyage en Italie (1603–1612)* (Moncalieri: Centro

Interuniversitario di Ricerche sul Viaggio in Italia, 2005), 31–38.
14. Henri Condé, *Voyage de Monsieur le prince de Condé en Italie depuis son partement du camp de Montpellier, jusques à son retour en sa maison de Mouron, ensembl les remarques des choses veuës en sondit voyage* (Paris, 1634) (hereafter cited as *Condé*).
15. Henri de Rohan, *Voyage du Duc de Rohan faict en l'an 1600: En Italie, Allemaigne, Pays-bas Uni, Angleterre, & Escosse* (Amsterdam: Louis Elzevier, 1646), 1 (hereafter cited as *Rohan*).
16. See Usher, "La France et ses frontières,"in *Errance et cohérence: Essai sur la littérature transfrontalière à la Renaissance* (Paris: Classiques Garnier, 2010), 11–21. See also my chapter 2.
17. Colette Beaune, *Naissance de la nation française* (Paris: Gallimard, 1985); Marcus Keller, *Figurations of France: Literary Nation-Building in Times of Crisis (1550–1650)* (Newark: University of Delaware Press, 2011); Vincent Ilardi, "'Italianità' among Some Italian Intellectuals in the Early Sixteenth Century," *Traditio* 12 (1956).
18. Rosanna Gorris, ed., *Les montagnes de l'esprit: Imaginaire et histoire de la montagne à la Renaissance: Actes du colloque international, Saint Vincent (Vallée d'Aoste), les 22–23 novembre 2002* (Vallée d'Aoste, Italy: Quart, 2005, 2002).
19. Pierre Du Val, *Le voyage et la description d'Italie: Montrant exactement les raretez [et] choses remarquables qui se trouvent es provinces [et] en chaques villes, les distances d'icelles; avec un dénombrement des places [et] champs de batailles qui s'y sont donées; ouvrage dressé pour la commodité des François [et] estrangers* (Paris: Clouzier, 1656), 7 (hereafter cited as *Du Val*).
20. Ibid., 8.
21. Ibid., 9.
22. Ibid., 9–10.
23. Ibid., 12. See also Théodore de Mayerne-Turquet, *Sommaire description de la France, Allemagne, Italie et Espagne, avec la Guide des chemins pour aller et venir par les provinces, et aux villes plus renommées de ces quatre regions* (Cologne: Jacob Stoer, 1618), 74. Du Val lists Mongenèvre as the route most used by the French due to its use for military expeditions. Mont Cenis was by far the most popular route for travelers from Paris to Rome, having been used by Bergeron, Du Gua, Neufville, Sirmond, Audebert, Villamont, and the authors of the *Discours viatiques*, *Provence*, and *1606*. Vinchant and Montaigne passed through Cenis on their return trips. Mongenèvre, taken by Henri de Condé (from Montpellier), Jacques-Auguste de Thou (Foix), Pierre Duval, and the Duc de Bouillon (Grenoble), comes in second. The route passing through Lausanne and Geneva to Vercelli, Novara, and Milan is a distant third.
24. *Audebert*, I, 129.
25. Ibid.
26. *Discours viatiques de Paris à Rome et de Rome à Naples et Sicile (1588–1589)* (Geneva: Slatkine, 1983), 48–49.
27. François Vinchant, *Voyage de François Vinchant en France & en Italie du 16 septembre 1609 au 18 février 1610* (Bruxelles: Société générale d'imprimerie, 1897), 186–87 (hereafter cited as *Vinchant*).
28. Pierre Du Gua, *Récit des choses remarquables qui sont en Italie* (Lyon, 1624), 2 (hereafter cited as *Du Gua*).
29. Jacques de Villamont, *Les Voyages du Seigneur de Villamont* (Paris: Claude de Montroeil and Jean Richer, 1600) (hereafter cited as *Villamont*).
30. *1606*, 39.
31. Ibid.
32. *Audebert*, I, 132.
33. Ibid., I, 125.

34. Banditi live outside the law and are thus excluded from its protection after their names appear on the *bando*.
35. *Discours viatiques*, 48.
36. *Du Val*, 4–5.
37. *Jacobi Sirmondi Hodoeporicum ab urbe Lutetia Romam usque anno MDXC*, vv. 315–16, in Monga, "L'Hodoeporicon de Jacques Sirmond, S.J.," *Humanistica Lovaniensia* 42 (1993): 320.
38. *Audebert*, I, 124.
39. Ibid., I, 121.
40. Ibid., 128.
41. *Discours viatiques*, 49.
42. *Villamont*, 5.
43. *Discours viatiques*, 50.
44. Ibid.
45. A silver coin minted throughout Italy valued as one quarter of a gold scudo.
46. *Audebert*, 137.
47. Carignano was, in effect, the old border between French and Savoy territory. In 1536, Galeotto Pico della Mirandola and Cesare Campofregoso conquered Carignano for the French, using the munitions to restock Turin and occupying Saluzzo, Pinerolo, Chieri, and Carmagnola. In 1544, imperial forces led by Del Vastoretook the town. Michael Mallett and Christine Shaw, *The Italian Wars, 1494–1559* (Harlow: Pearson, 2012), 232–42. A sixteenth-century drawing of Carignano's fortifications from the Turin archives can be seen at Carignano turismo, http://www.carignanoturismo.it/files/fortificazioni.pdf.
48. *Audebert*, I, 138.
49. *Villamont*, 9.
50. *Condé*, 4.
51. *Audebert*, I, 137.
52. "Qui si parla ordinariamente Francese; e paiono tutti molto divoti alla Francia. La lingua popolesca è una lingua la quale non ha quasi che la pronunzia Italiana: il restante sono parole delle nostre" (224). (Here they ordinarily speak French, and they all appear very devoted to France. The language of the people is a language that has almost nothing to do with Italian but the pronunciation, the rest of it is French words) (1036).
53. Audebert notes that this custom symbolized men rising to take the sword in defense of the faith, Du Gua (3) appears to copy this anecdote from Audebert's *Observations*.
54. Most travelers mention the vineyards "à l'Italienne," a practice still used in Campania, as attached to trellises tied to trees in a way that allowed grain, wine, and fruit to be produced on a single plot of land.
55. *Discours viatiques*, 52.
56. *Villamont*, 9.
57. Montaigne, *Journal de Voyage* (Paris: Presses universitaires de France, 1992), 223.
58. *Discours viatiques*, 54.
59. *Villamont*, 10 v.
60. *1606*, 43.
61. *Discours viatiques*, 54.
62. *Condé*, 11–12.
63. *1606*, 43.
64. *Villamont*, 11.
65. *1606*, 44.
66. Ibid., 44–5.
67. *Du Gua*, 3.
68. *Du Val*, 90.
69. Georg Braun and Franz Hogenburg, *Civitates orbis terrarum* (Antwerp: Gallaeus, 1572), 192–3.
70. *Audebert*, II, 235.
71. *Condé*, 13.
72. Pierre Bergeron, *Voyage en Italie (1603–1612)* (Moncalieri: Centro Interuniversitario di Ricerche sul Viaggio in Italia, 2005), 64 (hereafter cited as *Bergeron*).
73. *Audebert*, II, 236.
74. Nicolas Bénard, *Le voyage de Hierusalem et autres lieux de la Terre-Sainte, ensemble son retour par l'Italie, Suisse, Allemagne, Hollande, Flandre*

en la tres-fleurissante et peuplé ville de Paris (Paris: Moreau, 1621), 583 (hereafter cited as *Bénard*).
75. *Rohan*, 39.
76. *Discours viatiques*.
77. *1606*, 44.
78. *Villamont*, 11 v.
79. The Prince of Condé stayed in the palace and his servants in the "Faucon." The author of the *Voyage* of 1606 and François Vinchant stayed in the famous Osteria dei Tre Re, located in the historic Via dei Tre Re, later Via dei Tre Alberghi, a street destroyed in the 1930s to make way for Via Flavio Baracchini. Antonio Calzoni, *32 pagine d'un buongustaio milanese: Per una gara fra le osterie milanesi* (Milan: Alfieri e Lacroix, 1932), 27.
80. *Condé*, 13. The author of the *Discours viatiques* also had the "carraches" (carriages) of the Duke of Terranova, Don Carlos d'Aragona Tagliavia, governor of Milan from 1583 to 1592. *Discours viatiques*, 60.
81. *Claveson*, 305.
82. *Discours viatiques*, 58.
83. There is, in fact, no sign in any of the travelers' accounts of a humanist preference for classical architecture over gothic styles. All the French travelers admire the Cathedral of Milan, perhaps because of its gothic style but more probably because of its size and use of marble.
84. *Bénard*, 584.
85. *1606*, 46–47.
86. *Claveson*, 306.
87. *Bergeron*, 67.
88. *Bénard*, 587.
89. Villamont and Bénard use the same words. *Villamont*, 12; *Bénard*, 587.
90. *Bergeron*, 67.
91. *Bénard*, 587.
92. *Du Val*, 97. Rohan writes that the French had also built the second defensive wall around the castle. *Rohan*, 41–42.
93. Rohan insists he could have entered, had he wanted to, by pretending to be from Lorraine, and François Vinchant claims that "avec la clef de leur langage je pourrois facilement entrer." *Vinchant*, 49.
94. *Discours viatiques*, 57.
95. *Rohan*, 42.
96. The Venetian ducato was the most common currency throughout the sixteenth and early seventeenth century, replacing the fiorino. It weighed 3.44 g of twenty-four-karat gold. Ugo Tucci, "Il Rinascimento. Società ed economia—lavor. La ricchezza. Le coesistenze: Monete e banche nel secolo del ducato d'oro."
97. *Vinchant*, 58.
98. Ibid.
99. Ibid., 57.
100. The Battle of Marignano is one of the most remembered of the wars. The newly crowned François I entered Italy at the head of fifty thousand troops, recapturing Milan and defeating the Swiss at Marignano. Mallet and Shaw, *Italian Wars*, 126–32.
101. *Vinchant*, 60.
102. Ibid.
103. The statue of Crostolo was said to represent the Gaulish king. J. R. McCulloch, *A Dictionary, Geographical, Statistical and Historical of the Various Countries, Places and Principal Natural Objects in the World. Illustrated with Maps*, 2 vols., vol. 2 (London: Longman, Brown, Green and Longmans, 1842), 573.
104. *Vinchant*, 60.
105. *Bénard*, 558.
106. *Provence*, 100.
107. *Vinchant*, 66.
108. *Audebert*, I, 163.
109. French travelers identify the Flemish sculptor as Jean de Boulogne. Vinchant considers him French, from Picardy.
110. *Claveson*, 279–80.
111. *Bergeron*, 80.
112. *Claveson*, 279.

113. Claude Enoch Virey, *Vers itinéraires: Allant de France en Italie. 1592; allant de Venise à Rome* (Paris: Société des Textes Français Modernes, 1999), 66–67, vv. 595–98.
114. Rebuilt as a laboratory for ceramics and other artistic objects from 1570 to 1574, the Casino di San Marco was the new Grand Duke Francesco de' Medici's preferred pastime. Audebert visited in 1576.
115. *Audebert*, I, 249.
116. Ibid., I, 259. The duke's laboratory produced many of these objects. One of the more famous ones, by Cristofano Gaffuri, representing the harbor of Livorno, was completed in 1604.
117. *Vinchant*, 74.
118. *Villamont*, 17.
119. *1606*, 58.
120. Ibid.
121. 150 vertical meters over 13 kilometers.
122. *Virey*, II, vv. 608–9, p. 67.
123. 514 meters vertical over a distance of only 17 kilometers.
124. *Vinchant*, 72.
125. *Discours viatiques*, 72–73.
126. 426 meters over 12 kilometers.
127. Jacques-Auguste de Thou, *Memoires de la vie de Jacques-Auguste de Thou, conseiller d'état et président à mortier au parlement de Paris* (Rotterdam: Reinier Leers, 1711), 22.
128. *Vinchant*, 74.
129. *Audebert*, I, 246.
130. Ibid.
131. Ibid., I, 247.
132. François de Belleforest and Sebastien Münster, *La cosmographie universelle de tout le monde* (Paris: Michel Sonnius, 1575), 723 v.
133. Claveson's shows the degree to which the Medici domination had brought the city back to its former prosperity, whose surrounding countryside, in 1550, is described by Leandro Alberti as abandoned and destroyed after the devastating invasion by Charles V in 1529. Alberti writes, "Erano intorno a questa Città gia alquanti belli Borghi, liquali se fossero stati congiunti insieme, ne sarebbe risultato una Città forse non minore di Fiorenza, liquali tutti rovinati furono l'anno mille cinquecento nove" (There were as many towns around this city that, if counted together, would have made up a city as large as Florence, which were all destroyed in 1509). Leandro Alberti, *Descrittione di Tutta Italia di F. Leandro Alberti Bolognese, Nella quale si contiene il Sito di essa, l'origine, et le signorie delle città, e delle castella, co i nomi antichi et Moderni, i Costumi de Popoli, le Condicioni de Paesi: Et piu gli huomini famosi che l'hanno illustrata, i monti, i laghi, i fiumi, le fontane, i bagni, le minere, con tutte l'Opre maraviglose dalla Natura prodotte* (Bologna: Anselmo Giaccarelli, 1550), 41.
134. *1606*, 59.
135. Gilles Deleuze and Félix Guattari, "Treatise on Nomadology" and "The Smooth and the Striated," in *A Thousand Plateaus, Capitalism and Schizophrenia*, trans. Brian Massumi (Minneapolis: University of Minnesota Press, 1987), 351–423, 74–500.
136. *Condé*, 173.
137. *Fontenay-Mareuil*, 96.
138. *Audebert*, I, 249.
139. Francesco Bocchi, *Le Bellezze della città di Fiorenza dove è pieno di pittura, di scultura* (Florence, 1591).
140. *Claveson*, 84.
141. Saul Levine, "The Location of Michelangelo's David: The Meeting of January 25, 1504," *Art Bulletin* 56, no. 1 (1974); J. Huston McCulloch, "*David*: A New Perspective," http://www.econ.ohio-state.edu/jhm/arch/david/David.htm.
142. *Vinchant*, 65. Villamont (1595) writes, "Hercules qui massacre un

Roy à ses pieds" (19v); Bergeron, "Un Hercules tuant Anthée" (Hercules killing a king at his feet) (256).
143. *Audebert*, I, 256.
144. *Condé*, 174.
145. *1606*, 59.
146. Montaigne, *Journal*, 82.
147. *Audebert*, I, 250.
148. *Du Val*, 324.
149. *Claveson*, 81.
150. *Audebert*, I, 249.
151. "Par lequel regardant en bas, droit au milieu du choeur, où pour lors psalmodioint les chanoines, ne pouvions juger d'eux ce que ce pouvoit estre, bien quils fussent parés de leurs surplis blancs" (by which, looking down, straight into the choir, where at that time certain canons were singing, we could not judge what they were, even though they were wearing their white habits). *Claveson*, 81.

CHAPTER 6

1. From Rovereto to Rome, the troop stayed extra days in Padua (2 nights), Venice (7), Ferrara (2), Bologna (3), Florence (2), and Siena (2).
2. See Olivier Pot, "Lieux, espaces et géographie dans le *Journal de voyage*," *Montaigne Studies* 15 (2003): 63–104.
3. The "ora italica" of twenty-four hours began with midnight at sunset, making Montaigne's arrival, in August, four hours prior to sunset. For a description of the Italian clock, see TAGES, "Archeostronomia: Medioevo e Rinascimento," http://www.tages.eu/medioevo-e-rinascimento/.
4. Schneikert, *Montaigne dans le labyrynthe: De l'imaginare du Journal de voyage à l'écriture des Essais* (Paris: Champion, 2006), 419.
5. Eric MacPhail, *The Voyage to Rome in French Renaissance Literature* (Stanford: Stanford French and Italian Studies, 1990).
6. On Montaigne's conflicted "vision" of Rome, see Margaret M. McGowan, "Contradictory Impulses in Montaigne's Vision of Rome," *Renaissance Studies: Journal of the Society for Renaissance Studies* 4, no. 4 (1990); Margaret McGowan, *The Vision of Rome in Late Renaissance France* (New Haven: Yale University Press, 2000), 228–50.
7. Tom Conley depicts the *Essais'* "Political Geography of the Self" as "cosmographic in its universal appeal and its relation to a long span of time, but quasi-Ortelian in an exact representation of local spaces and history." Conley, *The Self-Made Map: Cartographic Writing in Early Modern France* (Minneapolis: University of Minnesota Press, 1996), 250.
8. The spatial layout of Rome thus provokes, in its extension, temporal and spatial depth, or what Lawrence Kritzman calls Montaigne's "desire to see and to imagine the self from a variety of vantage points." Kritzman, *The Fabulous Imagination: On Montaigne's Essays* (New York: Columbia University Press, 2009), 2. For Olivier Pot, Montaigne seeks identity in difference in a way that imitates a baroque theatricality in its multiplicity. Pot, *L'inquiétante étrangeté. Montaigne: La pierre, le cannibale, la mélancolie* (Paris: Champion, 1993), 126–39. See also Elizabeth Hodges, *Urban Poetics in the French Renaissance* (Aldershot: Ashgate, 2008), 102–30.
9. Pompeo Ugonio, *Historia Delle Stationi di Roma: Che si celebrano la Quadragesima; Dove Oltre Le Vite De Santi Alle Chiese de quali È Statione, si tratta delle Origini, Fondationi, Siti . . . die esse Chiese, antiche & moderne* (Roma: Bonfadino, 1588); Church Catholic, Manlio

Sodi, and Achille M. Triacca, *Missale Romanum: Editio princeps (1570)* (Città del Vaticano: Libreria editrice vaticana, 1998).
10. Most travelers depict this arrival with emotion and attempt to describe Rome's grandeur before entering the city. "Qui est celuy qui ne tressaillit de joye et ne rende graces à Dieu, se voyant à chef d'un grand voyage arrivé au desiré lieu où il vouloit parvenir?" (Who does not tremble with joy at the end of a long journey when they arrive in the desired place they so wanted to go?). *Voyage d'Italie (1606)* (Geneva: Slatkine, 1982) (hereafter cited as *1606*), 72.
11. Nicolas Audebert, *Voyage d'Italie (1574–78)*. (British Museum, Ms. Lansdowne 720) (Roma: Lucarini, 1981) (hereafter cited as *Audebert*), I, 264–81. The Campagna Romana was in fact relatively uninhabited, having been converted to a system of large-scale farms known as *casali* during the late Middle Ages. See Sandro Carocci and Marco Vendittelli, *L'origine della Campagna Romana: Casali, castelli e villaggi nel XII e XIII secolo* (Roma: Società romana di storia patria, 2004).
12. Montaigne's secretary describes their negotiation of this difficult road: "Nous reprismes nostre chemin lendemain bon matin le long d'une fondriere pierreuse, où nous passames et repassames cent fois un torrent qui coule tou le long" (88) (The next morning early we resumed our trip along a very stony bottom, where we crossed and recrossed a hundred times a torrent which runs all the length of it [934]). Audebert mentions crossing the Paglia "30 or 35 times." *Audebert*, I, 269.
13. The current altitudes of the final stretch leading to Rome are Montefiascone (566 m), Viterbo (330), Vico (517), Ronciglione (444), Monterosi (250), Baccano (241), La Storta (159), and Rome (8).
14. Jacques de Villamont, *Les Voyages du Seigneur de Villamont* (Paris: Claude de Montroeil and Jean Richer, 1600), 22r–v.
15. Florisel de Claveson, *Voyage d'Italie (1608–1609)* (Moncalieri, Italy: Centro Interuniversitario di ricerche sul viaggio in Italia, 2001), 93. See Livy, Book 5.
16. Claveson (*Voyage d'Italie*, 94–95) and Claude Énoch Virey (*Vers itinéraires: Allant de France en Italie. 1592; allant de Venise à Rome* [Paris: Société des Textes Français Modernes, 1999], I, vv. 1906–9) both cite this event.
17. Pierre Bergeron, *Voyage en Italie (1603–1612)* (Moncalieri: Centro Interuniversitario di Ricerche sul Viaggio in Italia, 2005), 110 (hereafter cited as *Bergeron*).
18. Duval Fontenay-Mareuil, *Voyage faict en Italie* (Paris: L. Boulanger, 1643), 122 (hereafter cited as *Fontenay-Mareuil*).
19. On the importance of Brennus to French national identity in the Renaissance, see Colette Beaune, *Naissance de la nation française* (Paris: Gallimard, 1985), 30–34.
20. *Bergeron*, 111.
21. Ibid., 93.
22. Henri de Rohan, *Voyage du Duc de Rohan faict en l'an 1600: En Italie, Allemaigne, Pays-bas Uni, Angleterre, & Escosse* (Amsterdam: Louis Elzevier, 1646), 57.
23. *Fontenay-Mareuil*, 120.
24. Montaigne uses this expression seven times in the *Essais*, five of which are related to the Italian Wars. "The Montaigne Project," http://www.lib.uchicago.edu/efts/ARTFL/projects/montaigne/; Richard Keatley, "'Du temps de nos peres': The Italian Wars in the Journal de Voyage," *Montaigne Studies: An Interdisciplinary Forum*.

Montaigne et ses historiens 29 (2017): 47–58.
25. Frame translates the Louis Lautrey edition of 1906, replacing "de celle-là" with "de Ciaia." Frame, *Montaigne: A Biography* (New York: Harcourt, Brace and World, 1965).
26. The Tolomei and Piccolomini were notably Guelph. The Cerretani trace their family to Charlemagne. Luca Fusai, *Mille anni di storia attraverso le vicende della famiglia Cerretani Bandinelli Paparoni* (Pisa: ETS, 2010). By the sixteenth century, the distinction of Guelphs as supporters of the empire and Ghibellines as supporters of the papacy had morphed into a complex political geography in which Guelphs (the Pepoli of Bologna, the people of Florence and the city of Siena) generally supported the French cause and Ghibellines (the Malvezzi of Bologna and Medici in Florence) supported the Spanish cause. See *Guelfi e ghibellini nell'Italia del Rinascimento* (Roma: Viella, 2005).
27. "La Cacciata della guardia spagnola da Siena, d'incerto autore, 1552," in *Archivio storico italiano*, tom. 2 (1842); Nerina Bartoli, "Le Congiure di Siena e la cacciata degli Spagnoli nel 1552," *Bollettino senese di storia patria* I (1930); Roberto Cantagalli, *La Guerra di Siena (1552–1559)* (Siena: Accademia Senese degli Intronati, 1962).
28. The same situation could be said of Perugia, where Pope Paul III built the Rocca Paolina on top of the city after the so-called Guerra del Sale. See Simon Pepper and Nicholas Adams, *Firearms and Fortifications: Military Architecture and Siege Warfare in Sixteenth-Century Siena* (Chicago: University of Chicago Press, 1986).
29. Montaigne, *Les Essais* (Paris: Quadrige/PUF, 1992), I, 42, 265; Frame, *Montaigne*, 194.
30. Pierre Villey misstates the date of the maréchal de Brissac, Charles I de Cossé, who took Casale Monferrato in 1555, and confuses him with his brother, Artus de Cossé-Brissac, "grand panetier de France." This second figure was still alive in 1580, while his brother was one of France's most important war heroes. Blaise de Monluc, whose son Montaigne met in Bologna and Rome, was inducted into the Order of Saint Michael because of his heroic actions. See Michael Mallett and Christine Shaw, *The Italian Wars, 1494–1559* (Harlow: Pearson, 2012), 269–71.
31. Montaigne, *Essais*, I, 26, 153; Frame, *Montaigne*, 112.
32. Donald Frame translates "sur les vingt heures" (90) as "at eight in the evening." Frame, *The Complete Works of Montaigne: Essays, Travel Journal, Letters* (Stanford: Stanford University Press, 1958). The "ora italica" of twenty-four hours began with midnight at sunset, making Montaigne's arrival, in August, four hours prior to sunset. For a description of the Italian clock, see TAGES, "Archeostronomia: Medioevo e Rinascimento."
33. Antonio Tempesta, *Roma al tempo di Clemente VIII la pianta di Roma* (Vatican City: Biblioteca Apostolica Vaticana, 1932), Map.
34. Antoine Du Pérac Lafréry, *Roma prima di Sisto V: La pianta di Roma, Du Pérac-Lafréry del 1577 riprodotta dall'esemplare esistente nel museo britannico* (1908).
35. Anna Esposito, "Roma e il Tevere," in *Le calamità ambientali nel tardo Medioevo europeo: Realtà, percezioni, reazioni* (Florence: Firenze University Press, 2008).
36. See Jessica Maier's excellent chapter on Bufalini's drawing of the city and its imaginative impact on the viewer. Maier, *Rome Measured and Imagined:*

Early Modern Maps of the Eternal City (Chicago: Chicago University Press, 2015).

37. Mariano Armellini, *Le chiese di Roma dal secolo IV al XIX* (Vatican City: Tipografia Vaticana, 1891), 332–33.

38. "Vis a vis, Contrà, Adversum, Ex adverso, In aspectu, E regione, Ex adversum, Adversus, In conspectu. *Il est vis a vis d'orient*, Spectat orientem." Estienne, *Dictionnaire Francoislatin, contenant les motz et manieres de parler Francois, tournez en Latin* (Paris: Robert Estienne, 1539), 518.

39. On the general development of Rome during this period, see Giorgio Simoncini, *Roma: Le trasformazioni urbane nel Cinquecento: II: Dalla città al territorio* (Florence: Olschki, 2008).

40. The church had owned pieces of land around it, and at least as late as the thirteenth century, it possessed a college of canonical priests (penelope.uchicago.edu through Wikipedia under S. L. della Tinta). The earliest documents speak of a pig's sty and vineyard "in loco qui dicitur carcer" (Tor di Nona).

41. Despite its presentation as a 3D portrait of the city, Du Pérac does make certain rhetorical or technical distortions. The Palazzo Aragona, a three- or four-story structure, is represented with two levels of windows, making it possible that the one-story buildings surrounding it are also larger.

42. Virginio Prinzivalli, *Torquato Tasso a Roma* (Rome: Libreria Desclée Lefebvre E C, 1895), 45–46.

43. Ibid., 40.

44. See Philippe Desan, *Montaigne: Une biographie politique* (Paris: Odile Jacob, 2014).

45. On the economic and social structure of Rome and the foreign population in its various rioni in the time of Montaigne, see Jean Delumeau, *Vie économique et sociale de Rome dans la seconde moitié du XVIe siècle* (Paris: De Boccard, 1957), 315–20.

46. Nicolas de Pellevé, Cardinal of Sens, bishop of the church of Santi Giovanni e Paolo.

47. Pirro Ligorio, *Antiquae urbis imago accuratissimae ex vetusteis monumenteis* (Venice: Michele Tramezzino, 1561). Emory University has placed their copy online at http://disc.library.emory.edu/viewsofrome/about-us/.

48. Lucio Mauro and Ulisse Aldrovandi, *Le antichità de la città di Roma, brevissimamente raccolte da chiunque ne ha scritto, ò antico ò moderno; per Lucio Mauro, che ha voluto particularmente tutti questi luoghi vedere: Onde ha corretti di molti errori, che ne gli altri scrittori di queste antichità si leggono. Et insieme ancho, Di tutte le statue antiche, che per tutta Roma in diversi luoghi, e case particulari si veggono, raccolte e descritte, per M. Ulisse Aldroandi, opera non fatta piu mia da scrittore alcuno* (Venice: Giordano Ziletti, 1558).

49. Lucio Fauno, *Delle antichità della città di Roma* (Venice: Michele Tramezzino, 1548). See Gennaro Tallini, *"Roma trenta miglia." Il viaggio in Italia di Michel de Montaigne e Le antichità di Roma di Lucio Mauro* (in press).

50. See Leandro Alberti, *Descrittione di Tutta Italia di F. Leandro Alberti Bolognese, Nella quale si contiene il Sito di essa, l'origine, et le signorie delle città, e delle castella, co i nomi antichi et Moderni, i Costumi de Popoli, le Condicioni de Paesi: Et piu gli huomini famosi che l'hanno illustrata, i monti, i laghi, i fiumi, le fontane, i bagni, le*

minere, con tutte l'Opre maraviglose dalla Natura prodotte (Bologna: Anselmo Giaccarelli, 1550).
51. These included Marliani's *Topographia*, translated in 1548 by Ercole Barbarasa; Andrea Fulvio's *Antiquitates Urbis*, translated in 1543 by Paolo Rossi; and Flavio Biondo, translated in 1542 by Lucio Fauno (Giovanni Tarcagnota).
52. Tallini, *"Roma trenta miglia."*
53. Tallini remarks that this fact is original to Montaigne, appearing in none of the Roman guidebooks. Tallini, *"Roma trenta miglia."*
54. Mauro and Aldrovandi, *Antichità di Roma*, 6–7.
55. See also MacPhail, *Voyage to Rome*, 174–78.
56. Montaigne's signed copy of Lucio Mauro's guide is, in fact, devoid of even the slightest annotation or sign of study. "MONLOE: Montaigne à l'oeuvre," https://montaigne.univ-tours.fr/centaine-de-livres/.
57. "Chez moy, je me destourne un peu plus souvent à ma librairie, d'où tout d'une main je commande à mon mesnage. Je suis sur l'entrée et vois soubs moy mon jardin, ma basse court, ma court, et dans la pluspart des membres de ma maison. Là, je feuillette à cette heure un livre, à cette heure un autre, sans ordre et sans dessein, à pieces descousues; tantost je resve, tantost j'enregistre et dicte, en me promenant, mes songes que voicy." Montaigne, *Essais*, III, 3, 828. See my first chapter.
58. The secretary makes entries on December 2, 25, 29, 31; January 3, 11, 14, 26, 28; and February 7, 8, 12, for a total of 12 entries in 83 days, or one entry every 6.92 days. Not counting his absence December 2–25, his entries total 11 in 50 days, or 1 entry every 4.54 days. Montaigne writes on February 16, March 1, 6, 13, (14), 15, 16, 17, 18, 19, 20, 22, 23, 25, 29, 31 and April 2 for a total of 17 entries in 45 days, or 1 entry 2.65 days.
59. The so-called Stational Masses were, as they still are today, a religious practice particular to Rome that centered on the period of Lent and brought the pilgrim, through a series of processions and Masses, to churches all over the city. The practice dated from the first centuries of Christianity in Rome, when the persecuted faithful would hold Mass in a different household each day. The location of these "stationes" eventually became fixed on certain churches and was well established in the Middle Ages and codified by the Council of Trent, which published the schedule of masses in the *Missale Romanum* of 1570. I thank Monsignor Renzo Marzorati, Canonico Bibliotecario of the Milan Cathedral, and Monsignor Claudio Antonio Fontana, Canonico Maestro delle Cerimonie of Milan Cathedral, for their provision of the official list taken from the *Missale Romanum* of 1570.
60. The saint refused to worship the pagan gods, "rispondendo [. . .] che i Dei delle genti eran Demonii" (answering that the gods of the people were demons). Ibid., K.
61. Ibid., K 4.
62. "Statione Vigesimaseconda, Chiesa di San Sisto in Piscina," ibid., 167 v–72.
63. "Statione XXXIX, Sabbato doppo la quinta Domenica di Quadragesima, à San Giovanni à porta Latina," ibid., 292 v–96 v.
64. Ibid., 296 v.
65. Ibid., 316 v.

CONCLUSIONS

1. Foucault, "Des espaces autres (1967), Hétérotopies," *Architecture,*

Mouvement, Continuité 5 (October 1984): 47.
2. Conley, *The Self-Made Map: Cartographic Writing in Early Modern France* (Minneapolis: University of Minnesota Press, 1996), 7.
3. Du Val, *Le voyage et la description d'Italie* (Paris: Clouzier, 1656), unnumbered.

BIBLIOGRAPHY

Abrougui, Olfa. *Du Bellay et la poésie de la Ville: Rome n'est plus Rome*. Paris: L'Harmattan, 2013.

Abulafia, David. *The Western Mediterranean Kingdoms, 1200–1500: The Struggle for Dominion*. London: Longman, 1997.

Alberti, Leandro. *Descrittione di Tutta Italia di F. Leandro Alberti Bolognese, Nella quale si contiene il Sito di essa, l'origine, et le signorie delle città, e delle castella, co i nomi antichi et Moderni, i Costumi de Popoli, le Condicioni de Paesi: Et piu gli huomini famosi che l'hanno illustrata, i monti, i laghi, i fiumi, le fontane, i bagni, le minere, con tutte l'Opre maraviglose dalla Natura prodotte*. Bologna: Anselmo Giaccarelli, 1550.

Alberti, Leon Battista. *Descriptio urbis Romae*. Geneva: Droz, 2000.

Anquez, Léonce. *Histoire des assemblées politiques des Réformés de France (1573–1622)*. Paris: Auguste Durand, 1859.

Archives nationales. "Inventaire de la Collection de Chastellux." *Bulletin de la Société des sciences historiques et naturelles de l'Yonne* 58 (1904).

Armellini, Mariano. *Le chiese di Roma dal secolo IV al XIX*. Vatican City: Tipografia Vaticana, 1891.

Armstrong, E. *The French Wars of Religion: Their Political Aspects*. New York: Russell and Russell, 1971 (1892).

Audebert, Nicolas. *Voyage d'Italie (1574–78)*. British Museum, MS Lansdowne 720. Rome: Lucarini, 1981.

Bal, Mieke. *Narratology, Introduction to the Theory of Narrative*. 2nd ed. Toronto: University of Toronto Press, 1997.

Balsamo, Jean. *Les rencontres des muses: Italianisme et anti-italianisme dans les lettres françaises de la fin du XVIe siècle* (in French). Geneva: Editions Slatkine, 1992.

———. "Le Voyage d'Italie et la formation des élites françaises." *Renaissance and Reformation / Renaissance et Réforme* 27, no. 2 (2003): 9–21.

Bartoli, Nerina. "Le Congiure di Siena e la cacciata degli Spagnoli nel 1552." *Bollettino senese di storia patria* 1 (1930): 361–421, 47–88.

Beaune, Colette. *Naissance de la nation française*. Paris: Gallimard, 1985.

Beik, William. *A Social and Cultural History of Early Modern France* (in English). Cambridge: Cambridge University Press, 2009.

Belleforest, François de, and Sebastien Münster. *La cosmographie universelle de tout le monde*. Paris: Michel Sonnius, 1575.

Bénard, Nicolas. *Le voyage de Hierusalem et autres lieux de la Terre-Sainte, ensemble son retour par l'Italie, Suisse, Allemagne, Hollande, Flandre en la tres-fleurissante et peuplé ville de Paris*. Paris: Moreau, 1621.

Benveniste, Emile. *Problèmes de linguistique générale*. Bibliothèque des sciences humaines. Paris: Gallimard, 1966–74, 1966.

Bergeron, Pierre. *Voyage en Italie (1603–1612)*. Moncalieri: Centro Interuniversitario di ricerche sul viaggio in Italia, 2005.

Bettoni, Anna. "Introduction." In *Claude Enoch Virey: Vers itineraraires: Allant de France en Italie. 1592; allant de*

Venise à Rome. 1593, 1–161. Paris: Société des Textes Français Modernes, 1999.

Bhabha, Homi K. *The Location of Culture*. London: Routledge, 1994.

Biancardi, Silvio. *La Chimera di Carlo VIII (1492–1495)*. Novara: Interlinea, 2009.

Bideaux, Michel. "La description dans le *Journal de voyage* de Montaigne." In *Études seiziémistes offerts à M. le Professeur V.-L. Saulnier par plusieurs de ses anciens doctorants*, 405–22. Geneva: Droz, 1980.

Bizer, Marc. *Les lettres romaines de Du Bellay*. Montreal: Les Presses de l'Université de Montréal, 2001.

———. "'Qui a païs n'a que faire de patrie': Joachim Du Bellay's Resistance to a French Identity." *Romanic Review* 91, no. 4 (2000): 375–95.

Blum, Claude. "Montaigne, écrivain du voyage: Notes sur l'imaginaire du voyage à la Renaissance." In *Autour du Journal de voyage de Montaigne, 1580–1980*, edited by François Moureau and René Bernoulli, 3–11. Geneva: Slatkine, 1982.

Bocchi, Francesco. *Le Bellezze della città di Fiorenza dove è pieno di pittura, di scultura*. Florence, 1591.

Boiardo, Matteo Maria. *Orlando innamorato*. Turin: Einaudi, 1974.

Bordo, Susan. *The Flight to Objectivity: Essays on Cartesianism and Culture*. Albany: State University of New York Press, 1987.

Bouchard, Jean-Jacques. *Les Confessions, suivies de son Voyage de Paris à Rome en 1630, publiées pour la première fois sur le ms. de l'auteur*. Paris: Liseaux, 1881.

Braun, Georg, and Franz Hogenburg. *Civitates orbis terrarum*. Antwerp: Gallaeus, 1572.

Broc, Numa. *La geografia del Rinascimento*. Ferrara: Panini, 1986.

Brown, Cynthia. "Books in Performance: The Parisian Entry (1504) and Funeral of Anne of Brittany." *Yale French Studies, No. 110: Meaning and Its Objects Material Culture in Medieval and Renaissance France* 110 (2006): 75–91.

———. "Du manuscrit à l'imprimé en France: Le cas des Grands Rhétoriqueurs." In *Les Grands Rhétoriqueurs: Actes du Ve Colloque International sur le Moyen Français. Milan, 6–8 mai 1985*. Vol. 1, 103–23. Milan: Pubblicazioni della Università Cattolica del Sacro Cuore, 1985.

———. "The Evolution of André de la Vigne's *La Ressource de la Chrestienté*: From the Manuscript Tradition to the Vergier d'Honneur Editions." *Bibliothèque d'Humanisme et Renaissance* 45, no. 1 (1983): 115–25.

———. "Introduction." In *La Ressource de la Chrestienté*, 1–106. Montreal: CERES, 1989.

Brush, Craig B. "La composition de la première partie du *Journal de voyage* de Michel de Montaigne." *Revue d'Histoire Littéraire de la France* 71 (1971): 369–84.

———. "The Secretary, Again." *Montaigne Studies: An Interdisciplinary Forum* 5, nos. 1, 2 (1993): 113–38.

Bufalini, Leonardo, Franz Ehrle, vaticana Biblioteca apostolica, and Medesima Biblioteca. *Roma al tempo di Giulio III: La pianta di Roma di Leonardo Bufalini del 1551: Riprodotta dall'esemplare esistence nella Biblioteca vaticana* (in Italian). Vatican City: Biblioteca Apostolica Vaticana, 1986.

Cabo Aseguinolaza, Fernando. "The Spatial Turn in Literary Historiography." *CLCWeb: Comparative Literature & Culture: A WWWeb Journal* 13, no. 5 (2011): 1–9.

Calder, Ruth. "Montaigne as Satirist." *Sixteenth Century Journal* 17, no. 2 (1986): 225–35.

Calzoni, Antonio. *32 pagine d'un buongustaio milanese: Per una gara fra le osterie milanesi*. Milan: Alfieri e Lacroix, 1932.

Cantagalli, Roberto. *La Guerra di Siena (1552–1559)*. Siena: Accademia Senese degli Intronati, 1962.

Carignano turismo. "Le fortificazioni di Carignano." http://www.carignano turismo.it/files/fortificazioni.pdf.

Carocci, Sandro, and Marco Vendittelli. *L'origine della Campagna Romana: Casali, castelli e villaggi nel XII e XIII secolo* (in Italian). Rome: Società romana di storia patria, 2004.

Carter, Erica, James Donald, and Judith Squires. *Space and Place: Theories of Identity and Location*. London: Lawrence & Wishart, 1993.

Catasto Alessandrino. State Archive of Rome. 1666. http://www.cflr .beniculturali.it/Alessandrino/ales sandrino_intro.html.

Catholic Church, Manlio Sodi, and Achille M. Triacca. *Missale Romanum: Editio princeps (1570)* (in Italian and Latin). Vatican City: Libreria editrice vaticana, 1998.

Catin, Joseph. "De l'Antiquité de Pezoles." Biblioteca Marciana, 1573.

———. "Tombeau du hault et puissant seigneur, Monseigneur de Clermont, decedé pour l'honneur de Dieu au service du Roy devant la Rochelle ceste année 1573, À Madame de Clermont, sa Vefve," fol. 70–79, 1573.

Catin, Joseph, and Luigi Monga. *Voyage aux champs phlégréens (1568) (de l'Antiquité de Pezoles)* (in Italian). Moncalieri: Centre interuniversitaire de recherche sur le Voyage en Italie, 1997.

Cavallini, Concetta. *L'italianisme de Montaigne*. Paris: Schena/Presses de l'Université de Paris–Sorbonne, 2003.

Cavallo, Jo Ann. "*L'Orlando innamorato*: Un romanzo per la corte ferrarese." In *Boiardo*, edited by Silvano Vinceti, 15–29. Rome: Armando, 2003.

Cave, Terence. *The Cornucopian Text: Problems of Writing in the French Renaissance* (in English). Oxford: Clarendon, 1979.

Certeau, Michel de. *The Practices of Everyday Life*. Berkeley: University of California Press, 1984.

Chantrel, Laure. "Les Notions de richesse et de travail dans la pensée économique française de la seconde moitié du XVIe et au début du XVII siècle." *Journal of Medieval and Renaissance Studies* 25, no. 1 (1995): 129–58.

Claveson, Florisel de. *Voyage d'Italie (1608–1609)*. Moncalieri, Italy: Centro Interuniversitario di ricerche sul viaggio in Italia, 2001.

Cocula, Anne-Marie, and Alain Legros. *Montaigne aux champs*. Bordeaux: Éditions Sud Ouest, 2011.

Commynes, Philippe de. *Mémoires*. Geneva: Droz, 2007.

Condé, Henri. *Voyage de Monsieur le prince de Condé en Italie depuis son partement du camp de Montpellier, jusques à son retour en sa maison de Mouron, ensembl les remarques des choses veuës en sondit voyage* (in French). Paris, 1634.

Conley, Tom. *The Self-Made Map: Cartographic Writing in Early Modern France*. Minneapolis: University of Minnesota Press, 1996.

Cooper, Richard. "Rabelais and the Topographia Antiquae Romae of Marliani." *Etudes Rabelaisiennes* 14 (1977): 71–87.

———. "Triumphal Entries under Henri II." In *Court Festivals of the European Renaissance: Art, Politics and Performance*, 51–75. Aldershot: Ashgate, 2004.

Cosgrove, Denis. *Social Formation and Symbolic Landscape*. Totowa, NJ: Barnes and Noble Books, 1984.

Cottrell, Robert D. *Sexuality/Textuality: A Study of the Fabric of Montaigne's Essais* (in English). Columbus: Ohio State University Press, 1981.

Croce, Benedetto. "Il primo descrittore di Napoli, Benedetto di Falco." In *Nuove curiosità storiche*, 1–20. Naples: Riccardo Ricciardi, 1922.

Dahlem, Andreas. "The Wittelsbach Court in Munich: History and Authority in the Visual Arts (1460–1508)." PhD diss., University of Glasgow, Faculty of Arts, 2009.

Deleuze, Gilles, and Félix Guattari. *A Thousand Plateaus, Capitalism and Schizophrenia*. Translated by Brian Massumi. Minneapolis: University of Minnesota Press, 1987.

Delumeau, Jean. *Vie économique et sociale de Rome dans la seconde moitié du XVIe siècle* (in Italian). Paris: De Boccard, 1957.

Département de Maine-et-Loire. *Inventaire sommaire des archives départementales antérieures à 1790*. Angers, n.d.

Desan, Philippe. *Les commerces de Montaigne: Le discours Èconomique des Essais* (in French). Paris: Libr. A.-G. Nizet, 1992.

——. "De la poésie de circonstance à la satire: Du Bellay et l'engagement poétique." In *Du Bellay*, edited by Georges Cesbron, 421–38. Angers: P de l'Univ. d'Angers, 1990.

——. *Montaigne: Une biographie politique*. Paris: Odile Jacob, 2014.

——. "The Public Life of Montaigne." In *The Oxford Handbook of Montaigne*, 117–37. Oxford: Oxford University Press, 2016.

——. "Work in the Renaissance." *Journal of Medieval and Renaissance Studies* 25, no. 1 (1995): 1–15.

Dickinson, G. *Du Bellay in Rome*. Leiden: Brill, 1960.

"Dictionnaire du Moyen Français (1330–1500)." Analyse et traitement informatique de la langue française. http://www.atilf.fr.dmf.

Di Falco, Benedetto. *Descrittione dei luoghi antichi di Napoli e del suo amenissimo distretto*. Napoli: Giovanni Francesco Sugganappo, 1549.

Discours viatiques de Paris à Rome et de Rome à Naples et Sicile (1588–1589) (in French). Geneva: Slatkine, 1983.

Doiron, Normand. *L'Art de voyager: Le déplacement à l'époque classique*. Sainte-Foy: Les Presses de l'Université Laval, 1995.

——. "L'Art de voyager. Pour une définition du récit de voyage à l'époque classique." *Poétique* 73 (1988): 83–108.

Du Bellay, Joachim. *Les Regrets et autres œuvres poëtiques suivis des Antiquitez de Rome, plus un Songe ou Vision sur le mesme subject*. Edited by Michael Screech. Geneva: Droz, 1979.

——. *The Regrets with The Antiquities of Rome, Three Latin Elegies and The Defense and Enrichment of the French Language*. Translated by Richard Helgerson. Philadelphia: University of Pennsylvania Press, 2006.

Du Gua, Pierre. *Récit des choses remarquables qui sont en Italie* (in French). Lyon, 1624.

Du Pérac Lafréry, Antoine. *Roma prima di Sisto V: La pianta di Roma, Du Pérac-Lafréry del 1577 riprodotta dall'esemplare esistente nel museo britannico*. 1908.

Du Val, Pierre. *Le voyage et la description d'Italie: Montrant exactement les raretez (et) choses remarquables qui se trouvent es provinces (et) en chaques villes, les distances d'icelles; avec un dénombrement des places (et) champs de batailles qui s'y sont donées; ouvrage dressé pour la commodité des François (et) estrangers* (in French). Paris: Clouzier, 1656.

Esposito, Anna. "Roma e il Tevere." In *Le calamità ambientali nel tardo Medioevo europeo: Realtà, percezioni, reazioni*, 257–76. Florence: Firenze University Press, 2008.

Estienne, Charles. *La guide des chemins de France*. Paris: Estienne, 1552.

Estienne, Robert. *Dictionnaire Francois-latin, contenant les motz et manieres de parler Francois, tournez en Latin*. Paris: Robert Estienne, 1539.

Fauno, Lucio. *Delle antichità della città di Roma*. Venice: Michele Tramezzino, 1548.
Ferguson, Margaret W. "The Exile's Defense: DuBellay's La Deffence et illustration de la langue françoyse." *PMLA: Publications of the Modern Language Association of America* 93, no. 2 (1978): 275–89.
Finley-Crosswhite, Annette S. *Henry IV and the Towns: The Pursuit of Legitimacy in French Society, 1589–1610*. Cambridge: Cambridge University Press, 1999.
Fontaine, Marie-Madeleine. "Rire comme Ulysse." In *La Naissance du monde et l'invention du poème*, edited by Jean-Claude Ternaux and Isamu Takata. Etudes et Essais sur la Renaissance (Etudes et Essais sur la Renaissance), 21, 345–67. Paris: Champion, 1998.
Fontenay-Mareuil, Duval. *Voyage faict en Italie par Monsieur le Marquis de Fontenay-Marueil (sic) ambassadeur du Roy près de Sa Saincteté en l'année 1641 . . . ensemble la façon d'eslire les Papes, le tout recueilli par le S.r de Vologer Fontenay* (in French). Paris: L. Boulanger, 1643.
Ford, Philip. "Du Bellay et le sonnet satirique." In *Le Sonnet à la Renaissance: Des origines au XVIIe siècle*, edited by Yvonne Bellenger, 205–14. Paris: Aux Amateurs de Livres, 1988.
Foucault, Michel. "Des espaces autres (1967), Hétérotopies." *Architecture, Mouvement, Continuité* 5 (October 1984): 46–49.
———. *Les mots et les choses*. Paris: Gallimard, 1966.
Foucault, Michel, and Paul Rabinow. "Space, Knowledge and Power." In *The Essential Works of Michel Foucault, 1954–1984*. Vol. 3, 349–64. London: Penguin, 2002.
Frame, Donald Murdoch. *Montaigne: A Biography* (in English). New York: Harcourt, Brace & World, 1965.
Fulvio, Andrea. *Antiquaria urbis*. Rome, 1513.
———. *Antiquitates urbis Romae*. Rome, 1527.
Fusai, Luca. *Mille anni di storia attraverso le vicende della famiglia Cerretani Bandinelli Paparoni* (in Italian). Pisa: ETS, 2010.
Genette, Gérard. *Figures III* (in French). Paris: Éditions du Seuil, 1972.
Gorris, Rosanna, ed. *Les montagnes de l'esprit: Imaginaire et histoire de la montagne à la Renaissance: Actes du colloque international, Saint Vincent (Vallée d'Aoste), les 22–23 novembre 2002*. Vallée d'Aoste, Italy: Quart, 2005, 2002.
Gray, Floyd. *La poétique de Du Bellay* (in French). Paris: Nizet, 1978.
Greenblatt, Stephen. *Marvelous Possessions: The Wonder of the New World* (in English). Chicago: University of Chicago Press, 1991.
———. *Renaissance Self-Fashioning from More to Shakespeare*. Chicago: University of Chicago Press, 1980.
Greene, Thomas M. *The Light in Troy: Imitation and Discovery in Renaissance Poetry* (in English). Elizabethan Club series. New Haven: Yale University Press, 1982.
Greimas, Algirdas Julien. *Dictionnaire de l'ancien français: Le Moyen Age* (in French). Paris: Larousse, 1994.
Guelfi e ghibellini nell'Italia del Rinascimento (in Italian with two contributions in English). Rome: Viella, 2005.
Guicciardini, Francesco. *Storia d'Italia*. 3 vols. Vol. 1. Turin: Einaudi, 1971.
"Historisches Lexikon Bayerns." https://www.historisches-lexikon-bayerns.de/Lexikon/Kesselbergstraße.
Hodges, Elizabeth. *Urban Poetics in the French Renaissance*. Aldershot: Ashgate, 2008.
Hoffmann, George. *Montaigne's Career*. Oxford: Clarendon, 1998.

Horace. *Satires, Epistles and Ars Poetica*. Translated by H. Ruston Fairclough. Loeb Classics. Cambridge, MA: Harvard University Press, 2005.

Iannone, Pablo. *Dictionary of World Philosophy*. New York: Routledge, 2001.

Ilardi, Vincent. "'Italianità' among Some Italian Intellectuals in the Early Sixteenth Century." *Traditio* 12 (1956): 339–67.

Internet Encyclopedia of Philosophy, a Peer-Reviewed Academic Resource. https://www.iep.utm.edu.

Jacks, Philip Joshua. *The Antiquarian and the Myth of Antiquity: The Origins of Rome in Renaissance Thought / Philip Jacks*. Cambridge: Cambridge University Press, 1993.

Jakob, Michael. *Il paesaggio*. Bologna: Il Mulino, 2009.

Jameson, Fredric. *Postmodernism, or, The Cultural Logic of Late Capitalism*. Post-contemporary Interventions. Durham: Duke University Press, 1991.

Katz, Richard. *The Ordered Text: The Sonnet Sequences of Du Bellay*. Berne: P. Lang, 1985.

Keating, L. Clark. *Joachim du Bellay*. New York: Twayne, 1971.

Keatley, Richard. "'Du temps de nos peres': The Italian Wars in the Journal de Voyage." *Montaigne Studies: An Interdisciplinary Forum. Montaigne et ses historiens* 29 (2017): 48–57.

———. "Lo spazio campano dei viaggiatori francesi di fine Cinquecento." In *Viaggio e comunicazione nel Rinascimento*, edited by Luisa Rotondi Secchi Tarugi, 301–10. Florence: Franco Cesati, 2017.

———. "Le statut du valet dans le *Journal du voyage de M. de Montaigne en Italie, par la Suisse et l'Allemagne en 1580 et 1581*." Master's thesis, Univeristé de Paris IV–Sorbonne, 1997.

Keller, Marcus. *Figurations of France: Literary Nation-Building in Times of Crisis (1550–1650)*. Newark: University of Delaware Press, 2011.

Kemp, Martin. *Seen and Unseen: The Visual Ideas behind Art and Science* (in English). New York: Basic Books, 2001.

Knecht, Robert J. *The French Renaissance Court*. New Haven: Yale University Press, 2008.

Krause, Virginia. *Idle Pursuits: Literature and Oisiveté in the French Renaissance* (in English). Newark: University of Delaware Press, 2003.

Kritzman, Lawrence D. *The Fabulous Imagination: On Montaigne's Essays*. New York: Columbia University Press, 2009.

Kuhn, Thomas S. *The Structure of Scientific Revolutions* (in English). Chicago: University of Chicago Press, 1970.

Labande-Mailfert, Yvonne. *Charles VIII et son milieu (1470-1498): La jeunesse au pouvoir*. Paris: Klincksiek, 1975.

"La Cacciata della guardia spagnola da Siena, d'incerto autore, 1552." In *Archivio storico italiano*, tom. 2, 479–524, 1842.

Langer, Ullrich. "Le Discours de la souveraineté dans Les Regrets." In *Du Bellay*, edited by Georges Cesbron, 377–90. Angers: P de l'Univ. d'Angers, 1990.

Laureys, Marc, and Anna Schreurs. "Egio, Marliano, Ligorio, and the Forum Romanum in the 16th Century." *Humanistica Lovaniensia* 45 (1996): 385–405.

Lautrey, Louis, and Michel de Montaigne. *Journal de Voyage*. Paris: Hachette, 1906.

La Vigne, André de. *La Ressource de la Chrestienté*. Montreal: CERES, 1989.

———. *Le vergier d'onneur nouvellement imprimé à Paris. De l'entreprise de Napples. Auquel est comprins comment le roy Charles huitiesme de ce nom a banyere desployee passa et repassa de journee en journee depuis Lyon jusques à Napples et de Napples jusques à Lyon. Ensemble plusieurs austres choses faictes et composées par reverend pere en dieu monsieur Octovien de sainct Gelais evesque d'Angoulesme et par Maistre Andry de la Vigne secretaire de la Ryone et de monsieur le duc de Savoye avec autres.* Paris, n.d., ca. 1500.

———. *Le Voyage de Naples.* Milan: Pubblicazioni della Università Cattolica del Sacro Cuore, 1981.

Lefebvre, Henri. "La production de l'espace." *L'Homme et la société* 31–32 (1974): 15–32.

———. *The Production of Space.* Cambridge, MA: Blackwell, 1991.

Le Fur, Didier. *Charles VIII.* Paris: Perrin, 2006.

Legros, Alain. "Comme un désir de Grèce." In *Montaigne à l'étranger: Voyages avérés, possible et imaginés*, edited by Philippe Desan, 99–113. Paris: Classiques Garnier, 2016.

———. "Inscriptions du 'cabinet' et dédicace perdue de la librairie." MONLOE: MONtaigne à L'Œuvre. 2015. https://montaigne.univ-tours.fr/autres-inscriptions-de-la-tour/.

Le Roux, Nicolas. "The Politics of Festivals at the Court of the Last Valois." In *Court Festivals of the European Renaissance: Art, Politics and Performance*, 101–17. Aldershot: Ashgate, 2004.

Lestringant, Frank. "André de la Vigne et *Le Vergier d'honneur*." In *Le poète et son oeuvre: De la composition à la publication*, edited by Jean Eudes, 199–214. Geneva: Droz, 2004.

———. *L'Atelier du cosmographe: Ou l'image du monde à la Renaissance.* Paris: Albin Michel, 1991.

———. "Chorographie et paysage à la Renaissance." In *Le Paysage à la Renaissance*, edited by Yves Giraud, 9–26. Fribourg: Eds. Universitaires, 1988.

———. *Le huguenot et le sauvage: L'Amérique et la controverse coloniale en France, au temps des guerres de religion (1555–1589)* (in French). Paris: Klincksieck, 1990.

Levine, Saul. "The Location of Michelangelo's David: The Meeting of January 25, 1504." *Art Bulletin* 56, no. 1 (1974): 31–49.

Ligorio, Pirro. *Antiquae urbis imago accuratissimae ex vetusteis monumenteis.* Venice: Michele Tramezzino, 1561.

Lipsius, Justus. "Epistola de ratione cum fructu peregrinandi et praesertim in Italia." In *Miscellanea litteraria*, edited by Adam Heinrich Lackmann. Hamburg, 1721.

Lipsius, Justus, and John Stradling. *A Direction for Travailers taken (by Sir J. Stradling) out of J. Lipsius and enlarged for the behoofe of . . . the young Earle of Bedford, being now ready to travell.* London, 1592.

Losse, Deborah N. *Sampling the Book: Renaissance Prologues and the French Courtiers.* Lewisburg: Bucknell University Press, 1994.

Low, Setha M. "Towards an Anthropological Theory of Space and Place." *Semiotica* 175 (2009): 21–37.

MacPhail, Eric. "Nationalism and Italianism in the Work of Joachim Du Bellay." *Yearbook of Comparative and General Literature* 39 (1990): 47–53.

———. *The Voyage to Rome in French Renaissance Literature.* Stanford: Stanford French and Italian Studies, 1990.

Maier, Jessica. *Rome Measured and Imagined: Early Modern Maps of the Eternal City* (in English). Chicago: University of Chicago Press, 2015.

Mallett, Michael, and Christine Shaw. *The Italian Wars, 1494–1559.* Harlow: Pearson, 2012.

Marliani, Giovanni Bartolomeo. *Antiquae Romae Topographia.* Rome: Bladus, 1534.

Marliani, Giovanni Bartolomeo, and Ercole Barbarasa. *L'Antichità di Roma di M. Bartholomeo Marliano tradotti in lingua volgare per M. Hercole Barbarasa.* Rome, 1548.

Martinet, Marie-Madeleine. *Le voyage d'Italie dans les littératures européennes.* Paris: Presses universitaires de France, 1996.

Matoré, Georges. *L'Espace humain: L'expression de l'espace dans la vie, la pensée et l'art contemporains.* Paris: La Colombe, 1962.

Mauro, Lucio, and Ulisse Aldrovandi. *Le antichità de la città di Roma, brevissimamente raccolte da chiunque ne ha scritto, ò antico ò moderno; per Lucio Mauro, che ha voluto particularmente tutti questi luoghi vedere: Onde ha corretti di molti errori, che ne gli altri scrittori di queste antichità si leggono. Et insieme ancho, Di tutte le statue antiche, che per tutta Roma in diversi luoghi, e case particolari si veggono, raccolte e descritte, per M. Ulisse Aldroandi, opera non fatta piu mia da scrittore alcuno.* Venice: Giordano Ziletti, 1558.

Mayerne-Turquet, Théodore de. *Sommaire description de la France, Allemagne, Italie et Espagne, avec la Guide des chemins pour aller et venir par les provinces, et aux villes plus renommées de ces quatre regions.* Cologne: Jacob Stoer, 1618.

McCulloch, J. Huston. "*David*: A New Perspective." http://www.econ.ohio-state.edu/jhm/arch/david/David.htm.

McCulloch, J. R. *A Dictionary, Geographical, Statistical and Historical of the Various Countries, Places and Principal Natural Objects in the World. Illustrated with Maps.* 2 vols. Vol. 2. London: Longman, Brown, Green and Longmans, 1842.

McDonough, Jeffrey K. "Leibniz's Philosophy of Physics." In *The Stanford Encyclopedia of Philosophy*, edited by Edward N. Zalta. Spring 2014. http://plato.stanford.edu/entries/leibniz-physics/#Aca.

McGowan, Margaret M. "Contradictory Impulses in Montaigne's Vision of Rome." *Renaissance Studies: Journal of the Society for Renaissance Studies* 4, no. 4 (1990): 392–409.

———. *The Vision of Rome in Late Renaissance France.* New Haven: Yale University Press, 2000.

Mela, Pomponius, Joachim Vadianus, and Joannes Camers. *Pomponii Melae De orbis situ libri tres.* Paris: C. Wechelum, 1540.

Monga, Luigi. "L'Hodoeporicon de Jacques Sirmond, S.J." *Humanistica Lovaniensia* 42 (1993): 301–22.

———. "Travel and Travel Writing: An Historical Overview of Hodoeporics." *Annali d'Italianistica* 14 (1996): 6–54.

"MONLOE: Montaigne à l'oeuvre." https://montaigne.univ-tours.fr/centaine-de-livres/.

Montaigne, Michel de. *The Complete Works of Montaigne: Essays, Travel Journal, Letters.* Stanford: Stanford University Press, 1958.

———. *Les Essais.* Paris: Quadrige/PUF, 1992.

———. *Journal de Voyage.* Edited by Fausta Garavini. Paris: Gallimard, 1983.

———. *Journal de Voyage.* Edited by François Rigolot. Paris: Presses universitaires de France, 1992.

———. *Journal du voyage en Italie (1774).* Photographic reproduction established and presented by Philippe Desan. Paris: Société des Textes Français Modernes, 2014.

———. *Journal du voyage en Italie, par la Suisse et l'Allemagne en 1580 et 1581.* Edited by Meunier de Querlon. Rome: Le Jay, 1774.

———. *Journal de voyage: Partie en Italien.* Edited by Élisabeth Schneikert and Lucien Vendrame. Paris: Classiques Garnier, 2012.

"The Montaigne Project." http://www.lib.uchicago.edu/efts/ARTFL/projects/montaigne/.

Moussa, Sarga. "Une rhétorique de l'altérité: La représentation de la Suisse dans le *Journal de voyage* de Montaigne." In *Montaigne, Journal de voyage en Alsace et en Suisse (1580–1581); Actes du colloque de Mulhouse/Bâle*, 3–29. Paris: Champion, 2000.

Negri, Stefano. *Dialogus in quem quicquid apud Pausaniam scitu dignum legitur quem diligentissime congessit Stephanus Niger tam graece quam latine opidoque, eruditus*. Milan: Minutianus, 1517.

Nicot, Jean. "Le Thresor de la langue francoyse, tant ancienne que moderne." Paris: David Douceur, 1606.

Offenberg, Adri K. "The Printing History of the Constantinople Hebrew Incunable of 1493: A Mediterranean Voyage of Discovery." *British Library Journal* 22, no. 2 (Autumn 1996): 221–35.

Panici, William Franklin. "Du Bellay's Regrets and Magny's Souspirs: Satire or Vituperation?" *Romance Notes* 23, no. 1 (1982): 34–43.

———. "Rejection and Indirection: Du Bellay's *Regrets*." *Journal of Evolutionary Psychology* 9, nos. 1–2 (1989): 185–95.

Peakware. *World Mountain Encyclopedia*. http://www.peakware.com/peaks.html?pk=1012.

Pepper, Simon, and Nicholas Adams. *Firearms and Fortifications: Military Architecture and Siege Warfare in Sixteenth-Century Siena* (in English). Chicago: University of Chicago Press, 1986.

Posner, David. *The Performance of Nobility in Early Modern European Literature*. Cambridge: Cambridge University Press, 1999.

Pot, Olivier. *L'inquiétante étrangeté. Montaigne: La pierre, le cannibale, la mélancolie*. Paris: Champion, 1993.

———. "Lieux, espaces et géographie dans le *Journal de voyage*." *Montaigne Studies* 15 (2003): 63–104.

Prinzivalli, Virginio. *Torquato Tasso a Roma*. Rome: Libreria Desclée Lefebvre E C, 1895.

Priscianese, Francesco. *Descrittione della illustre e generosa città di Napoli e suoi contorni*. Rome: Priscianese, 1544.

Provini, Sandra. "Les Entrées de Charles VIII à Chieri et à Florence en 1494 vues par André de La Vigne." In *Vérité et fiction dans les entrées solennelles: À la Renaissance et à l'Age classique*, edited by John Nassichuk. Collections de la République des Lettres: Symposiums (Collections de la République des Lettres: Symposiums), 63–86. Quebec: PU Laval, 2009.

Rabelais, François. "Franciscus Rabelaesus Medicus Cariss. doctissimóque viro D. Ioanni Bellaio Parisiensi Episcopo, Regísque in sanctiori consessu consiliario S.P.D." In *Topographiae antiquae Romae*. Lyon: Gryphius, 1534.

———. *La quart livre*. Geneva: Droz, 1947.

Recueil des lettres missives de Henri IV. Paris: Imprimerie Royale, 1843.

Rigolot, François. "Du Bellay et la poesie du refus." *Bibliotheque d'Humanisme et Renaissance* 36 (1974): 489–502.

———. "La situation énonciative dans le *Journal de voyage de Montaigne*." In *Poétique et Narration. Mélanges offerts à Guy Demerson*, 463–78. Paris: Champion, 1993.

Roger, Alain. *Court traité du paysage*. Paris: Gallimard, 1997.

Rohan, Henri de. *Voyage du Duc de Rohan faict en l'an 1600: En Italie, Allemaigne, Pays-bas Uni, Angleterre, & Escosse* (in French). Amsterdam: Louis Elzevier, 1646.

Rostand, Julie-André. "*L'ekphrasis* ou de l'efficacité de la description dans les relations d'entrées françaises." In *Vérité et fiction dans les entrées solennelles: À la Renaissance et à l'Age classique*, 137–49. Quebec: PU Laval, 2009.

Said, Edward W. *Orientalism* (in English). New York: Vintage Books, 1979.
Saint-Sulplice, Jean de. *Guerres de religion dans le Sud-Ouest et principalement dans le Quercy*. Geneva: Slatkine Reprints, 1975.
Sanudo, Marino. *La Spedizione di Carlo VIII in Italia*. Venice, 1883.
Saulnier, V. L. *Du Bellay*. Paris: Boivin, 1951.
Savransky, Martin. "Will There Be a Place for My Life? Cities, Subjectivities and Geographies of Resistance / ¿Habrá un Lugar mi Vida? Ciudades, Subjectividades y Geografias de Resistencia." *Athenea Digital* 12, no. 1 (2012): 191–206.
Sayre, Robert. *Solitude in Society: A Sociological Study in French Literature* (in English). Cambridge, MA: Harvard University Press, 1978.
Schneikert, Élizabeth. *Montaigne dans le labyrynthe: De l'imaginare du Journal de voyage à l'écriture des Essais*. Paris: Champion, 2006.
———. "Montaigne et l'appel de la Pologne." In *Montaigne à l'étranger: Voyages avérés, possible et imaginés*, edited by Philippe Desan. Paris: Classiques Garnier, 2016.
Schudt, Ludwig, and Oskar Pollak. *Le guide di Roma: Materialien zu einer Geschichte der römischen Topographie, unter Benützung des Handschriftlichen Nachlasses von Oskar Pollak, hrsg. von Ludwig Schudt*. Quellenschriften zur Geschichte der Barockkunst in Rom. Wien: B. Filser, 1971.
Schwartz, Jerome. "The Poet in Bivio: Du Bellay's Spiritual Itinerary in the Regrets." In *Lapidary Inscriptions: Renaissance Essays for Donald A. Stone, Jr.*, edited by Barbara C. Bowen and Jerry C. Nash. French Forum Monographs (FrFM), 74, 61–71. Lexington, KY: French Forum, 1991.
Screech, Michael, ed. "Introduction." In *Joachim Du Bellay, Les Regrets et autres oeuvres poëtiques*, 9–41. Geneva: Droz, 1966.
Simoncini, Giorgio. *Roma: Le trasformazioni urbane nel Cinquecento: II: Dalla città al territorio*. Florence: Olschki, 2008.
Sozzi, Lionello. "La polémique anti-italienne en France au XVIe siècle." *Atti della Accademia di scienze di Torino* 189 (1972): 90–190.
TAGES. "Archeostronomia: Medioevo e Rinascimento." http://www.tages.eu/medioevo-e-rinascimento/.
Tallini, Gennaro. *"Roma trenta miglia": Il viaggio in Italia di Michel de Montaigne e Le antichità di Roma di Lucio Mauro*. In press.
Tarde, Jean. *À la rencontre de Galilée: Deux voyages en Italie* (in French). Geneva: Slatkine, 1984.
Tempesta, Antonio. *Roma al tempo di Clemente VIII la pianta di Roma*. Vatican City: Biblioteca Apostolica Vaticana, 1932. Map.
Thou, Jacques-Auguste de. *Memoires de la vie de Jacques-Auguste de Thou, conseiller d'état et président à mortier au parlement de Paris* (in French). Rotterdam: Reinier Leers, 1711.
Tinguely, Frédéric. *L'Écriture du Levant à la Renaissance: Enquête sur les voyageurs français dans l'empire de Soliman le Magnifique* (in French). Geneva: Droz, 2000.
———. *Les ruses de l'écriture à la Renaissance*. Paris: Champion, 2014.
Todorov, Tzvetan. *The Conquest of America: The Question of the Other* (in English). New York: Harper and Row, 1987.
Trisolini, Giovanna. Introduction to *Le Voyage de Gênes by Jehan Marot*. Geneva: Droz, 1974.
Tucci, Ugo. "Il Rinascimento. Società ed economia—lavor. La ricchezza. Le coesistenze: Monete e banche nel secolo del ducato d'oro."
Tucker, George Hugo. *The Poet's Odyssey: Joachim Du Bellay and the Antiquitez de Rome*. Oxford: Clarendon, 1990.

Turler, Jerome. *De peregrinatione, et agro neapolitano. Libri II. Scripti ab Hieronymo Turlero. Omnibus peregrinantibus utiles ac necessarii: Ac in eorum gratiam nunc in primum editi.* Strasbourg, 1574.

———. *The Traveiler of Jerome Turler, Devided into Two Bookes . . . Conteining a Notable Discourse of the Maner, and Order of Traviling Oversea, or into Straunge and Forrein Countreys. The Second Comprehending an Excellent Description of the Most Delicious Realme of Naples in Italy*. Gainseville: Scholars' Facsimiles and Reprints, 1951 (1575).

Ugonio, Pompeo. *Historia Delle Stationi di Roma: Che si celebrano la Quadragesima; Dove Oltre Le Vite De Santi Alle Chiese de quali Ë Statione, si tratta delle Origini, Fondationi, Siti . . . die esse Chiese, antiche & moderne* (in Italian). Rome: Bonfadino, 1588.

Usher, Phillip John. *Errance et cohérence: Essai sur la littérature transfrontalière à la Renaissance*. Paris: Classiques Garnier, 2010.

Vacher, Antoine. *Le Berry. Contribution à l'Etude géographique d'une région française*. Paris: Armand Colin, 1908.

Villamont, Jacques de. *Les Voyages du Seigneur de Villamont de l'ordre de Hierusalem, Gentilhomme ordinaire de la chambre du Roy. Divisez en trois livres, comme il se voit dans la page suivante. Derniere edition reveuë, corrigee, et cotee par l'autheur* (in French). Paris: Claude de Montroeil and Jean Richer, 1600.

Vinchant, François. *Voyage de François Vinchant en France & en Italie du 16 septembre 1609 au 18 février 1610* (in French). Brussels: Société générale d'imprimerie, 1897.

Virey, Claude Enoch. *Vers itinéraires: Allant de France en Italie. 1592; allant de Venise à Rome* (in French, Middle).

Paris: Société des Textes Français Modernes, 1999.

Voyage de Provence et d'Italie: Ms. fr. 5550, BN Paris (in French). Geneva: Slatkine, 1994. Perseus Digital Library, 1890.

Voyage d'Italie (1606). MS 841, Bibliothèque Nationale, Paris (145r–157v). Geneva: Slatkine, 1982.

Williams, Wes. *Pilgrimage and Narrative in the French Renaissance: The Undiscovered Country* (in English). Oxford: Clarendon, 1998.

Wolfzettel, Friedrich. *Le discours du voyageur: Pour une histoire littéraire du récit de voyage en France, du Moyen Age au XVIIIe siècle* (in French). Paris: Presses universitaires de France, 1996.

VOYAGES D'ITALIE (1568–1656)

Alincourt, marquis d'. See Charles de Neufville.

Audebert, Nicolas. *Voyage d'Italie*. British Museum, MS Lansdowne 720. Edited by A. Olivero. Rome: Lucarini, 1981.

———. *Le Voyage et Observations de plusieurs choses diverses qui se peuvent remarquer en Italie, tant de ce qui est naturel aux hommes et aux pays, comme des coustumes et façons, soit pour le general ou particulier, et des choses qui y sont rares, enrichi de figures*. Paris: Clouzier, 1656.

Bénard, Nicolas. *Le voyage de Hierusalem et autres lieux de la Terre-Sainte, ensemble son retour par l'Italie, Suisse, Allemagne, Hollande, Flandre en la tres-fleurissante et peuplé ville de Paris*. Paris: Moreau, 1621.

Bergeron, Pierre. *Voyages en Italie (1601–1612)*. Edited by Luigi Monga. Moncalieri: Centro Interuniversitario di ricerche sul viaggio in Italia, 2005.

Bouchard, Jean-Jacques. *Les Confessions, suivies de son Voyage de Paris à Rome en 1630, publiées pour la première fois*

sur le ms. de l'auteur. Paris: Liseaux, 1881.
Bouillon, Duc de. See Pierre Du Val.
Brackenhoffer, Élie. *Voyage de Paris en Italie, 1644–1646*. Paris: Berger-Levault, 1927.
Catin, Joseph. *Voyage aux champs Phlegreens (1568), De l'antiquité de Pezoles*. Cod. Franc., App. 15 (280) Bibl. Marciana de Venise. Édition critique et annotée par Luigi Monga. Moncalieri: Centro Interuniversitario di ricerche sul viaggio in Italia, 1997.
Claveson, Florisel de. *Voyage d'Italie (1608–1609)*. Moncalieri: Centro Interuniversitario di ricerche sul viaggio in Italia, 2001.
Condé, Henri de Bourbon. *Voyage de Monsieur le Prince de Condé en Italie depuis son partement du Camp de Montpellier, jusques à son retour en sa maison de Mouron, ensemble les remarques des choses les plus notables qu'il a veuës en sondit voyage*. Bourges, 1624; Paris, 1634, 1635, 1666; Lyon, 1665.
De Thou, Jacques-Auguste. *Mémoires de la vie de Jacques-Auguste de Thou, conseiller d'état et président à mortier au parlement de Paris*. Rotterdam, 1711.
Discours viatiques de Paris à Rome et de Rome à Naples et Sicile (1588–89). MS 222 R 424, Bibliothèque Méjanes, Aix-en-Provence. Edited by Luigi Monga. Geneva: Slatkine, 1983.
Du Gua, Pierre. *Récit des choses remarquables qui sont en Italie*. Lyon (1624). Bibliothèque Nationale de France.
Du Val, Pierre. *Le voyage et la description d'Italie, montrant exactement les raretez et choses remarquables qui se trouvent és provinces et en châques villes, les distances d'icelles; avec un dénombrement des places et champs de batailles qui s'y sont données. Ouvrage dressé pour la commodité des François et estrangers: Avec la Relation du Voyage fait à Rome par le Duc de Bouillon en l'année 1644*. Paris, 1656. Bibliothèque Nationale de France.
Duval de Fontenay-Mareuil, François. *Voyage en Italie, par Monsieur le Marquis de Fontenay Marveil, Ambassadeur du Roy prés de sa Saincteté en l'année 1641. Où est compris tout ce qui se voit de remarquable de Paris jusquà Rome, les noms des villes, chasteaux, ports de mer, isles et autres lieux, leur antiquité, description et assiette, avec les réceptions qui y ont esté faictes audict ambassadeur, avec la façon d'eslire les papes: Le tout recueillis par le seigneur Vologer-Fontenay*. Paris: Boulanger, 1643.
Guise, Duc de. *Mémoire du voyage de M. le Duc de Guise en Italie, son retour . . . en 1556 et 1557*. In *Collection complète des Mémoires relatifs à l'Histoire de France*. Paris, 1819–1826.
Mayerne-Turquet, Théodore de. *Sommaire description de la France, Allemagne, Italie et Espagne, avec la Guide des chemins pour aller et venir par les provinces, et aux villes plus renommées de ces quatre regions*. Cologne, 1618; Rouen, 1642.
Montaigne, Michel de. *Journal de voyage*. Edited by Fausta Garavini. Paris: Gallimard, 1983.
——. *Journal de voyage de Michel de Montaigne*. Edited by François Rigolot. Paris: Presses universitaires de France, 1992.
——. *Journal du voyage de Michel de Montaigne en Italie, par la Suisse et l'Allemagne en 1580 et 1581*. Paris: Le Jay, 1774.
Neufville, Charles de. *Mémoire de tout mon voyage fait en Italie (1583–1585)*. Bibliothèque Nationale de France, MS 14660.
Rigaud, Jean Antoine. *Brief Recueil de choses rares et notables, antiques, citez, forteresses principales d'Italie*. Aix: Jean Tolosan, 1601.
Rohan, Henri, Duc de. *Memoires du duc de Rohan, sur les choses advenuës en*

France, depuis la mort de Henry le Grand, jusques à la paix faite avec les reformez, au mois de juin 1629. Augmentez d'un quatrieme livre, et de divers discours politiques du mesme auteur, cy-devant non imprimez. Ensemble le voyage du mesme autheur, fait en Italie, Allemagne, Pays-bas-Uny, Angleterre, et Escosse, fait en l'an 1600. Paris, 1661; Paris, 1665; Amsterdam, 1693.

———. *Voyage du . . . faict en l'an 1600 en Italie, Allemaigne, Pays-bas uni, Angleterre et Escosse . . .* Amsterdam, 1646.

Simeoni, Gabriele. *Les illustres observations antiques du Seigneur Gabriel Symeon Florentin. En son dernier voyage d'Italie 1557.* Lyon, 1558.

Sirmond, Jacques. *Hodoeporicon ab urbe Lutetia ad Romam usque (1590)* in *Opera varia,* Paris, 1696, Venice, 1728. In Luigi Monga, "L'*Hodoeporicum* de Jacques Sirmond, S.J.: Journal poétique d'un voyage de Paris à Rome en 1590." *Humanistica Lovaniensia* 42 (1993): 301–322.

Tarde, Jean. *À la rencontre de Galilée, Deux voyages en Italie.* MS Périgord 106, Bibliothèque Nationale. Texte établi par François Moureau et Marcel Tétel. Geneva: Slatkine, 1984.

Villamont, Jacques de. *Les voyages du seigneur de Villamont, cheualier de l'Ordre de Hierusalem, gentil-homme du pays de Bretaigne. Divisez en trois liures . . . plus un abregé de la description de toute la France: Et les ordonnances des chevaliers du Sainct Sepulchre de Hierusalem.* Paris: Claude de Montroeil and Jean Richer, 1595.

———. *Les Voyages du Seigneur de Villamont de l'ordre de Hierusalem, Gentilhomme ordinaire de la chambre du Roy. Divisez en trois livres, comme il se voit dans la page suivante. Derniere edition reveuë, corrigee, et cotee par l'autheur.* Paris, 1600 (cited edition). Paris, 1604, 1609; Arras, 1598, 1602, 1606; Lyon, 1606, 1607; S. Rigaud, 1611; Rouen, 1607, 1608, 1610; Liege, 1608.

Vinchant, François. *Voyage en France et en Italie (1609–1610).* Brussels: Félix Hachez, 1897.

Virey, Claude-Énoch. *Vers itineraires. Allant de France en Italie. 1592. Allant de Venise à Rome. 1593.* Paris: Société des Textes Français Modernes, 1999.

Voyage de Provence et d'Italie (1588–89) (BN Paris, ms FR. 5550). Edited with introduction and notes by Luigi Monga. Geneva: Slatkine, 1994.

Voyage d'Italie (1606). MS 841, Bibliothèque Nationale, Paris (145r–157v). Introduction and notes by Michel Bideaux. Geneva: Slatkine, 1981.

RENAISSANCE GEOGRAPHICAL SOURCES

1. Ancient Authors

Dionysius Periegetes (ca. 2nd–3rd century), *De chorographia*

De situ orbis. Translated by Priscian. Venice, 1477, 1478, 1481, 1482, 1488, 1498; Rome, 1497; Cologne, 1499; Paris, 1499; Deventer, ca. 1497.

———. In *Cosmographia, sive de situ orbis,* by Pomponius Mela. Venice, 1482, 1498.

———. In *Pomponius Mela. Iulius Solinus. Itinerarium Antonini Aug. Vibius Sequester. P. Victor de regionibus urbis Romae. Dionysius Afer de situ orbis Prisciano interprete.* Venice, 1518, 1521; Florence, 1519, 1526; Toscolano, 1521.

Itinerarium Antonini Augusti. Paris: Henri Estienne, 1512.

———. In *Pomponius Mela. Iulius Solinus. Itinerarium Antonini Aug. Vibius Sequester. P. Victor de regionibus urbis Romae. Dionysius Afer de situ orbis Prisciano interprete.* Venice, 1518, 1521; Florence, 1519, 1526; Toscolano, 1521.

Itinerarium provinciarum Antonini Augusti. Vibius Sequester . . . Lyon, 1536 (s.d.), 1545, 1550.

Mela, Pomponius
Cosmographia, sive, de situ orbis. Milan, 1471; Venice, 1477, 1478, 1482, 1493, 1497, 1498, 1500; Salamanca, 1498.
Cosmographia, sive de situ orbis. Edited with a preface by Ermolao Barbaro. Venice, 1494, 1495, 1498, 1500, 1501, 1502; Wittenberg, 1509; Pesaro, 1510; Vienna, 1512; Basel, 1514; Leipzig, 1515; Paris, 1517.
De situ orbis. First century AD.
De totius orbis descriptione. Paris, 1507, 1508, 1513.
Libri de situ orbis tres. Edited with commentary by Joachim Vadianus. Vienna, 1518, 1540; Basel, 1522; Paris, 1530, 1540.
———. Edited by Petrus Joannes Olivarius. Paris, 1536, 1538, 1539, and in *Polyhistor*, 1543.
———. In *C. Iulii Solini Polyhistor*, edited by Sebastien Münster. Basel, 1538.
Pomponius Mela. Iulius Solinus. Itinerarium Antonini Aug. Vibius Sequester. P. Victor de regionibus urbis Romae. Dionysius Afer de situ orbis Prisciano interprete. Venice, 1518, 1521; Florence, 1519, 1526; Toscolano, 1521.
Pomponius Mela's Description of the World. Ann Arbor: University of Michigan Press, 1998.
I tre libri di Pomponio Mela, del sito, forma e misura del mondo. Translated by Tommaso Porcacchi. Venice, 1557.

Pliny
Historiae Mundi Libri XXXVII. Edited by Pierre Regnaut. Paris, 1543.
———. *Historia naturalis.* Venice (Johann Spira), 1469; Rome (Sweynheym and Pannartz), 1470; Venice (Nicolaus Jenson), 1472. Numerous editions published in Venice, Parma, Bologna, Cremona, Treviso, Rome.
———. *Historia naturalis.* Edited by Nicolas Maillard. Paris, 1511, 1514, 1516.
———. *Historia naturalis.* Annotations by Ermolao Barbaro and Jean Petit. Paris, 1526.
———. *Historia naturalis.* Edited by Antoine Augereau and Galliot du Pré. Paris, 1532.
———. *Natural History.* Cambridge, MA: Harvard University Press, 1991 (1938) (Books 1–2); 1998 (1942) (Books 3–7).

Priscian
Verse translation of Dionysius Periegetes in *Opera.* Venice, 1470, 1476. Also printed in many editions, often with Mela's *De situ orbis.*

Ptolemy
Cosmographia (Geography). Venice, 1475; Bologna, 1477; Rome, 1478, 1490; Florence, 1482; Vicenza, 1486.
———. Translated in *terza rima* by Francesco Berlinghieri. Florence, 1480, 1481, 1482. See Berlinghieri.
Geography. Annotated translation of the theoretical chapters. Princeton: Princeton University Press, 2000.
Historia naturale. Italian translation by Cristoforo Landino. Venice, 1476.

Solinus, Gaius Julius (3rd century)
De memoralibus mundi. Venice, 1491, 1493, 1498, 1501; Paris, 1503; Speyer, 1512, 1515; Pesaro, 1512; Cologne, 1520.
De mirabilibus mundi. Brescia, 1498.
De situ et memorabilibus orbis capitula (Polyhistor). Venice, 1473; Rome, 1474.
Polyhistor. Paris, 1533; Lyon, 1538, 1539, 1541; Poitiers, 1554; Antwerp, 1572.
Polyhistor, rerum toto orbe memorabilium thesaurus locupletissimus. Edited by Sebastian Münster. Basel, 1538, 1543.
———. In *Pomponius Mela. Iultus Solinus. Itinerarium Antonini Aug. Vibius Sequester. P. Victor de regionibus urbis Romae. Dionysius Afer de situ orbis Prisciano interprete.* Venice, 1518, 1521; Florence, 1519, 1526; Toscolano, 1521.

———. In *Pomponius Mela . . . Iulius Solinus*. Paris, 1536; Basel, 1540.
———. In *De situ orbis*, by Pomponius Mela. Edited by Petrus Joannes Olivarius. Basel, 1536; Paris, 1586.
Solino delle cose maravigliose del mondo. Translated by Giovanni Belprato. Venice, 1557, 1559.
———. In *Antiquitatum variorum autores*. Edited by Archolochus Myrsilus. Lyon, 1560.
———. In *Pomponii Melae De orbis situ . . . et C. Ulii Solini Polyhistor*. Basel, 1576, 1595.
———. In *Dionysii Alex. Et Pomp. Melae Situs orgbis description*. Paris: Henri Estienne, 1577.
The worthie work of Iulius Solinus Polyhistor containing many noble actions of humaine Creatures, with the secretes of nature in beastes, Fishes, Foules, and serpents: Trees, Plants, and the virtue of precious Stones: with divers countryes, citties and people: Verie Pleasant and full of recreation for all sorts of people. Translated by Arthur Golding. London, 1587.
———. In *The rare and singular worke of Pomponius Mela*, by Pomponius Mela. Translated by Arthur Golding. 1590.

Strabo
Geographia. Translated by Guarino and Tifernate. Rome, 1469. Many editions and commentaries published throughout the Renaissance.
Geography. Loeb Classical Library. Cambridge, MA: Harvard University Press, 1997 (1917).

Victor, Publius
De regionibus urbis Romae. 1500. Paris, 1507.
———. In *Itinerarium provinciarum Antonini Augusti. Vibius Sequester . . .* Lyon, 1536 (s.d.), 1545, 1550.
———. In *Pomponius Mela. Iulius Solinus. Itinerarium Antonini Aug. Vibius Sequester. P. Victor de regionibus urbis Romae. Dionysius Afer de situ orbis Prisciano interprete*. Venice, 1518, 1521; Florence, 1519, 1526; Toscolano, 1521.

2. Renaissance Cosmographers and Geographers

Belleforest, François de. *La cosmographie universelle de tout le monde . . . par Sébastien Munster, ed par François de Belleforest*. Paris: Michel Sonnius, 1575.
Berlinghieri, Francesco. *Septe giornate della geographia di Francesco Berlingeri fiorentino allo illustrissimo genma sultan*. Turin: Consiglio regionale del Piemonte, 2006.
Boccaccio, Giovanni. *De montibus, silvis, fontibus, lacubus, fluminibus, stagnis seu paludibus, et de nominibus maris*. Venice, 1473, 1494, 1495, 1497.
———. *Dizionario geografico: De montibus, silvis, fontibus, lacubus, fluminibus, stagnis seu paludibus et de nominibus maris*. Turin: Fògola, 1978.
———. In *Genealogiae Joannis Boccatii: Cum demonstrationibus in formis arborum designatis. Eiusdem de montibus & siluis de fontibus: Lacubus: & fluminibus. Ac etiam de stagnis & paludibus; necnon & de maribus: Seu diuersis maris nominibus*. Venice, 1494, 1495, 1497; Paris, 1511; Basel, 1532.
———. In *Opera dell' huomo dotto et famoso Giovan Boccaccio da Certaldo*. Venice, 1520, 1530, 1550.
Braun, Georg, and Franz Hogenburg. *Civitates orbis terrarum*. Antwerp: Gallaeus, 1572, 1588; Cologne, 1577, 1588, 1593, 1597, 1612; s.l., Bertram, 1590, 1606.
Giovio, Paolo. *Descriptiones quotquod extant, regionum atque locorum*. Basel, 1561, 1571, 1578.
Münster, Sebastian. *Cosmographia*. German edition. Basel, 1544.
———. *Cosmographia universalis lib. VI. in quibus iuxta certioris fidei scriptorium*

traditionem describuntur. . . . Basel, 1550, 1552, 1554, 1559.
———. *La cosmographie universelle, contenant la situation de toutes les parties du monde, avec leurs proprietez et apartenances: La description des pays et regions d'iceluy*. Paris, 1556; Basel, 1568.
———. *Sei libri della cosmografia universale*. Basel, 1558.
Romain, Adrien. *Parvum theatrum urbium sive Urbium praecipuarum totius orbis brevis et methodica descriptio*. Frankfurt, 1595.
Terraube, Guillaume de. *Brief discours des choses plus necessaires et dignes d'estre entendues en la Cosmographie, reveu et corrigé de nouveau*. Paris: Frédéric Morel, 1569.
Uberti, Fazio degli. *Opera chiamato Ditta mundi vuolgare*. Venice, 1501.
Vadianus, Joachim. Commentary of Pomponius Mela, *De situ orbis*. [Cited under Pomponius Mela.]

3. Italy

Alberti, Fra Leandro. *Descriptio totius Italiae qua situs, origines, imperia civitatum et oppidorum nominibus* . . . Cologne, 1556.
———. *Descrittione di tutta Italia*. Bologna, 1550; Venice, 1551, 1553, 1557, 1561, 1567, 1568, 1577, 1581, 1588, 1596; Cologne, 1566, 1567.
———. *Isole appartenenti alla Italia*. Venice, 1567, 1588.
Alunno, Francesco. *La fabrica del mondo: Nella quale si contengono tutte le uoci di Dante, del Petrarca, del Boccaccio, & d'altri buoni autori, con la dichiaratione di quelle, & con le sue interpretationi Latine, con le quali si ponno scriuendo isprimere tutti i concetti dell'huomo di qualunque cosa creata*. Venice, 1548.
Bertelli, Pietro. *Theatrum urbium Italicarum*. Venice, 1599.
Bovio, Benedetto. *Itinerari Italiae*. Vicenza, 1600.

Ens, Kaspar. *Deliciae Italiae et index viatorius ab urbe Roma ad omnes in Italia, aliquas etiam extra Italiam civitates et oppida*. . . . Leipzig, 1599; Frankfurt, Cologne, 1609.
Fabricius, Georgius. *Itinerum liber unus*. Basel, 1544, 1550, 1587.
———. In *Roma antiquitatum libri duo: Ex aere, marmoribus, saxis membranisue veteribus collecti ab eodem et Itinerum*. Basel: Oporinus, 1550, 1560, 1587.
———. *Roma: Liber ad opt. autorum lectionem apprime utilis . . . Eiusdem Itinerum liber unus*. Basel, 1551.
Landi, Ortensio. *Commentario delle più notabili, et mostruose cose d'Italia, et altri luoghi: Di lingua aramea in italiana tradotto, con un breve catalogo de gli inventori delle cose che si mangiano et bevono, novamente ritrovato*. Venice, 1548, 1553; Bologna: Pendragon, 1994.
———. *Forcianae quaestiones: In quibus varia Italorum ingenia explicantur, multaque alia scitu non indigna*. Naples, 1535, 1536; Louvain, 1550.
———. In Pyrckmair et al. *De arte peregrinandi*. Nuremberg, 1591.
Mores Italiae. Manuscript with illustrations produced in Venice, 1575.
Musato, Giovanni Pietro. *Itinerario da Venetia a Bologna composto in stil dantesco*. Venice, 1554.
Reusner, Nicolaus. *De Italia, regione Europae nobilissima libri duo*. Strasburg, 1585.
Schott, André. *Italiae illustratae, seu Rerum, Urbiumque Italicarum scriptores varii, notae melioris*. Frankfurt, 1600.
Schottus, Franciscus. *Italy in its Original Glory, Ruine, and revival being an extract and survey of the whole Geography and history of that Famous Country, with the adjacent islands of Sicily, Malta, etc.* London, 1660.
———. *Itinerarii Italiae Germaniaeque libri III*. Cologne, 1620.

———. *Itinerari Italiae rerumq(ue) Romanarum libri tres.* Antwerp, 1600, 1625; Vicenza, 1601, 1610; Amsterdam (1655); Padua, 1615.

———. *Itinerario, overo nova descrittione de'viaggi principali d'Italia, nella quale si hà piena di notitia di tutte le cose più notabili, et degne d'essere vedute, di Andres Scoto. Novamente tradotto dal Latino in lingua Italiana, et accresciuto di molte cose, che nel Latino non si contengono.* Venice, 1610; Padua, 1615; Rome, 1650, 1700, 1737, 1747, 1761; Padua, 1621–22, 1628–1629, 1638, 1643, 1647–1649, 1654, 1659, 1670, 1688; Venice, 1665, 1675, 1679; Bologna, 1747.

Solis, Giulio Cesare. *L'origine di molte città del mondo, et particularmente di tutta Italia, con prencipi et fondatori di quelle, con la longhezze et larghezza di essa, confini, sito, et provincie . . . et la descrittione dell'Africa, Asia et Europa.* Venice, 1593.

4. The Alps

Signot, Jacques. *La division du monde, contenant la declaration des provinces et regions d'Asie, Europe, et Affrique: Ensemble les passages, par lequels on peut passer des Gaules és parties d'Italie—traitant de plusieurs belles matieres, par lesquelles on pourra facilement avoir la description de la Carte Gallicane.* Paris, 1539, 1540, 1544, 1547; (s.l.) 1555, 1564; Lyon, 1555, 1560, 1566, 1590.

———. *La totale et vraie description de tous les passaiges, lieux, destroictz par lesquelz on peut passer et entrer des Gaules es Ytalies, et signament par où passèrent Hannibal, Julius César, . . . et très puisssans roys de France Charlemaigne, Charles VIII, Louys XII, et le très illustre roy François à présent regnant premier de ce nom item plus est contenu le nombre et tiltres des cardinaulx et patriarches, l'ordre et les noms des archeveschez et eveschez estans en luniversel monde: Item les archeschez, esveschez, abbayes et aultres benefices reservez au sainct siège apostolique: Avec la carte ordinaire estans au royaume et seigneuries de la couronne de France.* Paris, 1515, 1518, 1520, 1522, 1523.

5. Milan and Lombardy

Merula, Gaudenzio. *De Gallorum Cisalpinorum antiquitate, ac origine.* Lyon, 1538; Bergamo, 1592, 1593.

6. Venice

Bardi, Girolamo de (and Francesco Sansovino). *Delle cose notabili della città di Venetia, libri II. Ne i quali si contengono usanze antiche. Habiti & vestiti. . . . Nuouamente riformati, accresciuti, & abbelliti con l'aggionta della dichiaratione delle istorie, che sono state dipinte ne i quadri delle sale dello Scrutinio, & del gran Consiglio del palagio Ducale. . . . Fatta da Girolamo Bardi fiorentino.* Venice, 1587, 1592, 1601, 1606.

De aedificatione Venetiarum. In *Ruffi Sexti Viri consularis rerum gestarum.* Venice, 1472; Rome, 1474, 1478, 1490, 1491.

Goldioni, Leonico, and Francesco Sansovino. *Le cose meravigliose dell'inclita città di Venezia.* Naples: Liguori, 2003.

———. *Le cose meravigliose et notabili della città di Venetia, reformate, accommodate, et grandemente compilate da Leonico Goldioni.* Venice, 1624.

Guisconi, Anselmo. *Tutte le cose che sono in Venetia (1556).* Venice, 1861.

———. *Tutte le cose notabili e belle che sono in Venetia, cioè usanze antiche, pitture e pittori, sculture e scultori, fabriche e palazzo, uomini illustri, i principi di Venetia, e tutti i patriarchi.* Venezia, 1556.

Sabellicus, Marcus Antonius. *Del sito di Venezia città.* Venice: Filippi, 1985.

———. In Biondo Flavio, *La seconda parte de le historie*. Venice, 1544.

Sansovino, Francesco. *Dialogo di tutte le cose notabili che sono in Venetia, cioè: Pittori et pitture, scultori e scolture, usanze antiche, fabriche e palazzo, huomini virtuosi, principi di Venetia, con la prima origine della edificatione di essa città*. Venezia, 1560, 1561, 1561, 1563 (anonymous), 1566, 1567, 1569, 1575, 1583, 1587, 1592.

———. *Venetia città nobilissima et singolare*. Venice, 1581, 1604.

Sansovino, Francesco, and Leonico Goldioni. *Le cose meravigliose dell'inclita città di Venezia*. Naples: Liguori, 2003.

Ugoni, Giovanni Andrea. *Discorsi del Magnifico Signor Ugoni gentilhuomo Bresciano della dignità et eccellenza della gran città di Venetia con una bellissima essortatione del medesimo autore, all'honorato consiglio dela città sua di Brescia*. Venice, 1562.

7. Verona

Querini, Carlo. *Orazione in laude della mag. Città di Verona*. Verona, 1597.

Tinto, Giovanni Francesco. *La nobiltà di Verona*. Verona, 1592.

Valerini, Adriano. *Le bellezze di Verona nuovo ragionamento*. Verona, 1586.

8. Genoa

Bracelli, Giovanni Battista. *Genuensis De bello Hispaniensi libri quinque, eiusdem De claris Genuensibus libellus; Orae Ligusticae descriptio*. Rome, 1573.

9. Bologna

Grimoard, Anglic de. *La "Descriptio civitatis Bononie eiusque comitatus" del Cardinale Anglicus (1371)*. Bologna: Deputazione di storia patria per le province di Romagna, 1990.

———. *Un volto riemerso di Bologna medievale: La "Memoria" smarrita*. Bologna: Pàtron, 1999.

10. Florence and Tuscany

Albertini, Francesco. *Memoriale di molte statue et picture di Florentia*. Florence, 1510. In *Five Early Guides to Rome and Florence*. Upper Saddle River: Gregg, 1972.

Bocchi, Francesco. *Le bellezze della città di Fiorenza: Dove à pieno di pittura, di scultura, di sacri templii, di palazzi I più notabili artifizii, et più preziosi si contengono*. Florence, 1591.

Miniati, Giovanni. *Narrazione, e disegno della terra di Prato di Toscana: Tenuta delle belle terre d'Europa*. Florence, 1596.

———. *Narrazione, e disegno della terra di Prato di Toscana: Tenuta delle belle terre d'Europa*. Prato, 1827.

Rutilius, Claudius. *De laudibus urbis, Etruriae, et Italiae*. Bologna, 1520.

Scanello, Cristoforo. *Cronica universale de l'antica regione di Toscana*. Florence, 1572.

11. Rome

Alberti, Leon Battista. *Descriptio Urbis Romae*. Critical edition. Translation and commentary by Martine Furno and Mario Carpo. Geneva: Droz, 2000.

Albertini, Francesco. *De Roma prisca et nova varii auctores*. Rome, 1523.

———. *Opusculum de mirabilibus novae et veteris urbis Romae*. Rome, 1510, 1515; Basel, 1519; Lyon, 1520.

———. *Opusculum de mirabilibus novae et veteris urbis Romae*. In *Five Early Guides to Rome and Florence*. Upper Saddle River: Gregg, 1972.

———. *Septem mirabilia orbis et urbis Romae et Florentinae civitatis*. Rome, 1510.

Biondo, Flavio. *De Roma instaurata, de Italia illustrata, . . . de gestis venetorum*. Venice, 1503, 1510.

———. *De Roma instaurata . . . de Italia illustrata . . . de gestis venetorum*. Turin, 1527.

———. *De Roma triumphante*. Brescia, 1503.
———. *De Roma triumphante*. Venice, 1511.
———. *De Roma triumphante . . . Romae instauratae . . . Italia illustrata . . . Decades*. Basel, 1531, 1559.
———. *Italy Illuminated*. Edited and translated by Jeffrey A. White. Cambridge, MA: Harvard University Press, 2005.
———. *Roma instaurata*. Rome, 1471.
———. *Roma instaurata. De origine et gestis venetorum. Italia illustrata*. Verona, 1482.
———. *Roma instaurata et gestis venetorum*. Verona, 1481.
———. *Roma instaurata / Rome restaurée*. Edited with introduction by Anne Raffarin-Dupuis. Paris: Belles lettres, 2005 (volume 1); 2012 (volume 2).
———. *Roma ristaurata et Italia illustrata*. Translated by Lucio Fauno. Venice, 1542, 1543, 1548, 1558.
———. *Roma trionfante*. Translated by Lucio Fauno. Venice, 1544, 1548, 1549.
Boissard, Jean-Jacques. *Romanae urbis topographia et antiquitates*. Frankfurt, 1597, 1603, 1627.
Calvo, Marco Fabio. *Antiquae urbis Romae cum regionibus simulachrum*. Basel, 1532, 1556, 1558.
Contarini, Luigi. *L'antiquità di Roma: Sito, imperadori, famiglie, statue, chiese, corpi santi, reliqiuie, pontefici, et cardinali di essa*. Venice, 1575.
———. *L'antiquità, sito, chiese, corpi santi, reliquie et statue di Roma. Con l'origine e nobiltà di Napoli*. Naples, 1569.
Le cose Marauigliose della Citta di Roma con le Indulgentie Reliquie & Stationi che sono in tutte le Chiesie di Ella. Translated by Alvisio de Doricho. Rome, 1532.
Le cose maravigliose de l'alma città di Roma: Doue si tratta delle chiese, stationi, indulgentie & reliquie de i corpi santi, che sono in essa.
Le cose maravigliose de l'alma città di Roma: Dove si tratta delle chiese, stationi, indulgentie & reliquie de i corpi santi, che sono in essa. Various authors: Franzini, Palladio, Giulio Accolti. Rome, 1563; Venice, 1565, 1576, 1585, 1588, 1591, 1596, 1600, 1619, 1636, 1640, 1650, 1675.
Le cose Marauigliose della Citta di Roma con le Indulgentie Reliquie & Stationi che sono in tutte le Chiesie di Ella.
La Edifichation de molti palazzi et tempii de Roma. Venice, 1480. In *Five Early Guides to Rome and Florence*. 1972.
Fabricius, Georgius. *Itinerum liber unus*. Basel, 1544, 1550, 1587.
———. *Itinerum liber unus*. In *Roma antiquitatum libri duo: Ex aere, marmoribus, saxis membranisue veteribus collecti ab eodem et Itinerum*. Basel: Oporinus, 1550, 1560, 1587.
———. *Roma: Liber ad opt. autorum lectionem apprime utilis . . . Eiusdem Itinerum liber unus*. Basel, 1551.
Fauno, Lucio. *De antiquitatibus Urbis Romae*. Venice, 1549.
———. *Delle antichità della città di Roma*. Venice, 1548, 1552, 1553.
———. *Roma ristaurata, et Italia illustrata*. Translated by Flavio Biondo. Venice, 1542, 1543, 1548, 1558.
Francini, Girolamo. *Le cose meravigliose dell'alma città di Roma*. Rome, 1566, 1568, 1588.
———. *Palatia procerum Romane urbis*. Rome, 1589.
———. *Stationi delle chiese di Roma: Per tutta la quaresima, con una breve narratione della fondatione et consacratione di esse; et delle reliquie, che in quelle sono; con la vita di tutti li santi e sante*. Rome, 1595.
———. *Templa Deo et Sanctis eius Romae dicata*. Rome, 1596, 1599.
Fulvio, Andrea. *L'antichità di Roma di Andrea Fulvio antiquario Romano, di nuovo con diligenza corretta e ampliata, . . .* Venice, 1588.
———. *Antiquaria Urbis*. Rome, 1513.
———. *Antiquitates Urbis*. Rome, 1527, 1545.
———. *Opera di Andrea Fulvio delle antichità della città di Roma*. Venice, 1543.

Gamucci, Bernardo. *Le antichità della città di Roma*. Venice, 1565, 1569, 1580, 1588.

(Indulgentiae ecclesiarum urbis Romae). *In isto opusculo dicitur, quomodo Romulus et Remus nati sunt en educati*. Rome, 1489, 1492, 1494, 1499, 1504, 1511, 1516, 1515, 1519, 1520, 1522, 1523.

I nomi antichi et moderni dell'antica città di Roma, et de tutti i popoli, provincie, città, fiumi, monti, selve, et altri luochi di tutta Italia, come al presente si adimandano. Venice, 1552.

In questa opereta ... Italian translation of *In isto opusculo*, a.k.a. *Mirabilia, vel potius historia et descriptio*. Rome, 1493, 1499, 1500, 1504, 1510, 1511.

———. *L'Antichità di Roma: Raccolta brevemente da gli autori antichi et moderni*. Rome, 1558, 1568, 1570.

———. *Descriptio brevissima priscae urbis Romae*. Venice, 1544.

———. *Descritione de le chiese de Roma*. Rome, 1554. In *Five Early Guides to Rome and Florence*. 1972.

Leto, Giulio Pomponio. *De antiquitatibus urbis Romae*. Lyon, 1552, 1560; Frankfurt, 1568, 1578; Paris, 1573.

———. *De antiquitatibus urbis Romae libellus*. In *Opera*. Strasburg, 1510, 1515; Paris, 1520.

———. *De antiquitatibus urbis Romae libellus*. In *Opuscula*. Paris, 1511.

———. *De antiqvitatibvs vrbis Romæ libellus... Topographiae veteris Romae Io. Bartholomæi Marliani... epitome, nunc primum in lucem edita. P. Victoris De vrbis Romae regionibus & locis libellus*. Basel: Thomas Platter, 1538.

———. *De vetustate urbis*. Rome, 1538.

———. *L'antiquità di Roma*. Rome, 1550.

———. *Opera... varia. Quorum catalogum in sequent reperies pagella*. Mainz, 1521.

Ligorio, Pirro. *Libro di M. Pyrrho Ligori napolitano, delle antichità di Roma: Nel qvale si tratta de' circi, theatri, & anfitheatri: Con le paradosse del medesimo auttore, quai confutano la commune opinione sopra uarii luoghi della città di Roma*. Venice, 1553.

Lipsius, Justus. *Della grandezza di Roma et del suo imperio di Giusto Lipsio lib V*. Rome, 1600.

Marliani, Bartolomeo. *L'Antichità di Roma*. Translated by Ercole Barbarasa. Rome, 1548.

———. *L'Antichità di Roma*. In *Antiqvitatvm variarvm avtores, quorum catalogum sequens continet pagella*. Lyon, 1560.

———. *L'Antichità di Roma*. In *Onuphrii Panuinii, Bartholomaei Marliani, Petri Uictoris, Iani Iacobi Boissardi Topographia Romae cum tabulis geographicis*. Edited by Jean-Jacques Boissard et al. Frankfurt, 1597.

———. *Antiquae Romae topographia, libri septem*. Rome, 1534.

———. *Antiquae Romae topographia, libri septem*. With manuscript notes by Pietro Corsi. Beinecke Library, Yale University. Rome, 1534.

———. *Topographia Antiquae Romae*. Edited by François Rabelais. Lyon, 1534.

———. *Topographiae veteris Romae Io. Bartholomaei Marliani Patricii Mediolanensis, Epitome*. Basel, 1538; Paris, 1573; Frankfurt, 1578.

———. *Urbis Romae Topographia*. Rome, 1544, 1549, 1560; Basel, 1550; Lyon, 1552; Venice, 1558, 1588.

The Marvels of Rome: Mirabilia Urbis Romae. New York: Italica Press, 1986.

Mauro, Lucio, and Aldrovandi, Ulisse. *Le Antichità della città di Roma brevissimamente racolte da chiunque ha scritto, ò antico, ò moderno... Et insieme anco di tutte le statue antiche, che per tutta Roma in diversi luoghi, e case particolari si uegonno, raccolte e descritte*. Venice, 1556, 1558, 1562, (1580), 1584.

Mazzocchi, Giacomo. *De Roma prisca et nova varii auctores*. Rome, 1523.

Les Merveilles de Rome (Texte imprimé): Two Medieval French Versions of the

"Mirabilia Urbis Romae." Edited by David J. A. Ross. Copenhagen: Gyldendal, 1969.

Mirabilia Romae. Rome: Adam Rot, 1472. Treviso: 1475. Rome, 1475, 1482, 1491, 1492, 1494, 1495, 1499, 1500, 1524 (1475 Morgan Library; 1482).

———. In Solinus, Polyhistor, sive De mirabilibus mundi. Add. Mirabilia Romae. Venice: Theodorus de Ragazonibus, 1491.

Mirabiliae Romae vel potius historia et descriptio urbis Romae. Sant'Orso: Giovanni de Reno, 1475; Rome, 1484, 1485, 1487, 1489, 1491, 1492, 1493, 1494, 1496, 1499, 1500, 1506, 1511, 1518, (1475 Yale). See also (Indulgentiae), In isto opusculo . . .

Mirabilia urbis Romae nova recognita et emendata. Rome: Bladus, 1524, 1550.

Palladio, Andrea. L'Antichità di Roma. Rome, 1554, 1587; Venice, 1555, 1565, 1570, 1576. In Five Early Guides to Rome and Florence. 1972.

Panciroli, Guido. I tesori nascosti nell'alma città di Roma. Rome, 1600, 1625.

Panvinio, Onofrio. De praecipuis urbis Romae santioribusque basilicis quas septem ecclesias vulgo vocant liber. Rome, 1570; Cologne, 1584.

———. Le sette chiese principali di Roma. Rome, 1570.

Ponto, Antonino. Mirabilia urbis Romae nova recognita et emendata . . . Rome, 1524, 1530, 1550.

———. Rhomitypion . . . Vbi dum omnia, quæ notatu sunt digna Vrbis Romane & noua, & uetera breuiter . . . scribuntur. Ingeniose et depingit huius Mundi uarietas, Insania, & fragilitas. Habet hic quoque totius terræ Situs, Aeris, & superiorum oium cognitio. Quicquid est ab ultima circuferetia ad centru uniuersi. Et demum breuissima Cosmographia . . . Rome, 1524.

Roma cita santa: Capo del mondo. Rome, 1500.

Scamozzi, Vincenzo. Discorsi sopra l'antichità di Roma. Venice, 1581, 1582, 1583.

———. Discorsi sopra l'antichità di Roma. Milan: Il Polifilo, 1991 (1582).

Schottus, Franciscus. Italy in its Original Glory, Ruine, and revival being an extract and survey of the whole Geography and history of that Famous Country, with the adjacent islands of Sicily, Malta, Etc. London, 1660.

———. Itinerarii Italiae Germaniaeque libri III. Cologne, 1620.

———. Itinerari Italiae rerumq(ue) Romanarum libri tres. Antwerp, 1600, 1625; Vicenza, 1601, 1610; Amsterdam, (1655); Padua, 1615.

———. Itinerario, overo nova descrittione de'viaggi principali d'Italia, nella quale si hà piena di notitia di tutte le cose più notabili, et degne d'essere vedute, di Andres Scoto. Novamente tradotto dal Latino in lingua Italiana, et accresciuto di molte cose, che nel Latino non si contengono. Venice, 1610; Padua, 1615; Rome, 1650, 1700, 1737, 1747, 1761; Padua, 1621–22, 1628–1629, 1638, 1643, 1647–1649, 1654, 1659, 1670, 1688; Venice, 1665, 1675, 1679; Bologna, 1747.

Serlio, Sebastiano. Le antiquità di Roma: Libro 4. Venice, 1537.

———. Il terzo libro di Sebastiano Serlio bolognese, nel quale si figurano e descrivono le antiquità di Roma. Venice, 1540, 1544, 1545, 1551, 1559, 1562.

Soranzo, Girolamo. Breve naratione del viagio et peregrinatione fatta da me Hier(oni)mo Soranzo . . . l'anno del jubilee 1575 a Roma et in altri luogi (ca. 1575).

Stella, Cherubino di. Itinerario delle poste per diverse parti del mondo. Et il viaggio di San Iacomo di Galitia. Con tutte le fiere notabili che fanno per tutto il mondo. Con una narratione delle cose di Roma, et massime delle sette chiese *brevemente ridotta*. Venice, 1564, 1576, 1585 1598; Lyon, 1588.

Ugonio, Pompeo. *Historia delle stationi di Roma, che si celebrano la quadragesima, dove oltre le vite de santi, alle chiese, de quali è statione, si tratta delle origini, fondationi, siti, restauratione, ornamenti, reliquie e memorie di esse chiese antiche e moderne*. Rome, 1588.

Vittore, Publius. *See* Ancient Authors: Publius Victor.

Las yglesias indulgencias y stacio(n)es de Roma co(n) los no(m)bres de las reliqas, y delos summos Po(n)tifices, Emperadores, y Reyes de Fra(n)cia, Napoles y Sicilia: Añadidas de nuevo algunas yglesias, las staciones de todo el año, y la guía romana, y otras cosas, todl eme(n)dado . . . Rome: (Valerio Dorico) a costa de Francisco y Faustino Hermanos libreros, 1561.

12. Naples and Pozzuoli

Accolti, Francesco. *Libellus de mirabilibus civitatius Putheolorum et locurum vicinorum: Ac de nominibus virtutibusque balneorum ibidem existentium*. Naples, 1475.

Di Falco, Benedetto. *Descrittione dei luoghi antichi di Napoli, e del suo amenissimo distretto*. Naples, 1549, 1568, 1580, 1589.

Di Stefano, Pietro. *Descrittione de i lvoghi sacri della citta di Napoli con li fondatori di essi, reliquie, sepolture, et epitaphii scelti che in quelle si ritrouano. L'intrate, & possessori, che al presente le possedeno, & altre cose degne di memoria. Opera non meno dilettevole, che utile*. Naples, 1560.

Elisio, Giovanni Battista. *Opusculum de balneis Puteolorum, et Pithecusarum*. (See Scipione Mazzella). Naples, 1591.

Griffolini, Francesco. *Libellus de mirabilibus civitatius Putheolorum et locurum vicinorum: Ac de nominibus virtutibusque balneorum ibidem existentium*. (Also attributed to Francesco Accolti). Naples, 1475.

Lombardi, Giovanni Francesco. *Synopsis authorum omnium, qui hactenus de balneis aliisque miraculis Puteolanis scripserunt*. Naples, 1559; Venice, 1566.

Mazzella, Scipione. *Descrittione del Regno di Napoli di Scipione Mazzella Napoletano*. Naples, 1586, 1601.

———. *Opusculum de balneis Puteolorum, Baiarum, et Pithecusarum*. Naples, 1591, 1593.

———. *Sito, et antichità della città di Pozzuolo, e del suo amenissimo distretto con la discretione di tutti i luoghi notabili, e degni di memoria, e di Cuma, e di Baia, e de gli altri luoghi convicini. Con le figure de gli edifici, e con gli epitafi che vi sono*. Naples, 1591, 1594, 1595.

Petrus de Ebulo. *I bagni di Pozzuoli. Poemetto napolitano del sec. XIV*. Naples, 1887.

———. *De balneis Puteolarum et Baiarum*. New York: Edition Medicina Rara, 1976.

———. *Nomina et virtutes balneorum; seu De balneis Puteolorum et Baiarum. Codice Angelico 1474*. Rome: Istituto poligrafico dello stato, 1962.

Priscianese, Francesco. *Descrittione della illustre et generosa città di Napoli e suoi contorni*. Rome, 1544.

Tarcagnota, Giovanni. *Del sito, et lodi della città di Napoli con una breve historia de gli re suoi, et delle cose più degne altrove ne' medesimi tempi avenute*. Naples, 1566.

Tyfernus, Augustinus. *Libellus de mirabilibus civitatis Puteolorum et locorum vicinorum; ac de nominibus virtuibusque balneorum ibidem existentium*. Naples, 1597.

13. South of Naples

Barri, Gabriele. *Antichità e luoghi della Calabria*. Cosenza: Brenner, 1985.

———. *De antiquitate et situ Calabriae libri quinque*. Rome, 1571.

Bascarini, Nicolo de. *La Descrittione dell'Isola di Sicilia*. Venice, 1546.

Fazello, Tommaso. *Rerum sicularum scriptores ex recentioribus praecipui, in unum corpus nunc primum congesti, diligentique recognitione plurimus in locis emendati*. Frankfurt, 1579.

14. Henri III

Benedetti, Rocco. *Discours des triomphes et resjouissances faicts par la sérénissime Seigneurie de Venise, à l'entrée heureuse de Henry de Valois, troisiesme de ce nom, treschrestien roy de France et de Pologne*. Lyon, 1574.

——. *Le feste, et trionfi fatti dalla serenissima signoria di Venetia nella felice venuta di Henrico III, christianissimo re di Francia*. Venice, 1574; Turin, 1574.

Della Croce, Marsilio. *L'historia della publica et famosa entrata in Vinegia del Serenissimo Henrico III, re di Francia et Polonia con la descrittione particolare della pompa, e del numero, et varietà delli Bregantini, Palaschermi, et altri vasselli armati, con la dechiaratione dell'èdificio, et arco fatto al Lido*. Venice, 1574.

La entrata che fece in Vinegia l'illustrissima et eccellentissima s. duca Alfonso II Estense, duca di Ferrara. Venice, 1562.

I gran trionfi fatti nella nobil città de Treviso, nella venuta del . . . Re di Francia, et di Polonia, Henrico Terzo. Venice, 1574.

Lucangeli, Niccolò. *Successi del viaggio d'Henrico III, christianissimo re di Francia, e di Polonia, dalla sua partita di Craccovia fino all'arrivo in Turino*. Venice, 1574.

Manzini, Gregorio. *Il gloriosissimo apparato fatto dalla serenissima Republica venetiana per la venuta, per la dimora, et per la partenza del christianissimo Enrico III re di Francia et di Polonia*. Venice, 1574.

Ordre de la réception . . . Henry III. Lyon, 1574.

Porcacchi, Tommaso. *Le attioni d'Arrigo Terzo, Re di Francia et Quarto di Polonia*. Venice, 1574.

15. Other

Stella, Cherubino di. *Itinerario delle poste per diverse parti del mondo. Et il viaggio di San Iacomo di Galitia. Con tutte le fiere notabili che fanno per tutto il mondo. Con una narratione delle cose di Roma, et massime delle sette chiese brevemente ridotta*. Venice, 1564, 1576, 1585, 1598; Lyon, 1588.

INDEX

Alberti, Leonbattista, 71
Alberti, Leandro, 91, 108, 137, 164
Albertini, Francesco. *See* Roman guidebooks
allegorical space, 33–37
Alps, the, 9–12, 20, 21–28, 108–17
   dangers of, 111–15
   passes through, 109
   sociological changes of, 113–14
Alpine guides (marrons), 110–11
Apennines, 135–39
   banditry, 136
Aragonia, palazzo, possible site of Montaigne's apartments, 161–62
Audebert, Nicolas, 106, 116, 133–34
authority, 75–77, 79–80
authorship, 48–50, 185

Bavaria (region), 9–13
Bavaria, Duke of, 9–10
Beauvoisin, bridge of (territorial marker between France and Savoy), 115–16
Belleforest, François de, cosmographer, 91, 108
Bergeron, Pierre, 107, 143, 151, 152, 156
Bhabha, Homi, 20
Biondo, Flavio, 73, 192
Bizer, Marc, 51
Bologna, 129–32
   border between Cisalpine Gaul and Etruria, 132
   Guelfs and Ghibellines in, 132–33
   Torre degli Asinelli, 131–32
   University, 131
borderlands, 19–21, 108–9
Bouchard, Jean-Jacques, 106
Brennus, Gaulish King, 130, 151, 188, 202
Bufalini, Leonardo. *See* Rome, maps of

Calvo, Fabio. *See* Roman guidebooks

Campagna Romana, 148–57
   Gallican readings of, 151–57
Campi Flegrei, the. *See* Catin, Joseph
Carignano, castle of, 119
Cartaro, Mario. *See* Rome, maps of
Casale Monferrato, 48, 155
categories in the description of Rome, use of, 72–73
Catin, Joseph, 7, 75–86, 174
Cenis, Mont, 40, 98, 105, 107, 109, 115, 117, 197
ceremonial entrances, 45–47
Charlemagne, 35, 36, 38, 119, 120, 130, 152
Charles V, Holy Roman Emperor, 129, 130, 137
Charles VIII, King of France, 32–37, 42–48, 119, 120, 129–30, 138, 182, 183
Chemins de France, Guide des. *See* Charles Estienne
Chieri, Charles VII's reception in, 45–47
Chivasso, 121
Chiusa, San Michele della, 119
citation, 77–84
Claveson, Florisel de, 107, 124, 125, 138, 139, 140, 143, 151, 156, 143
Condé, Henri, Prince of, 104, 107
Conley, Tom, 173
cosmographical framing, 90–94
cosmopolitanism, 26–27, 148, 170–71
courage, 97–101. *See also* heroism

Di Falco, Benedetto, 7, 77–79, 82–84
Discours viatiques, 1–3, 111, 114, 117, 126, 136
dreams, 33–40, 98–100
Du Bellay, Jean, cardinal, 52, 56
Du Bellay, Joachim, 6, 49, 51–69
   narrative of *Regrets*, 52–54
   work ethic, 54–60
   learning through travel, 61–66
Du Pérac, Antoine, *See* Rome, maps of

erotic space. *See* sexualized space
Estienne, Charles, 15
Estienne, Robert, 54–55, 84–85, 177
Estissac, Charles de, 9
experience, 88–90

Florence, 133–45
　arrival from Bologna, 134–39
　Duomo (Santa Maria del Fiore), 141–43
　Montaigne's political reaction to, 143–45
　Palazzo Vecchio, 144
　suburbs , 137–39
　tours of, 139–41
　use of art, 140–41
Fontenay-Mareuil, François de, 106, 151, 152
Foucault, 85–87, 172, 174, 188
framing, 87–97
France, passage through, 15–16
　history of, 16–17
　national identity, 32–50
François I, King of France, 129, 141–42, 199
Fulvio, Andrea, 73–74, *See* also Roman guidebooks

Galileo (Galilei), 172
Gallic space, Italy as a, 108
gardens (*pourpris*), 40–41, 91–94, 100–101
goiters, 114
Gondi family, 144
Guicciardini, Francesco, Florentine historian, 36, 129, 143
guidebooks, 107–8, *See also* Bibliography, "Renaissance Geographical Sources," 219–229

Harlay, Achille de, 101, 104, 189
Henri de Navarre, *See* Henri IV, King of France
Henri III, King of France, 15, 101
　return from Poland, 116
Henri IV, King of France, 7, 68–69, 101, 103
heroism, 35–36, 55–60, 75, 98–101, 119–20, 144, 154–55
heterotopy, 172
history, reading of, 16–17
Hotman, François, 20

industry, *See* work

Italian Wars, 3–4, 18, 32–37, 105, 108, 152
itineraries of the Italian journey, 105–8

Katz, Richard, 52
Kesselberg Pass, 9–13
Königsdorf, 9
Krause, Virginia, 3

labor, *See* work
landscape, 9–11, 177
La Vigne, André de, 32–50
Lefebvre, Henri, 4
leisure, performed, 3, 12–13, 54
Leto, Pomponio, *See* Roman guidebooks
Ligorio, Pirro, 73, 164. *See also* Rome, maps of
Losse, Deborah N., 79
Loubenx de Verdalle, Cardinal Hugues, 2–3
Lyon, 33, 94–96

Marignano, battle site, 129
Marliani, Bartolomeo, 70–75, 164, 191
marrons, *See* Alpine guides
Mattecoulon, Bernard de, 9
Method, Travel, 66–68
Milan, 121–128
　battlements, 122
　Duomo, 126–127
　modernity 127
　Sforza castle, 125
　similarity to Paris, 123–24,
　size and wealth, 122–24
　strength, 127–28
　surrounding countryside, 122
Mirabilia Romae (twelfth-century guides of Rome), 73, 192
Missal, Roman, 169–70
monstrosity, 98–99
Montaigne, Michel de, 9–31, 146–71
　disease, 14–15
　father of (Pierre de Montaigne), 17–19
　in Florence, 143–145
　home of, 13–15, 179
　idea of Italy, 17–19
　location of apartments in Rome, 157–62
　love of freedom, 154–57
　participation in religious festivities, 168–71

Montaigne, Michel de *(continued)*
  in Rome, 146–71
  scorn for erudition, 156
  secretary of the *Journal*, 21–31
  study of Rome, 162–68
Montalcino, 154–55
Münster, Sebastien, 84–85, 91

Naples, 75–79
Naples, kingdom of, 4, 6, 33–35
narration, 72–75
Navarre, Henri de, *See* Henri IV, King of France
Novalesa, 118–119
  beginning of Piedmontese dialect, 120
Novara, 122

Parma, 129
Pausanias, 73, 191
Pellevé, Nicolas de, Cardinal of Sens, 163
performance, 3, 12–13, 28–31, 42–47, 75–77, 90–91, 181–82
Petrarch, 82–83, 100, 195
Piacenza, 129
Pliny, 84–86
political science, 88–90
politics, 68–9, 87–90, 101–4
Ponte, Antonio. *See* Roman guidebooks
Pozzuoli, *See* Joseph Catin

Rabelais, François, 70–73
racism, 37–39
reading, historical. *See* history
Regrets, The. See Du Bellay, Joachim
Ressource de la Chrestienté. See La Vigne, André de
Robert of Anjou, King of Naples, 82–83
Roche-Melon, 97–100, 195
Rohan, Henri de, 107, 128, 152
Roman guidebooks, 72–75
Rome, 146–71
  Arch of Septimius Severus, 165
  Capitoline Hill, 168–69
  Castel Sant'Angelo, 161, 162
  grandeur of 162–68
  maps of, 158–62
  palazzo Savelli (Theater of Marcellus), 166–68

Santa Lucia della Tinta, church of, 160–61
Schwartz, Jerome, 52
secretaries. *See also* secretary of Michel de Montaigne
sexualized space, 39–42
Sicily, 1–3
Siena, 146, 148, 149, 151, 152
  relationship to France and the Gauls, 151–52
  in Italian Wars, 152–56, 203
Sirmond, Jacques de, 105–6
social class, 2–4
Solfatara. *See* Vesuvius, Catin mistakes the Solfatara for
space, theory of, 4–5, 9–13, 178
spatial theory. *See* Space, theory of
staging, *See* performance
Strozzi, palazzo, 140
Strozzi, Piero, Marshal of France, 17–18, 144, 180
Strozzi family, 144
Susa, 118

Tarde, Jean, 106
Tempesta, Antonio. *See* Rome, maps of
tempests in travel literature. 63–64, 95–96
Ticino river, 122
topographical framing, 94–97
topography, 72–75, 192
tourism, 47–48
Turin, 117–21
Tuscany, fertility of, 149

Ugonio, Pompeo, author of *Historia delle Stationi*, 169–70
Ulysses, 60–65

Vasari, Giorgio, 139, 140, 144
Vercelli, 121–22
Vergier d'honneur, le. See, La Vigne, André de.
Vesuvius, Catin mistakes the Solfatara for, 84–86
Villamont, Jacques de, 87–104
  climb of Roche Melon, 97–101
  cosmographical framing, 91–94
  desire to serve his country, 87–90
  itinerary of, 90–91, 107

political career, 101–4
sources, 91
use of topography, 94–97
Virey, Claude-Énoch, 107
Virgil, 83–84
Viterbo, 146–48
Voyage de Naples, *See* La Vigne, André de
Voyage de Provence et d'Italie, 106
Voyages of Jacques de Villamont. *See* Villamont, Jacques

walking around, 72–73
wandering, 67–68
Wars, Italian. *See* Italian Wars
Wars of Religion, 15–17
work, 54–69, 187

www.ingramcontent.com/pod-product-compliance
Lightning Source LLC
Chambersburg PA
CBHW030300010526
44108CB00038B/940